Management Stripped Bare

UNDERSTANDING BUSINESS AS IT *REALLY* IS

JO OWEN

AMACOM
American Management Association
New York • Atlanta • Brussels • Buenos Aires • Chicago • London • Mexico City
San Francisco • Shanghai • Tokyo • Toronto • Washington, D.C.

This publication is designed to provide accurate and authoritative information in regard to the subject matter covered. It is sold with the understanding that the publisher is not engaged in rendering legal, accounting, or other professional service. If legal advice or other expert assistance is required, the services of a competent professional person should be sought.

Library of Congress Cataloging-in-Publication Data

Owen, Jo.
    Management stripped bare : understanding business as it really is / Jo Owen.—1st U.S. ed.
        p.   cm.
    Originally published: London : Kogan Page, 2002.
    Includes index.
    ISBN 0-8144-0776-5
    1. Management.   I. Title.

⌐HD31.O846   2003
    658'.003—dc21

                                                            2002155252

Printing number

10   9   8   7   6   5   4   3   2   1

To Gaie and Toby
Without whom, nothing

Contents

Acknowledgments   ix

Introduction   xi

A   1

An Age of Ambiguity. Agreement and Argument;
Alliances; Alphabet Soup; Altitude Sickness; Annual
Performance Appraisals; Association with Success;
Attrition Is Good; Averages and the Drunkard

B   14

Baselines and the Fallacy of Forecasting; Baselines and the
Salvation of Management; Battles; Benchmarking;
Bluffing; Boards and Executive Committees; Botched Jobs
and Blame; Boundaries; Branding; Budgets; Budget Codes;
Business Schools

C   27

Calculators; Change; Claims to Fame; The Client Rule;
Commercial Confidentiality; Committees; Competitive
Advantage for the Twenty-First Century; Competitive
Intelligence: Use It or Lose It; Compounding; Computer
Abuse; Conferences: The Survival Guide; Consultants;
Contracts; Control, Compliance, and Commitment;
Corruption, Bribery, and Skulduggery; Cost Cutting: The
Soldier's Boots; Cost Saving: The Red Dollar Syndrome;
Courtesy; Culture, Crabs, and the Death of the Tea Lady;
Customer Loyalty and the Moment of Truth; Customers
for Profits; Customer Research: Lies and Statistics;
Customer Service: Living with Reality; Customer Service
Lines and Contempt for the Customer

Contents _____

D   61

Delegation, Empowerment, and Deception; Democracy
and Dictatorship at Work; Diversity; Dress, Schizophrenia,
and the Caste System; Due Diligence

E   66

Easy Does It; E-Business: The Master and the Servant;
Emotional Cycle of Change and the Valley of Death;
Enthusiasm; Entrepreneurs, Business, and the Pact with
the Devil; Entropy and Excellence; Excess Capacity;
Excuses; Expatriates; Eyes of Management

F   77

Financial Accounting: The Road to Irrelevance; Financial
Accounting: Roads to Riches and Ruin; Flat Organizations,
Flat Results; Forecasting and Experts; Frequent Flyers

G   84

Glory and Lies: The Annual Report; Grass Is Greener on
the Other Side of the Fence; Guarantees: Promises and Lies

H   90

Headhunters; Head Office; Herd Instincts; Honest
Feedback; Humor and the Sense of Humor Test; Hustle:
Controlling Your Destiny

I   100

Information Inflation: Back to the Future; IT Consultants:
The Builder's Brick; IT: Intermediate Technology;
Innovation: Winning Without Fighting; Investing to Lose;
"-Ists"

J   107

Japan: Learning to Eat Sushi and Conquer the World; Job
Descriptions Versus the Psychological Contract

K   109

Killing Ideas; Knowledge Management

L   113

Language; Lawyers and the Revolution; Leadership;
Learning, Mistakes, and the B.S. Detector; Lies; Luck

M   **120**

Management: Who Is in Charge?; Management
Accounting: Death and Reincarnation; Management by
Walking Away; Management Information Systems; Mars
Bars, Utility, and the Salesperson; Meetings: The Good,
The Bad and the Ugly; Mergers and Acquisitions; The
Midas Touch; Multinationals and Multilocals; Myths of
Management

N   **135**

Negotiate to Win; New Economy Blues

O   **137**

Offices: Form Follows Function; One-Way Options;
Organization Charts; Overpay People

P   **143**

Pareto Principle; Parkinson's Law; Perfect Predators;
Planning Heaven and Hell; Political Correctness; Power
Games; Presentations; Pricing; Professionals and
Pyramids; Professors and the One-Night Stand; Project
Management; Punks, Hippies, Experts, and the Future

Q   **170**

Quality Zealots; Quick-Fix Fixation

R   **174**

Rational, Political, and Emotional Management;
Recruiting; Reengineering Reengineering; Required Rates
of Return; Resisting Insanity; Respect for the Individual;
Revenge; Reviewing Documents: The Art of Reading; Risk
and the Middle Layer; Rushing and Relaxing

S   **184**

Salaries and Secrets; Seagull Management; Secretaries;
Sell-By Dates: When to Move On; Selling; Sex and Drugs
and Rock and Roll; Shakespeare and Management; Sheriffs
and Cowboys; Skills: Stuff and People; Sorry; Spend,
Spend, Spend; Staff and the Masters of the Universe;
Status; Stewardship and Values; Strategy: War and Peace;
Stress Is Good

T   **202**

Team Players; Teflon-Coated Management: Turning Losses
into Investment; Teleworking: Myth and Reality; Thank-

Contents _____

You; Thinking; Time: Activity, Efficiency, and
Effectiveness; Titles; Training Versus Experience; The Trust
Equation

U   **215**
Understanding and Paraphrasing; Unfair Competition;
Unreasonable Management; Upward Management

V   **220**
Venting; Victimless Crimes; Vision Statements

W   **224**
What Do You Do?; Why Work?; Wishful Thinking;
Working Hours; Writing Skills

X   **229**
Theories X, Y, and Z

Y   **231**
Ygwyd; The Yogi and the Commissar

Z   **233**
Zones of Comfort and Discomfort

Summary   **235**

Index   **237**

Acknowledgments

We all learn from experience. This is to thank all of the organizations with which I have worked. Some I have worked with for days, others for years. But from all of them, I have learned something. I hope they got something out of it as well.

AIG
American Express
Accenture
Apple Computers
Armstrong Industries
Barclays Bank
BT (British Telecom)
Chase Group
Citibank
Cap Gemini
Diatech
Halifax
Hallmark Cards
HCA (Health Care Assoc.)
ICI (Imperial Chemical Industries)
ItoChu
Lloyds Bank
Merita Nordbanken
Merrill Lynch
MetLife
Mitsubishi Chemicals

Monsanto
NCB (National Commercial Bank)
National Air Traffic Service
NatWest
Netfoods
Norwegian Dairy Association
Peoples Choice
Philips
Procter & Gamble
Royal Sun Alliance
SABIC (Saudi Arabian Basic Industries Corp.)
SDP (Social Democratic Party, UK)
San Miguel
SWIFT
Teach First
Thorn rental
UBS (Union Bank of Switzerland)
Union Carbide
ZFS (Zurich Financial Services)

Aside from the many companies who have tolerated my presence, I would also like to thank those who have made this book possible. There are those exceptional individuals from whom I have learned so much: Professor Chan Kim at INSEAD, Professors Philip Kotler and Bob Duncan at Kellogg, and James Kelly and John Rolander at the MAC Group. Without Tony Johnson, who inspired this book, Frances Kelly who advocated it, and Hiromi, who endures my ramblings and rantings, there would have been nothing.

To everyone, my thanks for their support and my apologies for any faults, which are all mine.

Introduction

Managers the world over face the same problems. Bad meetings, boring presentations, political intrigue, difficult bosses, and unhelpful staff plague them. They are caught in the crossfire of unreasonable goals with inadequate resources, complex organizations, and an uncertain and changing outside world. Somehow managers are meant to make sense of this.

And yet, there is no training or guidance on how to deal with the problems that managers face. It is simply assumed that managers know instinctively how to run good meetings, how to write well, how to deal with the thousand tricky situations that crop up in the managerial year.

In the end, managers serve an informal apprenticeship where they learn from the successes and failures of all those around them. After some years, they end up with a model of how they think their world works and how they can survive in it.

The good news is that those patterns of success and failure are common to all managers in all industries. There is no single rule of success. Instead, there are a thousand small things that a manager can do right or wrong every day.

This book draws on 20 years' experience of serving different industries across the world to map out what consistently does, and does not, work in the situations managers face. It is not a grand theory of management. It is a practical guide to survival in the managerial world.

AN AGE OF AMBIGUITY

It used to be so simple: managers managed, workers worked. Thinking and doing were separate. People may not have liked it, but at least they knew where they were. Now, no one knows where he or she stands.

We work in a high-commitment but family-friendly environment. Passion is in, but loyalty is out. We have gigabytes of data, but no useful information. Organizations are flat, but we are now matrixed to two bosses where the old hierarchy gave us just one. We are meant to be empowered, but we have more reporting than ever. We are meant to be entrepreneurial, but are not meant to fail. It's not even clear what we are meant to wear. Conformity of the suit has been replaced by confusion of choice. The gurus have all the answers, but all the answers are different. No one knows the problem.

For the brave, ambiguity is great. It creates opportunities to ignore the rules, break the rules, change the rules as it suits. The brave enjoy career acceleration: they succeed fast or fail fast. For the rest of us, we are left searching for the few rocks of certainty and stability that we can call our own as the revolution gathers around us. This book is a survival guide for the revolution.

AGREEMENT AND ARGUMENT

Agreement is easy, and dangerous. Excessive agreement is positively unhealthy. Human nature dislikes conflict, so agreement is often the easy way out even when there is disagreement. The disagreement only becomes apparent after the meeting when people are chatting around the coffee machine. This is the wrong time to start the disagreement.

Excessive agreement is dangerous because:

- It rarely represents the best solution. When everyone agrees without discussion, this normally shows deference to the hierarchy or lack of interest rather than enthusiastic support.
- It fosters cynicism. The real discussion and disagreement starts outside the meeting.
- It wastes time: if the real opposition and discussion start outside the meeting, then huge effort has to be displaced to round up all the dissident ideas and deal with them.
- It reinforces hierarchy: that bosses tell and staff do, may have worked 50 years ago, but not today. An effective organization is one in which bosses do not have to pretend to have a monopoly on wisdom.
- It represents a postdated check for someone. Once something is agreed, it normally implies a next step or outcome for someone else. If it's you, be ready to have the check cashed.

Clearly, some organizations are more prone to the plague of agreement than others. Traditional, hierarchical organizations like government agencies and insurance companies are the worst. In creative industries, sometimes getting agreement on the day of the week is a challenge.

The main challenge is how to encourage positive discussion in which disagreement is seen as helpful, rather than disloyal. Both boss and staff are responsible for changing behavior. The boss has to signal that discussion is good, and to reinforce those signals both in private and in public.

For the staff member, the challenge is to frame the disagreement positively, so that it is not an objection but is supportive. Two habits help. First, state benefits (what you like about the idea) before concerns. This helps show you have listened to and understood the idea. Then, state the concerns as "how to." Instead of: "That's bloody stupid, we can't afford it," try "How do we build the financial case for this?" The same concern, but at least in the second case you are hinting that you could be part of the solution, not just part of the problem.

ALLIANCES

From the day we start our careers, we are forming alliances. A large part of the art of middle management is alliance making: successful managers know instinctively how to build, sustain, and leverage alliances across the organization.

Alliance building becomes more important as organizations become more complex, more matrixed, and less hierarchical. This means that most middle managers do not have the resources or authority to achieve their goals. And they cannot rely on the hierarchy to force other parts of the organization into cooperation.

In building alliances we are always either creating personal equity (helping someone else) or using personal equity (receiving help from someone else). It is worthwhile trying to keep a reasonably positive balance of equity: someone who always needs help and never gives it is a pain in the backside.

Ultimately, alliances rely on trust. There is a simple formula for thinking about trust: $T = (S \times C)/R$ where:

- T = Trust.
- S = Shared goals and interests. The more you have common interests, the more likely you are to be able to collaborate.
- C = Credibility. This is the credibility and the ability of both alliance partners to deliver on their commitments. There is no point in allying with someone who shares your goals, talks a great talk, but never delivers.
- R = Risk. The greater the risk, the more difficult it is to gain someone else's trust. Most alliances build up slowly through mutual help on small things. Where this has not happened before, working hard at taking away the risk, the time, and the effort that your proposed alliance partner has to expend makes all the difference between getting cooperation or not.

Never mistake alliances for friendship. Remember the dictum of British foreign policy when Britannia ruled the waves: "Great Britain has no friends: it only has some common interests." In other words, as soon as your interests diverge, it becomes increasingly difficult to hold together an alliance.

ALPHABET SOUP

The World of Jargon

Managers have forgotten how to speak or write English. In its place there has been an eruption of TLAs (Three-Letter Abbreviations), MLAs (Multi-Letter Abbreviations) and jargon.

In theory, jargon is shorthand that simplifies communication. In practice, it does not. It is used to differentiate insiders from outsiders. One retail chain refuses to refer to any of its branches by their location. Instead, it refers to the branch numbers, which only managers know. So if you don't know why 147 (West 48th Street) is outperforming 67 (East 96th Street), you do not belong to us.

Jargon is also used to impart a false sense of sophistication to the speaker: "Our P6MA at 95 on an msu basis is off the Q3 G7 forecast" sounds more sophisticated than: "We blew it: sales volume in the last six months is down 5 percent against the September forecast for the board."

Ban jargon. Force people to speak English and you may find out what they mean.

The Recipe for Success

The challenge of this game is simple. Pick any letter of the alphabet, and any number between one and seven. Then find a management theory for both the letter and the number, and use it to show how it will fundamentally transform the performance of the business. Try this a few times and you will find it is easy to be convincing. Do it well and you can become a consultant. Do it very well and you can become a partner and use the techniques to sell anything to clients.

There are nearly an infinite number of MLAs and TLAs for the management theory alphabet. Here is one version:

The Management Alphabet

▪ ABC. Activity-Based Costing. A way for consultants to make a lot of money by telling you that you are losing lots of money where you did not realize it.

▪ B2C, B2B. Business to Consumer: a fast way for venture capitalists to lose money in the dot-com world. Business to Business: a slow way for venture capitalists to lose money. When it all ends in tears it becomes Back to Banking and Back to Consulting for the dot-com managers.

▪ CRM. Customer Relationship Management. Consultants are very good at this, which is why you will pay them a lot of money to find out about it. Do not be deceived: CRM is not about customers, but about building vast computer files, which will tell you at vast expense what a chat with your customers would tell you in five minutes.

- DCF. Discounted Cash Flow analysis. A way of projecting the value of future cash flows. Normally used to justify making large short-term losses in favor of even larger long-term gains. Used well, this justifies lousy short-term performance, which will earn you a transfer before someone else is left to fulfill the postdated check of the big returns that have been promised. Can be used to justify CRM: big up-front expense followed by strictly theoretical results later.

- ERP. Enterprise Resource Planning. You pay a lot of money to consultants to come and take over your business.

- FTF. First Things First, one of the seven habits of highly effective people. Common sense, which will make you a star if you use it. Most people apparently put second and third things first.

- GIGO. Garbage In, Garbage Out. Applied to computers. Not a defense when disaster strikes as you obey some insane new management instruction. You should achieve GIEO: Garbage In, Excellence Out.

- HR. Human Resources. The only way to retaliate is to insist on still calling them Personnel. Watch them climb up the wall—and then fire you.

- IT. Information Technology in theory, Intermediate Technology in practice. The rate of obsolescence is so fast that management spend a fortune to catch up, only to find that after the three-year systems program is implemented, it represents a design at least three years out of date.

- JIT. Just In Time. All the rage when we thought that Japan would rule the world. Past its sell-by date. We are on to the next fad.

- KM. Knowledge Management. Another fad. Businesses coped by appointing knowledge czars: this absolved the rest of the organization from having to do anything about it. A harmless way of dealing with surplus management capacity.

- LIFO. Last In, First Out. Accounting tool for valuing stocks, and an HR tool for identifying who they will fire first.

- MBWA. Management By Wandering Around, extolled as a great route to excellence in *In Search of Excellence*. Management by walking away is better: it's called delegation and lets people get on with what they need to.

- NLP. Neuro Linguistic Programming, a way of using language to make people agree to things they should not agree to. But they feel good about it afterwards.

- OVA. Overhead Value Analysis. Overhead Value is an oxymoron.

OVA is a sophisticated way of reducing the amount you spend on overhead by spending a lot on consultants, who believe they are not overhead.

▪ P2P. Path to Profitability. This normally takes the shape of a deep hockey stick, which shows deep investment (losses) turning into profit. Management excels at fulfilling the first part of the hockey stick.

▪ QFD: Quality Function Deployment. A bureaucratic method of making sure that you get the wrong product to the wrong market at the wrong time, but that it will be technically excellent anyway.

▪ R. Four Rs of transformation: Restructuring, Renewing, Reframing, and Revitalizing. Otherwise known as an invitation for the consultants to come in and take over.

▪ SI–CC. Strategic Intent–Core Competence. Linked concepts that encourage businesses to stretch for the outrageously impossible. Everyone gets very excited for a few days dreaming the impossible. Then they realize it is impossible and return to business as usual.

▪ TQM. Total Quality Management: a triumph of process over results or relevance. Dangerous in the hands of zealots.

▪ USP. Unique Selling Proposition, also known as the better mousetrap proposition. Rarely found, and when it is found it is normally beaten by more ruthless competitors (Apple/Windows, Betamax/VHS, Broad Gauge/Standard Gauge).

▪ VR. Virtual Reality. Another name for CVs or résumés.

▪ WYSIWYG, pronounced "whizzywig." Around 1985, technologists made the astonishing discovery that when people are word processing they like What You See Is What You Get, not unintelligible gobbledegook. Management is still unsure if this principle should be applied to how they operate.

▪ Theories X, Y, and Z. Theory X takes you to the rationalist school of the time and motion men, theory Y takes you to the woolly sweater brigade examining your early childhood, Z integrates the two and finishes you off.

Managing by Numbers

Management theory in practice rarely gets beyond seven. Anything more than seven is too long to remember and too complicated to implement:

1. One-minute management.
2. Any two-by-two matrix, limited only by imagination. Try portfolio

analysis: prescribes where the CEO should be investing and divesting. If every CEO uses it, then the entire industry heads in the same direction and disaster ensues. At which point the consultants come in again to tell you where you went wrong, without mentioning the portfolio analysis they did for you.

3. The three Cs of marketing: Customers, Channels, and Competition. As with all good marketing people they omit the fourth C: Costs.

4. The four Ps of marketing: Product, Price, Promotion, and Place. Do not ask the marketing person to reconcile the four Ps and the three Cs: this will spoil a beautifully presented pitch.

5. Structure in fives (Mintzberg). Brilliant work on the organization, which has five parts: strategic apex, middle line, operating core, technostructure, and support staff. Nobody understands the theory, but everyone implements it in practice.

6. Six sigma quality: applied to the production of microchips and payment processing systems, which need to be fault-free. Normal managers struggle to achieve one sigma quality.

7. The seven habits of highly effective people. This is for much more sophisticated people than the one-minute manager: there are seven things to remember and do, not one. Most used by junior and middle management who are likely to stay that way.

ALTITUDE SICKNESS

This is a common management disease. Likely victims are junior managers getting exposed to senior management for the first time, or middle managers who find that they have been promoted higher than they can survive. The common symptoms include:

- Dumbstruck incoherence, followed by a flood of babble.
- Inappropriate dress, body language, and jokes.
- Presentations made by talking entirely to the screen, not to management.
- A complete failure to make any sensible contribution to the debate.

There are only three known remedies for this disease:

1. Proceed immediately back down the corporate mountain. You will find it easier to breathe. Once back down again, you will have three further choices:

- Rest while waiting to tackle the summit again (see options 2 and 3).
- Find another mountain to climb.
- Settle for a gentle life in the foothills of management.

2. Clone yourself: copy senior management and be like them. This is the most certain way to succeed, although it may involve selling your soul to the devil and having a brain transplant. The best way to achieve this is:

   - Find a sherpa who can guide you up the mountain. This will be a senior manager who will act as your sponsor. Senior managers like to play the sponsor role for good people: it appeals to their vanity. It gives them some good lieutenants on whom they can rely—and exploit.
   - Find out what is on the agenda of senior management. Mold your work to fit the agenda of the senior managers, make sure it has relevance and impact to them.
   - Find out the rules of the club: dress, language, body language. Senior managers preach diversity, but value intimacy. They want to deal with people they feel they can trust and understand. In other words, they want to deal with people like themselves. If you are a fat, 50-something white male this is easy. If you are a 30-year-old black female, this is tough. At crunch time, senior managers do not walk the talk on diversity.

3. Be true to yourself. This is the riskiest route. The chances of success may be the lowest, but the impact you can make will be the greatest if you are able to stick to your strengths. By definition, most great leaders are not ordinary people, but people who had the courage to follow their own path. Napoleon came from humble beginnings. Churchill spent many years in the wilderness until his finest hour came. It requires real talent at what you do, persistence, and luck. But you do retain your soul, whether you win, lose, or draw.

ANNUAL PERFORMANCE APPRAISALS

These are often exercises in equivocation. People do not like hurting other people's feelings, so the euphemisms and code words come flooding out. You need a cryptographer to find out what is really meant.

The result is disaster. The reviewee does not understand his or her position, does not understand what is really required in terms of future development. They are being set up for failure and disappointment, which will be all the worse when it comes because it will be a surprise to them. Meanwhile, promotion and bonus decisions become arcane exercises in trying to decipher what all the different evaluations mean. Different reviewers have different degrees of equivocation.

The truth only comes out when all the reviewers are sat in a room together and are asked exactly what they thought of all the reviewees. Here are some translations of the more common review comments:

- Outstanding performance: the reviewee saved the reviewer's butt on several occasions during the period in review.
- Above average performance: average performance.
- Average performance: barely acceptable performance. Ninety-five percent of staff always land up being average or above. Mathematically impossible, politically and emotionally inevitable.
- Below average performance: who hired this turkey?
- A challenging year: catastrophic performance, but I do not want to say so.
- Development challenges: no chance of developing or progressing.
- Needs to develop analytical skills: reviewee does not have a brain.
- Analytically outstanding: smarter than the reviewer.
- Needs to develop interpersonal skills: I never want this person on my team again.
- Strong interpersonal skills: political snake oil salesperson.

The list goes on forever. The question is how to avoid it. There are two responses. First, oblige reviewers to live with the consequences of their decisions. As long as staff and management are constantly being shuffled, the chances are that a reviewer will not have responsibility for a reviewee for long. That means that nasty problems can be shuffled off onto the next manager. In the meantime, the manager can focus on promoting the great performers, which makes everyone feel happy. Or, secondly, shift performance appraisals away from the traditional good/bad or below/above average evaluation. The very nature of these evaluations creates conflict and tension: it is difficult to tell another human being they are no good or below average. It is a judgment that invites denial and hostility, which does not move anyone forward.

There is an alternative. Map out the typical time it takes for some-one to progress to the next stage in their career, be it three, five or seven years. Show what sorts of skills, responsibilities and accom-plishments need to be achieved as the person progresses. Then assess their skills and performance in terms of progression, not an absolute good/bad judgment. No one who has just been promoted minds being told that their performance is consistent with someone who has only been one year into a five-year career step. The same person, just promoted, would be mortified to hear that their performance is below average. In performance terms, both messages say the same thing, but with radically different results. The growth maturity evaluation looks something like this:

Performance level

Criteria:	New	Developing	Maturing	Mature
interpersonal skills		x		
leadership		x		
analytical skills			x	
presentations	x			
sales results		x		
others . . .				

If this individual has been around a while, the messages would be clear, positive, and constructive about where he or she is strong and where he or she needs to develop. Note that most of the marks are in what would be a "below average" column if the individual were being judged against everyone at their level. The development approach works because:

■ It is less confrontational than the good/bad approach.
■ It is more constructive: you end up with an agenda about what to do about going forward.
■ It gives the reviewer a fighting chance of being honest and the re-viewee a fighting chance of being able to listen without too much angst.
■ It gives a good picture of who is ready for promotion and when. And if someone is not developing, it gives clear signals about who is at risk and why.

Even if the formal performance appraisal system is the good/bad one, using the development approach informally with reviewees will help build trust and understanding on both sides.

ASSOCIATION WITH SUCCESS

Beware of people who are associated with success. They will have a long list of successful initiatives with which they have been associated. What they really mean, is that at some point they offered some advice. It may or may not have been used, helpful, or positive but it was enough for them to then claim that they were associated with the initiative if it was a success. If it was a failure, then they can either claim that they were not responsible for it, or that the turkey who was responsible for it did not follow their advice. They have set themselves up with a win-win situation every time.

Of course, they have made zero contribution to the organization. They mainly exist in flat organizations where it is possible for people to jump on and off passing bandwagons at ease. All the risk lies with the person actually leading the bandwagon. If the leader succeeds, all his or her passengers will claim credit, if it fails they will all point the finger of blame at the leader. The only solutions are:

- Go back to a traditional functional hierarchy where responsibilities are clearer and hiding is more difficult.
- Set very clear MBO (Management By Objectives) criteria and enforce them.
- Kneecap anyone who claims to be "associated" with success. They either put themselves on the line, or they did not. Find out which is which.

ATTRITION IS GOOD

Planned headcount attrition is good, at all levels of the business. It keeps the corporate gene pool fresh, it keeps the performance bar high within the business, and it enables the business to manage changes in the shape and volume of demand smoothly.

The question is how to manage attrition effectively. Having seen it done spectacularly badly, the attrition disasters give some idea of how not to do it—and by implication, how it could be done. How not do it:

▪ Set a high, fixed attrition rate and force-rank everyone. Automatically lose those in the bottom 20 percent. It keeps the performance bar high, and it is a great way of encouraging competition, politics, and paranoia among those subject to the force ranking. And it encourages arrogance among those who survive.

▪ Set a low attrition rate that represents no more than natural wastage. If this is the case, the performance bar is not being maintained. The chances are that good people are leaving and average people are arriving.

▪ Exclude senior managers from the attrition targets. Encourage complacency, create an "us and them" set of rules, ensure that the gene pool of senior managers is not refreshed. Not smart.

▪ Have a single target for planned and unplanned attrition. Do not track the unplanned losses or the reasons for the losses. This is a good way to ensure that there is no useful information to manage performance or to minimize unplanned attrition.

▪ Have a weak performance appraisal system. This causes double chaos. It denies management any rational basis for making decisions, which will increasingly look political and irrational to outsiders. It fails to manage expectations of the individual. With a good evaluation system, the individual will see the way the wind is blowing and will jump, with plenty of goodwill all around, before being pushed involuntarily. The weak system leads to surprises and unenforceable decisions with the lack of data. It is also an invitation to legal action.

AVERAGES AND THE DRUNKARD

Statistics lie. Managers use statistics the way a drunk uses a lamp post: for support rather than illumination. Of all statistics, the average is the best liar. It sounds so reasonable that few want to question it. But any statistic that is an average or refers to an average should be questioned and challenged. Normally, a lie will be discovered lurking behind the average. The most common average lies are:

▪ People's performance relative to the average. In every consulting firm, about 95 percent of the staff are rated as "above average" performers. The remaining 5 percent are fired. Statistically, this is impossible, unless the benchmark is the general population, which is useless. Clearly, "above average" performance ratings make for an easy evaluation for the reviewer, and keeps the reviewee happy. But it simply stores up trouble when it comes to promotions and bonuses. Forced rankings at least create some clarity and help decision making. In a forced ranking, half the reviewees will be below average, and about half will be above. This clarifies where the performance bar is.

- Investment performance. Look at the financial pages of any paper. One hundred percent of the advertisements for established funds will claim above average performance. There is some self-selection in this: successful funds advertise, unsuccessful ones do not. Although for the most part this has the perverse effect of encouraging investors to move into asset types just as they hit their peak after a long run of outperformance: new investors can then look forward to a long period of underperformance. Above average performance is claimed by creative benchmarking of assets (versus bonds, cash, other markets) and over creative periods (6 months to 20 years). Most funds can claim overperformance by fudging the reference.

- Customer satisfaction. Customers always try to be nice in customer surveys. Satisfaction is only rated below average if it is truly awful. Even "average" performance normally reflects fairly deep dissatisfaction. These surveys can lull management into a false sense of security.

Averages are less useful to management than exceptions. The average consumer is probably 50 percent men and 50 percent women. This misleads. The exceptions are where both the insight and the money can be found. The customers who leave, or rejoin, or are particularly inactive or particularly active say more about what we are doing right or wrong than the average.

And it is the exceptions that are profitable. Procter & Gamble launched a toilet soap with a very strong fragrance. On average, it got a poor reception and some people hated it because of the fragrance. Then there were the exceptions: about 15 percent of the target market thought this soap and its fragrance was outstanding. They turned out to be very loyal customers willing to pay a high premium for the product.

BASELINES AND THE FALLACY OF FORECASTING

The fallacy of forecasting is based on the stable, historic baseline. The assumed baseline for next year's performance is last year's performance with some sort of historical trend extrapolated into the future. For a laugh, look at a five-year plan from five years ago. Its projections for today will bear no resemblance to the reality of today, unless you are a monopoly in a static industry.

Part of the problem comes from unpredictable external shocks, from the Internet, through takeovers, government intervention, and recessions. Inability to forecast these shocks is excusable. The purpose of scenario planning is to give a basis for looking at such shocks.

The greater part of the problem comes from assuming that current performance can be maintained without special management action. This is nonsense. The true baseline for any business is one of rapidly deteriorating performance. The reasons for this are obvious:

■ Operationally, everything tends to slide towards chaos. Anyone who has worked in a store sees how quickly displays, stock, and prices go awry. In professional service firms the constant loss of experienced talent and the introduction of inexperienced talent means that just maintaining the overall skills level is a major challenge.

■ The competition, on average, is likely to be as smart as you. Certainly, basing a plan on the assumption that they are stupid is unwise. And yet, this is the implicit assumption in most plans. They assume that the profit improvement program, cost savings, and new marketing plan will all lead to cost savings and share improvements. Then there is surprise when they don't. Somehow, the competition has a way of cutting costs and prices and creating marketing programs at the same rate as you do. Any successes tend to be short-lived.

- External pressures are rarely benign. Customers do not volunteer to pay higher prices, suppliers do not offer lower prices, employees do not work for less, and, for every dollar the government gives, it will take away another three.

Given this, any performance baseline must be assumed to be negative. In the extreme, over four years one company achieved cost savings equivalent to four times its profits. Over those four years, its profits declined. Clearly, without the cost savings the business would have been in dire straits, but the pace of change was nothing like what management had hoped for.

The only time that management understands the nature of the declining baseline is when it comes to setting budgets. At budget time management becomes expert at predicting all the problems and disasters that justify having a very low profit and revenue commitment, supported by an extraordinary increase in resources. Suddenly the stable baseline becomes the famous hockey stick. Normally management can deliver on the downward element of the hockey stick.

BASELINES AND THE SALVATION OF MANAGEMENT

This is the oldest trick in the book. Whenever you are given a new responsibility, dig out every last bit of dirt and disaster that you have inherited. Paint the bleakest picture possible of all the chaos you have inherited, of a business or project that is about to spin out of control and suffer fatal setbacks and losses. From there on, any performance will look like a relative improvement on the appalling situation you apparently inherited.

Conversely, your predecessor will have tried to stress how the business has been brought to the cusp of a breakthrough and everything is poised for the most sensational success. If this version of history is the accepted one, you are dead meat. You will struggle to fulfill what your predecessor has promised. If you do achieve it, it will be because of the groundwork of your predecessor. If you do not achieve it, it will be because you are a turkey. You cannot win, and the only surprises will be nasty.

This game playing is not just for scheming middle managers. Watch how often a change of CEO is followed shortly by results that include major provisions, write-offs and exceptional items. Done early, the CEO can implicitly blame it all on the previous regime. At the same time, the new CEO builds himself financial wriggle room against unforeseen disasters, like poor leadership from the CEO.

BATTLES

Corporate battles are a way of life. The most vicious battles are not between businesses, they are within the business. One department battling against another for resources. One manager against another, battling for recognition and promotion. The challenge for a manager is knowing which battles to fight and when. There are three rules to picking a fight. These rules are variously attributed to Admiral Nelson and to Sun Tsu. They are:

- Only fight if there is a prize worth fighting for. Don't fight over whether the coffee machine should be free of charge or not. Better to make your point and graciously concede. Don't waste personal capital on it.
- Only fight if you know you can win. In Wall Street, if you don't know who the fall guy is, you are. In corporate battles, if you don't know who the loser will be, you are. In other words, if you don't know if you can win, you will lose. This means that most battles are won and lost before they are fought. You must know before you start whether you have lined up all the political alliances and support, as well as the rational arguments, to win.
- Only fight if there is no other way of winning. If possible, give your opponents a way out. Don't back them into a corner where they are forced to fight. There is no point in incurring all the damage that a fight, even a victory, brings if you can avoid it. Remember, once a battle is fought and lost you have probably acquired an enemy for life.

People who fight battles too often and too obviously, eventually lose. And when they do, there will be no shortage of enemies waiting to come out of the woodwork and apply the *coup de grâce*. At the other extreme, avoiding all battles results in the agreement plague and very weak management.

BENCHMARKING

Benchmarking is better in theory than in practice. In theory, benchmarking helps identify where you are relative to competition, and can help guide and focus remedial action. In practice, it suffers severe challenges:

- Benchmarking results are totally deniable. At one large electronics group, benchmarking showed that they were hopelessly uncompetitive with Asian competition. The reaction was not to sort the problem, but to challenge the data. The essential argument was, you had to equalize the data; to allow for different accounting treatments, product specifications and product mix, different exchange rates, and so on. Ultimately, the agument was that if the competition was the same as us, it would have the same benchmark data as us. Logically true but practically useless. Meanwhile the business was hammered in the marketplace.
- Getting good benchmark data is difficult, unless competition cooperate in syndicated research—or you have excellent industrial espionage.
- Any strategy that is focused on catching up with competition is doomed to failure. By the time you get to where they were at the time of the benchmarking, they have already moved ahead. You never catch up, you are always in catch-up mode. Equally, if the data shows that you are ahead of competition, that will not be a call to arms: it will be a call to complacency.

At best, benchmarking can be a call to arms to mobilize the organization into making major change fast. At worst it is a charter for consultants to make money, and for management to plunge into arcane debate about the data while losing focus on the business. Benchmarking should be treated less as an intellectual analytical tool, and more as part of a process of mobilizing and focusing management.

BLUFFING

Never let someone bluff you. If they try it, call their bluff every time. Bluffing is just a power game. The moment you give in, you have lost. Typical bluffs worth calling include:

- "You must accept this job offer by Friday, or it will be withdrawn." Do you want to work for a company that bullies people even before they have joined? If they really want you, they will come back again.
- "If I don't get a 20 percent raise, I'll resign." Do you want the organization to discover that this is how salaries are negotiated? Even if the individual merits 20 percent, give 19 percent. Let them decide what to do.
- "If you don't change your decision, I'll take it up with the CEO." Pick up the phone and arrange the meeting with the CEO. If you are right, they will back down before you have gotten through. If you are wrong, you should not have made the decision in the first place.

BOARDS AND EXECUTIVE COMMITTEES

Boards and executive committees suffer from the plague of agreement, although for different reasons. At board level, too many non-executives are there because they are thought to be prestigious. These non-executives may be good for the corporate image; they are not good for corporate governance.

Effective corporate governance comes better from business practitioners: existing CEOs or senior directors of other businesses who have practical experience of running things. Someone who has chaired lots of prestigious public committees is unlikely to be ideally placed to understand the dynamics of running a rapidly evolving investment bank, retailer, or technology company.

Within the board meeting, there is great reluctance to challenge the executive too strongly. Partly, this is because it is "not the done thing" to rock the boat. But partly, it is because unqualified non-executives—who have no performance measures, no incentive compensation, no boss who evaluates their performance, and in many cases no experience of running things—do not feel well positioned to challenge effectively. All too often, the challenge to a chief executive comes far too late for the company, and the CEO only hears about it from a whispering campaign, which may surface in the press.

Executive committees also suffer the plague of excessive agreement. There is an unwritten rule in all executive committees: "I will not pee on your turf if you do not pee on mine." This mutual non-peeing contract is reinforced by the lack of expertise that each committee member has in regard to other committee members' responsibilities. In functional organizations, the marketing people do not understand technology and vice versa. In geographic organizations, the Europeans do not understand the Asian market and the Asians do not understand the American market.

In practice, this renders most executive committees useless. They rubber-stamp decisions. This is not necessarily bad, if the CEO has put in place an effective decision-making process outside the executive committee. But it puts huge pressure on the CEO. He or she is the only person in the organization who balances all the interest groups in the business. It also makes the business heavily dependent on getting the right CEO. It does not help with the process of developing and identifying the successor to the existing CEO, if the leadership team is based on functional silos.

BOTCHED JOBS AND BLAME

As long as there are people, there are botched jobs. Every bungle results in a vicious game called pin the blame. There is a hunt to find a victim, and to ensure that the blame is pinned elsewhere than on your own doorstep. This is natural: no one wants to wear the managerial equivalent of the dunce's cap.

Weak managers happily play the blame game. It is a way of ducking responsibility and simplifying, shuffling off a problem. But a witch hunt hardly helps improve levels of trust and cooperation among managers.

Strong managers do not play the blame game. They recognize that it is destructive to individuals and counterproductive to the business. When something goes wrong, it is normally a symptom of some more systemic problem in the organization. The hunt should focus on what went wrong with the system that enabled this fault to occur. By looking at the system first, not the individual, the hunt is depersonalized and managers have a fighting chance of finding out what actually happened, instead of being met with a wall of political fog and obfuscation. Once management knows what happened, it can then act to stop a reoccurrence.

Strong managers will also stand up when the fault lies in their own backyard. By standing up, the rest of the organization breathes a huge sigh of relief, and there is an implicit sense of gratitude for letting other people associated with the botched job off the hook. If the manager reports to enlightened senior managers, this act of statesmanship will tend to strengthen, not weaken, the manager. Provided the mistake is not fatal and does not occur again.

The message of this is simple: when there is a botched job, blame the system not the person. That way the business can learn and improve.

BOUNDARIES

Clear organization boundaries are essential for corporate success:

- Clear boundaries clarify roles and sharpen accountabilities. There is nowhere to hide. Everyone knows what they are meant to do. The ambiguities of flat organizations are eliminated.
- Clear hierarchy clarifies and simplifies the decision-making process: authority levels are well understood.
- Costs and budgets are easily managed if they live in well-defined departmental buckets.
- Time and effort are not wasted in the countless internal meetings needed to coordinate the efforts of flat organizations.
- Functional expertise is encouraged.

Clear organization boundaries are a disaster in Twenty-First-century business:

- Strong boundaries mitigate against crossfunctional cooperation. Most business problems and processes flow across functions and need crossfunctional cooperation.
- Strong boundaries encourage departments to focus on their functional goals at the expense of broader business goals.
- Hierarchy boundaries send the wrong messages about delegation, trust, and empowerment and lead to slow decision making as decisions flow up and down the hierarchy.
- True costs and profitability are obscured by the departmental focus: costs are driven by activities that run across departments (order fulfillment, new account acquisition and setup). And customers, not just products, drive profitability.
- General management expertise is fostered by encouraging people to work with and across functions.

You pays your money, you makes your choice.

BRANDING

Be True to Yourself

Every product, business, and person is a brand. Some are good, some are not. Strong brands have a good product and good values, which are well communicated. The product and how it is communicated and developed have to fit. Strong brands know their franchise, know themselves, and remain true to themselves.

Product Branding in Action

Product branding started by manufacturers putting their logo on their products. Procter & Gamble put their moon and stars stamp on blocks of soap, which acted as a quality guarantee to customers. Traditional product branding remains true to this custom. The traditional brand will communicate three things:

- A distinctive performance benefit.
- A reason why consumers should believe they benefit.
- A character for the brand.

Confusing the message with multiple benefits, or changing the message, is disaster. For instance, the detergent Tide is meant to be exceptionally good at stain removal. Woolite is meant to be good for caring for delicate fabrics and colors. Mixing the messages so that Tide blasts out all known dirt while caring for delicate fabrics would have low credibility. The products have to stay true to themselves. In a crowded marketplace, consumers will not remember complex messages: they will remember one simple thing about each brand. Lifestyle brands such as Nike or Louis Vuitton lead on the character and values of the brand, allowing people to aspire to a desired identity through their choice of clothes. They both have products that support their lifestyle claims. Neither could credibly try to occupy the other brand's territory. They have to stay true to themselves.

Corporate Branding

Every business is a brand. Some are highly indistinct and are known more to the recruiting market or shareholder constituency. Some are visible in the consumer market. In the United Kingdom (and to some extent in the United States) Virgin stands for a set of values that include fun, trust, value for money, and an antiestablishment proconsumer perspective. This allows the Virgin brand to stretch widely across records, Internet portals, airlines, drinks, telecommunications, and even wedding dresses. It also opens up unlikely markets. The savings market is one where Virgin had no competence. But it was an industry where all the brands said the same thing: trust me, your savings will do better with us. The Virgin brand brought a genuinely trusted name into the industry. Married to the technical expertise of AMP, the Australian insurer it was able to build scale rapidly in the market.

Personal Branding

Like the product brand, we should be able to answer three questions:

- What is distinctive about our performance for the business?
- What is our distinctive capability?
- What is the character or style we wish to convey?

In a large organization, we will not be remembered for all the small things we do day to day. We will be remembered for one thing. Make sure it is the right thing. And we cannot be what we are not. We have to stay true to ourselves.

Branding and the Advertising Agency

Unfortunately, everyone is an expert at advertising. Because we all see so much advertising, we have strong views on what we like and what we dislike. Advertising is not about what we like or dislike. It is about what works. This is a message that both advertising agencies and clients forget. The agency focuses on winning creative awards, and the client uses his or her "person in the street" expertise to pronounce judgment based on what he or she likes. This is not a recipe for results. There are three ways of working with agencies:

- The chairperson's way.
- The expert way.
- The third way.

The Chairperson's Way

Never let the chairperson, or even the CEO, get involved in choosing the advertising. Of course, the CEO needs to be involved in developing the strategy. But the execution of the strategy is a professional job. As soon as the CEO gets involved, with the best of intentions, judgment goes out of the window and prejudice comes in. The agency has to focus on what will keep the CEO happy, not on what will work. This is demoralizing for the agency and will not get its best talent focused on the job.

The Expert Way

This is potentially even more demoralizing for the agency, and only one or two businesses can do it. P&G arguably knows more about successful detergent advertising than its advertising agencies do. And its brand managers are all trained in the P&G way of brand advertising. This means that the brand managers can, and often do, argue the agency into submission and despair. The agency loves the huge fees it generates from the P&G account, but everyone runs a mile from working with the company. The good news is that the advertising works. The bad news is that the public hates it and the agency hates developing it. For better or for worse, not many businesses can do this.

The Third Way

Management focuses on the strategy with the agency. This may require an annual off-site meeting with the agency, where you will have to drink copiously. Do not ask what the creative team is drinking. You will also have to endure people with loud clothes and opinions speaking a lot of psychobabble and asking a lot of impossible questions such as "Who are we?" "If we were a flower/car/historical figure/decade, what would we be?" "Who do we want to be?"

Amidst this fog there is some important stuff. It is about getting some insight about the brand and the business and how it will be presented to the market. It helps the advertising strategy and management think more broadly about what they are trying to do with the business.

Once the strategy is in place, let the agency get on with it. Do not challenge them over their creative execution strategy. Do not give them the benefit of your advice about what you do or do not like. Focus the challenge on two things. How will success be measured and tracked? (Do not give up on this one, however hard the agency tries to palm you off with irrelevant tracking studies.) Challenge on points of fact, such as when they use the wrong logo.

Otherwise, accept what they offer or change agencies. This puts all the pressure on them to create something that works. They will not be making advertising to keep you happy or to second-guess you. And you are more likely to get the best talent in the agency working on your account.

Finally, invest properly. An underfunded brand campaign is money thrown away: the message does not get enough exposure to be heard, understood, and acted on in a crowded marketplace. Achieving this takes time, money, patience, and a very consistent, simple message.

Brand Advertising: Fair and Unfair Questions

Unfair Questions

Any questions that are based on what you or your spouse or family would like.

Fair Questions

Avoid a big philosophical debate with the agency about these questions. The agency will blind you with babble, and you will only demoralize them. Check the points below to make sure that the agency has not gone completely off the wall:

- Is the advertising in line with the strategy? In other words, do you clearly get the message? For TV advertising try listening to the sound alone, and then watching the pictures alone. Both should be clear in their own right.
- Is the brand the hero of the advertising? One commercial shows Claudia Schiffer, the supermodel, in a provocative pose. I have no idea what the brand is. In this case the hero is the personality, not the brand.
- Is the message distinctive? If you put one of your competitors in place of your brand, would it still be credible? No one will confuse Nike and Benetton advertising: they know how to stay distinctive. Most financial service brands are wholly interchangeable.
- Is the content accurate (and legal)? This is important detail: right logos, right colors, right uniforms, right packaging, and right product.
- Does it fit with the rest of the marketing strategy? Everything should coordinate.

BUDGETS

Why waste 11 months a year trying to meet an ambitious budget? It is much easier to play hardball for one month a year and agree to an unambitious budget that can then be beaten with ease. Then watch the bonuses and promotions flow your way.

Ultimately, budgeting is political. It represents a contract between two parts of management to deliver certain results for certain resources. Depending where you are in the negotiating chain you either want to maximize results and minimize resources or vice versa. All the data that is brought to the budget process is simply ammunition for the different points of view. Like the drunk using the lamp post, the data is used for support, not illumination. An effective budget process achieves the following:

■ It represents a stretching, but achievable, goal for the business.
■ The budget process itself helps managers understand the priorities, risks, and opportunities for the business: it creates a common management view of the business.
■ It is a process of generating management commitment to a course of action and goals. Without achieving the commitment objective, the budget process will have failed.

Achieving a stretching but doable budget requires unreasonable management. Reasonable management will listen to all the arguments about why next year's performance will be tough. The result will be a soft budget and low performance. Unreasonable management sees top-down the "must have" performance imperatives and sticks to them. If this forces management to think creatively about how to improve performance, the budget process will have served some purpose.

The most common fallacy with the budget process is to let staff functions dominate it. Staff functions have value in adding up the numbers and providing an umpiring service to the budget process. But when they take over they cause more trouble than they are worth:

■ They obstruct the process of developing management commitment.
■ They wear the organization down by looking for far greater detail than is reasonably required for making a management judgment.
■ They end up justifying a job for themselves with endless rounds of budget revisions and forecasts through the year, which again represent a drain on management time.

BUDGET CODES

Budget codes can be deployed effectively to demoralize staff, prevent cooperation between different parts of the business, stifle initiative, encourage power games, and escalate costs. The way to do this is to insist that everything has a budget code. Every photocopy, every hour of everyone's day should be accounted for by a budget code. This means that nothing can move without the say-so of the great panjandrum who holds all the budget codes. He or she should only let them out in small amounts to minimize an individual's discretion, and to maximize his or her own power. On no account should secretaries have purchasing cards or discretion to buy office supplies. Make them use budget codes and formal purchasing procedures: make sure they understand who is really the boss.

BUSINESS SCHOOLS

Business schools do three things for emerging management talent:

- They attract the best young talent and the top employers and act as a dating agency between the two. There is a market for a new school that drops all the grind of two years' tuition, charges half the fees and simply acts as the dating agency. The cost and time saving would delight graduates. Employers would still get the same quality, and the business school would make a fortune. Someone will figure this out, make it work, and make a fortune.
- They provide a core of business knowledge, not skills. This knowledge probably has a half-life of 18 months. Most of the knowledge is not directly usable to someone who becomes a bond salesperson. Even consultants use only a fraction of the knowledge they glean. This makes the non-studying MBA feasible for both graduate and employer: the knowledge simply is not that critical. It only becomes really important years later as the graduate enters general management. By then the knowledge has been forgotten and re-learned three times over.
- They give the graduates confidence. Just as a dating agency gives customers a structure and confidence to enter into a new environment with new people, business schools do the same.

The things that graduates really need to learn, like how to survive the management jungle on a day-to-day basis, are not taught at business schools. Business schools teach explicit knowledge, which can be codified. They do not teach the tacit skills of management survival. This is a business opportunity waiting to happen. Be the first corporate MBA: the corporate Marriage Bureau Agency for graduates and employers.

CALCULATORS

Throw them away. Use of a calculator is normally a way of ensuring that the math is right to eight decimal places, even when the logic is 100 percent wrong. Actuaries and accountants are experts at this problem. When looking at a page with data on it, there are better ways of testing it than using a calculator:

- Do the simple math test. Do the last digits in the column sum produce a result consistent with the last digits in the total?
- Do the reasonableness test. Most managers should have at their fingertips the key data for their business or department. If they see data that shows that share will suddenly double and costs halve, it's time to start asking questions, however robust the numbers may be.
- Test definitions. I used to work on a product called Flash. It had 40 percent market share, but was in terminal decline because the market was falling. This was because we defined our market as powdered household cleaners. Meanwhile liquid and cream cleaners were growing like crazy. We did not take the obvious action of introducing a cream or liquid product because it was not our market: if it *was* our market it would make our share look small and declining.
- Test assumptions. All forecast data is simply a reflection of assumptions made about the market, share, costs, and prices. Normally, the assumptions are made to produce the answer that is required. So the answer is meaningless unless the assumptions are good.

Using a calculator simply obscures the need to think about data. It does not help test for reasonableness, or for assumptions, or for definitions. It also helps people become innumerate. Better to use the brain than a calculator.

CHANGE

The Bell Curve

People have different levels of enthusiasm for change. The bell curve is a normal distribution. Ninety-five percent of the management population exists within two standard deviations of the mean in terms of their enthusiasm for change. They are neither openly hostile, nor are they actively supportive of change. It is this mass of the management population that needs to be shifted. Passive acceptance or resistance to change needs to be converted into willing support. They will never become change zealots, but their active cooperation is nevertheless required.

The interesting challenges lie with the outliers. There will be 2.5 percent who are change zealots and an equal number who will staff the barricades in defense of the status quo.

The Change Zealots

These are the shock troops of the change program. Theirs will be the glory if it succeeds, and they are also most exposed if it fails. Clearly, these troops are invaluable for leading the change program. The challenge is to find the right ones in the right places. Good change leaders are not just in powerful positions, although those are needed. They are people who have influence at all levels of the organization. They will work the grapevine with more credibility and authority than any official newsletter.

The right person may be the 50-year-old called Jack who is in a quiet staff job that apparently has no power. Because he has no power he is no threat; he is not seen as part of the official power structure. Because he has been around for ages, people tend to trust him. He is the person you want as a change leader. The acid test is when someone asks Jack what he thinks of the latest change program. If the answer is that it is the normal management B.S. that will float by, an opportunity is lost. If he perks up and says that for once management may be on to something worthwhile, the right message starts spreading to the 95 percent who are stuck in the middle. They will sit up and take notice.

Spending time gaining the commitment of these key influencers is a strong investment, which pays by giving the change program credibility and commitment with the majority of the business.

The Reactionaries

These people will fight change tooth and nail. They may be a tiny minority, but they will spread poison. The temptation is to spend countless hours trying to convert them. You may as well try to convert a Jesuit to Buddhism. If the reactionary is in a leadership position, it could be fatal. The choice for the reactionary leader is simple: get on the train, or try standing in front of it. Either way, the train will leave the station.

Elsewhere in the organization, the focus should be on gaining the support of the 95 percent, not dealing with the resistance of the 2 to 3 percent. As the minority see the majority board the change train, they will start to feel pretty lonely. They will then break into three camps: some will join the train, some will run away, and a couple of diehards will lie down on the tracks in front of the train. Let them come to their own conclusions. The train will move on.

The Change Equation

Change Equation for Business

Most normal human beings hate change. It takes effort, is risky, and you never quite know where things may end. And then there are consultants. They love change. Change equals revenues for consultants. A new IT system, a new strategy, a new organization: the consultants will be there to help. They get the revenues, and they do not have to live with the consequences. They get all the benefit and none of the risk.

How do you know if the organization is ready for change? After twenty years' use, the change equation still provides an accurate assessment of whether the organization is ready for change. Here it is, with all its spurious mathematical elegance: $(P \times V \times C \times F) > R$.

In English, the business is ready for change if there is pain (P) today, a vision (V) for the future coupled with the capability (C) to get there and some practical first steps (F). All of these together need to be greater than the perceived risks and costs of change (R). If a change program goes awry, it is normally because some or all of these preconditions have not been fulfilled:

■ P is for pain. There is no point in having a brilliant solution (reengineering, TQM, time-based management) if it does not solve a problem where the organization feels real pain. The first question to ask of any idea is: "What problem does it solve?" Without any pain there will be no interest in or commitment to change. At best, people will go through the motions.

■ V is for vision. The devil you know is better than the devil you don't. So the pain has to be linked to a vision of the future that is clear and has demonstrable benefits to the business. You must "size the prize." The benefits must be big to justify the costs of change that will be incurred. Don't play for small prizes. With no common vision, management change efforts will be like headless chickens running around in all directions. Time, effort, and morale will evaporate.

■ C is for the organization's capacity to change. This is partly about priorities: knowing what you will not do in order to free up people, time, and money to focus on the required change. It also requires the right skills, strong sponsorship, and credible managers who have a track record of delivering. If the organization lacks the capacity to change, launching another change effort is an invitation to cynicism all around as people wait for yet another management initiative to fail.

■ F is for practical first steps. People want instant gratification. Or, at least, they want to know that they are on the winning side, and to see a sense of momentum. Ensure that the change program gets some early easy and visible wins. It builds confidence. Without it, enthusiasm wanes and momentum evaporates.

■ R is for the risks and costs of change. These are high: financial costs are small relative to the opportunity cost of not doing other things while focusing priorities on the change effort. The more the risks and costs can be reduced, the more readily change will be accepted. If the risks are high, the opposition to change will be high, and will be both rational and political.

Change Equation for People

Ultimately, businesses cannot change unless people do. And people have strong emotional resistance to change. Fear of the unknown tends to outweigh greed for the opportunity. People are risk and loss averse. The change equation works for individuals as well as for businesses. People will change where $(P \times V \times C \times F) > R$.

■ P is for pain. When people are hurting, they are ready to change. This can be in the form of a risk (threat of takeover, redundancy) or simply unsatisfactory current conditions. If everyone is fat and happy, complacency rules and change will not happen. Occasionally, you need to create the crisis to stimulate change.

■ V is for vision. People want to know where they are going and what it means to them personally. They may listen to all the good stuff about how the business will be transformed by some change, but they will not be engaged. Tell them what it means to them in terms of their career opportunities and what they can get out of it, and you will have their full attention. Get personal.

■ C is for capacity to change. People don't know if they can handle change. They don't know what it will mean to them in terms of new skills and performance requirements. You are taking away what they can do and replacing it with something they do not know. They need reassurance that they either have the capability, or that they will get the capability to succeed in the new world.

■ F is for first steps. People want to know they have backed the right horse, they want to see some early results and early recognition of their personal contribution. Give it. Otherwise morale and momentum will go.

■ R is for risks. Change is risky to individuals. They do not know how or if they will succeed in the new world. The more you de-risk a change program, the more easily it will be accepted. Naturally, this can run counter to the need to stretch the organization to force it into new ways of working. Change needs to do a balancing act between risk and stretch.

CLAIMS TO FAME

Everyone needs a claim to fame. Simply doing the job as required is not enough. The larger the organization, the easier it is for people to become lost in it. The claim to fame brands people, gives them an identity that managers recognize. With hundreds or thousands of the people in the organization, it is a success to be known for one thing. To be known, the claim to fame has to be big.

Once an individual becomes known as an expert at something, or great for achieving something, then life changes. Instead of drifting between assignments, the individual is in demand from peers and managers alike. A good claim to fame will make the individual in demand. It will create choices about where to focus time and effort, and will give visibility when it comes to bonus and promotion time.

A claim to fame is about doing something that has impact and relevance at least two levels up the hierarchy. This is unlikely to come from doing business as usual. It comes from taking an extra risk, making an extra effort and finding out what really is on the agenda of management. Drifting is possible in some organizations, but it is the slow boat to nowhere.

Claims to fame are critical at promotion time. Promotion decisions should be rational, based on a proper understanding of a candidate's achievements and skills. Perhaps in some businesses this degree of detailed objectivity is achieved. In many businesses the decision is cruder and simpler.

Evaluations may be written by your immediate boss, who may put up a promotion recommendation. But the actual decision will be made by people two or three levels up the hierarchy. Their knowledge of each individual is sketchy and simplistic. So they will rely on three pieces of evidence to make up their mind. In each piece of evidence it is the exceptional, not the standard, that grabs attention and determines the outcome:

▓ The detailed promotion packages. They may be looking at 20 or 30 of these in a day. All of them will be persuasive and all will be about good candidates. They tend to cancel each other out, unless there is some outstanding achievement or problem associated with the candidate. Each candidate needs a claim to fame.

▓ The credibility and strength of advocacy of the person recommending the promotion. The strength of advocacy is a reflection of the individual's political skills as well as the strength of the advocate's opinion. The advocacy is always strongest when the advocate can point to a single, distinctive claim to fame that sets the candidate apart from the crowd.

▓ Personal knowledge of the candidate. This may be trivial, like a meeting that went well or badly. This trivial event can assume disproportionate significance. What will swing the decision comprehensively is if the decision makers have personal awareness of the individuals' claim to fame. With 20 or 30 candidates under review, and many more within their area of responsibility, most individuals will struggle to be known for just one claim to fame. The stronger it is, the more it will influence the decision.

THE CLIENT RULE

The client rule is: The client rules. There is one other client rule: He who owns the client, rules. The client rules applies to marketplace competition and to internal organizational competition.

The Client Rule in the Organization

In any firm there are power struggles between staff types, product people, marketing, finance, operations, and all the different functions. A matrix simply makes the contest between the functions more equal, more ambiguous, and more vicious. Ultimately, the winners are those who unambiguously own the clients.

In private banks, the relationship managers own the clients, that is, bring in the revenues. Ultimately, they have the power. In consulting, partners who own big clients have all the power. Greed (everyone wants to be on the big project) and fear (no one wants to lose the revenue stream) drive behavior.

Salespeople do not own the client. They come, they sell, they go. They are dispensable. It is the person on whom the client relationship depends that is indispensable. At bonus time, this helps.

The Client Rule in the Market

The business that owns the client is strong. Businesses that do not, are weak. This shows up in profitability. Ford owns the customer. Contractors are squeezed: they depend on Ford to deliver the volumes. And subcontractors get squeezed by the contractors. They are at the wrong end of the food chain. The same is true of suppliers to the big retailers: the only way of fighting back is through strong branding. This gives the chance of the brand owning the customer, not the retailer. Client ownership is a struggle of power and profit.

COMMERCIAL CONFIDENTIALITY

This is a useful panic button to press occasionally. It is used in particular by governments whenever they want to cover up some major bungle. Also used by management to avoid defending the indefensible.

A minor variation is the legal version of client privilege. This can be used to great effect by management. When asked for a reference for a litigious individual who has been fired, simply refer the matter to the lawyers and have them draft the response. This will kill the reference stone dead.

COMMITTEES

Committees are the land of the living dead. Put them out of their misery. Kill them. Committees normally suffer from four problems:

- Responsibility and accountability. A committee is a great way of diffusing accountability and responsibility. If a committee makes a decision, then it is hard to pin responsibility on any one individual. Even the chairperson can hide behind the excuse of expressing the will of the majority.
- Bad decisions. Committees make bad decisions. They tend to compromise. If there are two proposals to be judged, a committee will find a compromise designed to save face all round. You do not beat the competition by compromising.
- Speed. Committees tend to be slow and bureaucratic: they meet on a regular basis and need papers in advance. This means that if the new sales opportunity or credit request comes on the wrong day, you will be left waiting a week or a month for a reply. By then, the competition will have sewn up the opportunity.
- Performance metrics and rewards. Committees rarely have clear performance metrics, clear goals that are then measured and reflected in the evaluation and bonuses of the committee members.

There are two good alternatives to committees. First, give management responsibility to individual managers. If the manager then needs support from colleagues in executing that responsibility, he or she will find a way of doing it efficiently. But at least you retain clear accountability, with the flexibility to meet the demands of the situation.

Second, create a small task force with a time-limited objective that can be measured, and with a leader who has clear accountability for delivering the objectives of the task force. And, when the deadline is up, disband the task force with an appropriate celebration. The leader of the task force should also be responsible for implementing its suggestions: this encourages clearer, better, and more practical recommendations.

COMPETITIVE ADVANTAGE FOR THE TWENTY-FIRST CENTURY

Forget sustainable competitive advantage. The question is: how long can the advantage be sustained? Perhaps until the patents run out. Or, until the competition can copy your product. In investment banking that might be as long as it takes for your competitor to walk through your client's door.

Competitive advantage is becoming harder to find and sustain. Twenty-first-century competitive advantage is different from traditional twentieth-century competitive advantage in five key areas. These are the areas to focus on and to test your own position against.

From Tangible to Intangible Advantages for Customers

Traditional product marketing is based on demonstrable product advantages: Tide washes whiter. Now brands have to offer more than performance and a quality assurance. Coca-Cola loses taste tests against Pepsi, but wins on market share. It is not just selling dark fizzy liquid, it is selling youth and American values to the rest of the world. It is a rich brand. Nike clothing is not necessarily better than other sporting and leisure clothes. People buy not just clothes, but a lifestyle from the brand.

Intangibles are more than brand. The service industry promises and delivers intangible benefits that may or may not be bundled with a physical product. Restaurants offer food and ambience, overnight delivery is a time promise, consulting is an insight promise, aeroengines offer both a loss-making product and a profit-making service. The challenge is to demonstrate the value of these intangibles to the customer.

From Single Point to Multiple Advantages

In the past, the corporate Olympics included three events: better, faster, cheaper. Now there is just one event: betterfastercheaper. The market wants it all, and wants it now.

This is about layering one advantage on top of another over time. The Japanese auto manufacturers entered the U.S. market with cheap, but reliable cars. It was a new price/quality trade-off based on innovative production methods. Over time, they added new layers of advantage. First, they increased the level of features; then they moved upmarket into higher profit segments; then they started introducing new models up to three times faster than competition. Competition could not keep up with all the different layers of advantage the Japanese were introducing.

From Formulaic Advantages to Creative and Customized Advantages

The formulaic advantages of the twentieth century are not enough. These advantages were typically described as scale versus differentiation, price versus quality. Today the answer is as likely to be price and quality and scale and differentiation. Amazon.com started with a highly differentiated offering, which allowed for high customization. They are building scale and price, making it hard for competition to enter. They have thrown the formulaic trade-offs out of the window.

Other competitive advantages are likely to be more creative. Honda entered the U.S. motorbike market thinking it would have to compete head on with the traditional Harley type of bike business. It stumbled upon and developed the family leisure bike business, gained volume, and eventually outflanked the traditional players.

Creative thinking allows competitors to thrive in the same market. In the PC market, Apple invented a whole new market for personal computers. It has sustained a position based on design and ease of use, targeting the education and publishing sectors. IBM entered, trying to use its muscle in the corporate market and the implicit assurance of quality. Dell entered the market with a disintermediated mass-customized approach, which enables it to largely eliminate stocks and the hazards of forecasting. These are three totally different approaches to the same market.

From Sustainable to Temporary Advantage

Traditional thinking regards competitive advantage as sustainable. It is not sustainable any more. Perhaps in the past, you could build a railroad and no one could compete with that; or build a huge chemical plant and deter anyone else from following suit.

A good test of the strength of the business is the innovation index. This is the proportion of sales derived from products less than three years old. Traditional industries should be able to achieve 25 percent. The computer, fashion, consulting, and investment banking industries should be achieving nearer 100 percent, and they should be looking for a shorter time frame over which to measure innovation. The proportion of sales to new customers should also be high, especially for growth businesses.

From External to Internal and External drivers of Advantage

Advantage is no longer sustainable based on the strategic position of the business. Advantage is temporary. If the business is not moving ahead at least as fast as the competition, it is falling back in a relative way. Competition can reduce costs and raise quality by 25 percent each in three years. Our 20 percent improvement means we are falling back.

In this world, competitive advantage may be expressed in market-place performance, but it is driven by the internal strengths of the business. These strengths are not about a static core competence ("We are good at small motors."). They are about dynamic strengths that enable the business to innovate and move forward.

This is most notable in the talent-driven businesses. Investment banks and consulting companies find it easy to copy each other's products. There is no competitive advantage there. Advantage comes from having the right talent that can consistently innovate and brings those innovations to market.

COMPETITIVE INTELLIGENCE: USE IT OR LOSE IT

Forget the sleuths and the expensive consulting reports. If you know you will act on it, do it yourself. If you just want it for information, don't bother. There are other more creative ways of wasting the company's money.

Most of what you need to find out about the competition is readily available. It is simply a matter of focus. Paying consultants for competitor profiles has always been wasted money. It's a job either for the library or for a junior consultant as a test of his or her ability. There are no magic sources. Here are the real ones:

- Annual reports and stock exchange disclosures.
- Broker reports, media coverage (Internet).
- Trade associations.
- Special reports (existing benchmark data, syndicated research).
- Ex-employees of the competition on your payroll.

- Headhunters, suppliers, and customers—normally helpful and will tell you where you differ from the competition, what you can do better.
- Your own R&D (research and development) analysis of competitor product performance and costs.
- Sales force intelligence: sales finds out early about pricing changes, promotions, and new products and price lists often leak.

This is all very basic stuff. Even if you use consultants, they will need you to give them access to headhunters, customers, suppliers, sales, brokers, and employees. Once you have gone through the effort of giving them access, you should be able to complete the job yourself. The issue for most businesses is not about collecting the data: it is about using it. It normally lives in some remote staff functionary's office. Competitor intelligence is only worth collecting if it is acted on.

COMPOUNDING

Getting Rich Slowly

If there is one piece of math worth knowing, it is compounding. It is the way to wealth. The math is simple. Ten percent annual growth means roughly doubling every seven years. Seven percent growth means roughly doubling every 10 years. This may not sound dramatic, but it is the way to get rich slowly and surely. A return of 10 percent annually on a $10,000 investment will produce $1,170,000 over 50 years. That's a nice retirement fund at the age of 70 for the thrifty 20-year-old. The greedy 30-year-old wanting to retire at the age of 50 will only net $57,000 over 20 years for a $10,000 investment.

At the extreme, it would have been great if an ancestor could have invested one dollar for me at the time of Christ, at just 1.5 percent compound interest. I would now be inheriting $8,552 billion. Unfortunately, wars, fraud, taxes, governments, bankruptcies, not to mention the millions of other competing descendants and the complete absence of any such ancestor, have got in the way of this money-making scheme.

For businesses, the same logic of compounding applies. For decades, Procter & Gamble held to the ambition of doubling unit sales every 10 years. This represents just 7 percent real annual growth. But it enabled a $10 million business to grow to a $40 billion business over 160 years.

The same relentless logic applies to the growth of costs. At a personal level, the impact of charges on your savings make a vast difference. If the thrifty 20-year-old pays charges of 1.5 percent annually on his $10,000 savings, the return at the age of 70 reduces from $1,170,000 to just $590,000. Meanwhile, some fund manager will have gotten rich at the investor's expense.

Compounding for Business: Kaizen Versus Crisis

The math is simple. Reduce unit costs by 4 percent a year, and after 10 years they will have been reduced 34 percent, with effort but not with drama. This is the kaizen or continuous improvement way to cost cutting. Ideally, it is associated with growth that enables the surplus staff to be redeployed. If there is no growth, then there is the kaizen way of reducing headcount: open the back door and close the front door. Natural attrition will get the headcount down by at least 4 percent per year in most businesses.

There is an alternative approach. Mess around with alternating growth, quality, service, and product innovation strategies for eight years as different managers wander through the business with different quick fixes. Then in year nine, realize that you have a big productivity problem. Hire consultants, reengineer the business, cut costs by a dramatic 20 percent in two years and fire 20 percent of the staff. The cost cutter will be a hero, but the business will still be behind the kaizen company.

Reengineering is rarely about leaping ahead of the competition with discontinuous change. It is more normally a matter of trying to catch up and remediate past failures.

COMPUTER ABUSE

We use computers because we have them. This does not mean we should use them, or that we are wise in how we use them. For every one hour of time the computer saves, it wastes anything between five minutes and five hours. The most common abuses of the computer include:

▪ Managers acting as typists or production experts. I have seen a room full of consultants billing an average of $2,000 a day, busily producing graphics for a presentation. This is not their job. They are slow, and the results are low quality. For $400 a day, I could hire a great specialist who would produce far better quality at twice the speed. If you see consultants wasting your money like this, fire them.

■ Reporting by the gigabyte. Volume of reporting information does not equate to quality. More reporting data simply leads to more questions, more analysis, more data revision, and more managers chasing their tails. Reporting requirements should focus on what is needed, not on what is possible.

■ Upgrading to the latest gizmo. Senior managers are particularly prone to this because personal computers are not simply work tools, they are status symbols. So senior managers must have the latest and best computers, even though functionally they are way beyond their modest office requirements. The people who most need all the latest functionality are those on the front line: they are the last to get the upgrade.

■ The solitaire supremos. The blame should not be attached to the individuals who have enough spare time to start honing their chess, solitaire, or bridge skills on the computer. The real question is why there is so much spare capacity in the office, and why it is not being used more effectively.

■ Placing computers between you and the customer. Every day I can buy a newspaper from my local newsstand or from the corner drugstore. The newsstand knows me, and we exchange papers, money, and pleasantries in a moment. The drugstore has a computer that tracks stock. There is always a line because the clerk has to swipe each transaction through the till and there are always mistakes that then need to eliminated and reentered. Customers then have to wait while a receipt is printed out. The computer keeps the accountants happy. It drives the service staff and the customers crazy. Computers can enhance the customer buying experience, but only if it is designed for the customer and not for the accountants.

CONFERENCES: THE SURVIVAL GUIDE

Corporate conferences at least provide the opportunity to get out of the office, perhaps go somewhere nice and, hopefully, earn a few more air miles. You might also get a decent meal and a big drinking session. The price to pay is high: sitting in a dark, stuffy conference hall for hours on end listening to some self-important Big Cheese making an instantly forgettable speech. Most conferences have three elements, which the management survivalist can use to good advantage:

■ Plenary sessions. Many of these will be a waste of time. This is where important people get on the stage and, like dogs peeing to mark their territory, make speeches to show that they are big shots. Some of you may have to attend. But the schedule should reveal several sessions that have no relevance to you, and you will not be missed. This is a good opportunity to catch up with paperwork, phone calls, or your exercise program if there is a health club. You are doing no more than follow the example of the VIPs who believe they are too busy and important to attend all the plenary sessions. Make your exits and your entrances discreetly.
■ Break-out sessions. You know that any work you put into the break-out session will receive a short, garbled summary in the plenary session and will then be ignored. But the big shots like to think that because you have now been involved, you have therefore bought into whatever they are proposing. Because these groups are small, you will be missed and you should go. Survive them.
■ Informal time, coffee breaks, and meals. These are the most useful parts of conferences. Most people waste them. People only speak to people they already know: New York office speaks to the New York office, IT speaks to IT. But, if you have prepared, you will know there are some people out there with interesting ideas, or with interesting projects and career opportunities. Make a point of searching them out. Have your story ready. Do not try to negotiate your next career move there and then, but use the opportunity to put a marker down and ensure there is a promise of a follow-up after the conference. Then make sure you follow up. These opportunities are not just with bosses, but with your peer group and others with good ideas.

CONSULTANTS

You get the consultants you deserve. If you find that they have set up camp permanently in your building, charge outrageous fees, and produce little by way of results; tough. You know what you should do about it.

Essentially, most consultants are tarts. They will do anything for anyone, provided the customer can pay. It is worth knowing what may motivate the highly plausible consulting partner sitting opposite you:

■ He or she will be rewarded for making a sale, not for giving you best advice.

■ Consultants prefer to sell what they know, regardless of whether the solution fits your problem. The answer you get lies less in the nature of your problem than in the experience of the consultant you are talking to.

■ Once in your door, the consultant is aware that selling a project to a new client is roughly seven times more expensive, difficult, and risky than selling a second project to an existing client.

■ A consultant will expect to spend roughly one-third of his or her effort in the project finding the solution for you, one-third convincing you of the solution, and one-third of the time selling you on the next project.

■ Consultants want to swim upstream to the source of all power: the CEO. CEOs are the softest touch in terms of pricing, terms, conditions, and payment. They have the biggest budgets and give the best overview of where the next project might come from. Finally, CEOs give the consultants the most power within the organization.

■ No consultant will commit the consulting organization to any real liability concerning performance.

All of this is fairly self-evident. It means that consultants, for all their protestations, are not on your side. They are in it for the fees. This has some inevitable consequences:

■ They will do more or less of whatever you want, even if it is not the right thing.

■ They will represent that they have the right skills for your task: whether you ever see the person with the right skills beyond the pitch is doubtful; in all probability he or she is a very scarce resource much in demand elsewhere.

■ They will promise results based on the fallacy of the stable baseline: given the baseline is moving you will never be able to quantify their contribution to the business relative to all the other moving variables. Their performance promises are usually worthless.

- They all have great products to sell from time to time: reengineering, core competence, time-based competition, quality. They will apply this solution, regardless of what your problem is, because that is what they know how to sell and how to do.
- They will try to make themselves indispensable to the organization, which in effect means hollowing out and disempowering middle management.
- Forget confidentiality. No consulting firm will actually take your confidential plans and tout them round the market. But they will take all the experience they have gained from you and wrap it up in an anonymous case and start selling it to all your competitors. They will at least use another partner when selling your experience to your direct competition.

This leaves the challenge of how to use consultants effectively. There are a few principles that work:

- Make it very hard for the organization to take on consultants. It should be an executive committee decision and, more or less on principle, the board should turn down all first requests for consulting support. When the squeals of agony get very loud, then you might start listening.
- Managers must be able to prove that they do not have the technical skills that the consultants claim to bring: if it is simply a question of bodies and resources, then the discussion should be about corporate priorities, not about consultants.
- Managers must be able to show that the consultants are actually working on the right problem.
- Pick not just the right firm of consultants, but the right individuals. The partner you are talking to is probably having a struggle to identify and release the right people to work with you, and is under huge pressure to take new recruits (20 percent of the workforce annually) and weak performers onto his or her team. Your pressure is essential in getting to the A team, not the B team.
- Once the consultants are in, manage them effectively. This means being able to make rapid decisions. A good way to escalate IT implementation costs is to make decisions slowly and then reverse them.
- Keep the consultants hungry. Make them happy, dangle the carrot

of extra work in front of them: then they will put their best resources into the effort. Then kick them out.

If you are in middle management and you find that consultants are suddenly swirling around, don't fight. Be helpful, and quietly try to co-opt them in support of your agenda. They are also a useful source of finding out what the agenda is of senior management. Remember, consultants often have a direct line into the executive committee. This can be used to your advantage, but make them into enemies and it could be fatal. I have yet to meet a CEO who does not, at some point, pull one of the consultants to one side and ask for an opinion of his management team.

CONTRACTS

Contracts are scary. Lawyers often like to make them even more scary. They point out all the dangers and surround the contract with unintelligible gobbledegook. As the world becomes more legalistic, contracts are becoming more important. Contracts are a management reality.

From a management perspective, there are four things a manager should do about contracts. They are all common sense. This means that most managers will at some time have a personal or professional contract disaster because one of the four rules has not been followed:

▪ Know when you do and do not have a contract. Just because there is no written document, this does not mean there is no contract. There may be a duty of care. And, as soon as money is exchanged for services, there is a contract.

▪ Never sign a contract until you are ready. The moment you sign, your negotiating position evaporates and the obligations begin. This is normally discovered by new employees, when it is too late.

▪ Never sign a contract you do not understand. Good lawyers, who can translate legalese into plain English and can give practical as well as legal advice, are worth their weight in gold. Which is roughly how much they charge. But use them.

▪ Standard contracts are never in your favor. They favor the person offering the standard contract. Because it is standard, people think it is a take it or leave it proposition. I just go through the document striking out clauses I do not like and adding new ones in where I want them. If the contract bearer defends the contract on the basis that "It's what other people sign," he has no defense. The only good contract is one you are happy with.

CONTROL, COMPLIANCE, AND COMMITMENT

Every business needs to stay in control. If there are new tools for controlling the business, it is reckless not to use them. Except that control and commitment work in opposite directions. And, ultimately commitment is a more productive form of control than mere compliance. *Less* formal control is sometimes better than *more*.

There are five control levers open to management. Most managers use all five levers, in different proportions. The challenge is to get the balance right.

Rules and Hierarchy

This is the traditional command and control model. If the business is one where managers think and workers work, having checked their brains and souls out at the front door, command and control is fine. This is the land of the multivolume policy manual. The policy manual tells people what they cannot do. It is designed to stop disaster. But it does not tell people what they should do, it does not empower them, and it does not create a culture of trust and commitment. It is long on compliance, short on commitment.

Information and Reporting

The explosion of communications, information, and technology has led to an explosion in the frequency, breadth, and depth of management reporting. The volume of reporting is inversely proportional to the trust you have in your managers. The provincial governors in the Roman Empire had to be empowered and trusted to manage: they could not send a trireme back to Rome with a few hundredweight of stone tablets asking for guidance every time a problem came up in Judaea. The Roman Empire lasted longer and achieved more than most business empires can ever hope to. Just because the technology enables us to have mountains of reporting, it does not mean we should have it. Excessive reporting is a comfort blanket for insecure senior management.

Skills and Standards

The medieval guilds were a way of ensuring that all the butchers, bakers, and candlestick makers had the skills to produce goods to a standard that was acceptable to the community. It did not require long policy manuals: most candlestick makers were illiterate; nor was there much in the way of reporting. Today, the professions such as doctors, lawyers, and accountants maintain the same approach. This creates a curious mix of cultural conformity, control, and individual commitment. Making it work across a business encompassing multiple skills, trades, and cultures is close to impossible, unless you are a firm of accountants or lawyers.

Control of Outcomes

This is the classic conglomerate approach to business. Strong financial measures and rewards are put in place, together with tight financial control. Then management is left to get on with it, provided they are achieving their goals. This maximizes flexibility, and is a high commitment model, based on the twin human motivations of fear and greed. Within organizations, effective delegation is about controlling outcomes, not processes. It is fundamentally a high trust, high commitment form of control.

Cultural Control

This is a high commitment, but potentially low compliance form of management. In the extreme, millions of people have volunteered to die to defend communism, fascism, and democracy. They may have been brainwashed by years of propaganda, but from the leader's point of view, they got the result they needed: a highly committed and dedicated following. High commitment businesses normally have strong cultures. This does not need to be high energy passion, with 100-hour weeks in a new economy business. The traditional "job for life" company, still present in a few businesses in Japan, proves its commitment to the individual over a career and expects the same in return.

CORRUPTION, BRIBERY AND SKULDUGGERY

Some countries and industries are awash in corruption, bribery, and skulduggery. Managers and businesses can play this in one of four ways:

- Don't play in those countries and industries.
- Avert your gaze and shade the truth. This is popular. Your local sales agent works on 10 percent commission. Of course, you have no idea that the 10 percent mostly goes on kickbacks: that's not your business. Naturally, you should invite the clients to the trade show at Disney World, pay their expenses (first class) for them and assistants (significant others or family) and reimburse them through their travel company (which they own, and they are expensing both their employer and another company for the same trip). But you would never bribe them with a free trip for their family to Disney World, would you? Just don't expect the judge to understand the difference.
- Play to lose: enter those countries, avoid all the unethical and illegal activity and accept you will lose. But in 20 or 30 years' time, if the country cleans its act up, you may still have a reputation to build on.
- Play to the local rules of the game.

From an economic point of view corruption and bribery is irrational: it leads to poor allocation of resources and poor economic performance. This is why most advanced economies act strongly against skulduggery. The kindest thing to say about countries that still suffer corruption is that they are simply at an early stage of economic development. The UK at the start of the industrial revolution was still deeply corrupt in many areas: the running of the naval shipyards being best documented for its corruption.

But from the short-term point of view for individuals with power, corruption is highly profitable. They can sing while the country burns. Corruption will not disappear soon.

COST CUTTING: THE SOLDIER'S BOOTS

Cutting costs can be used to get thinner, or get fitter. Corporate fitness is preferable to corporate anorexia.

Cutting Costs to Get Thinner

This version of cutting costs is about spending less to achieve less. Companies do not shrink their way to greatness. In a crisis, or where the business is grossly bloated, cost cutting is fair game. There will be resistance. Every department will find a reason why they should be exempted from the cost cuts. Typical blocking tactics include:

- We have already cut our costs from last year's.
- We are growing: we can not cut costs and grow.
- Our benchmark costs are already lower than the competition.
- We will have to cut our marketing budget, so we will lose sales.

The list is endless. The most effective response is the shroud-waving response, which takes several forms:

- Army cost cuts: "No problem, of course we won't be able to buy the troops any more boots."
- Air traffic control: "Of course we can cut, but you do realize it could result in two 747s colliding over downtown Chicago?"
- Hospitals: "We can cut costs, but who takes responsibility when a patient dies because we cannot afford the nursing staff?"

The point is that across-the-board cost cutting targets will mobilize the organization in opposition to the management. The only reasonable response of management is to be unreasonable, and make no exceptions: "Read my lips: either you get 20 percent cost reductions, or you are part of the cost reduction."

Traditional cost cutting programs, like ZBB (Zero Based Budgeting) are focused on individual departments and businesses. This encourages department heads to protect their empires and discourages cooperation across the business. The greatest cost reductions are achievable not by looking within each department. They are made possible by looking at the systemic costs across the business, which raise the cost of work in every part of the business.

At the end of a traditional cost cutting exercise, the organization may be thinner but it is almost certainly weaker. And the business will be demoralized.

Cutting Costs to Get Fitter

The challenge here is to do more or better with less. The starting point is not the departmental budget. It is the marketplace. The first challenge is to focus on those products, services, and features that the market actually wants, and which are profitable.

ABC (Activity Based Costing) may be a painful exercise, but it gives a completely new perspective on where the business is making and losing money, and what is driving the costs of the business. ABC looks at the costs of activities (issuing invoices and collecting debts), rather than functions (accounting). Every customer and product uses these activities. Linking the activities to products normally shows the business has a long tail of marginal or unprofitable products and customers. This offers huge profit improvement opportunities. And, by looking at the cost of delivering different activities, departments are encouraged to collaborate to see how they can reduce the cost. ABC encourages working smarter, not working harder.

ABC is not perfect. It sounds like another consulting fad; it is yet another TLA (Three Letter Abbreviation) to add to the jargon dictionary. It is hard work, and does not produce instant results. It does not look like macho management. But sometimes boring detailed grind is better than the grand gesture. And it works.

COST SAVING: THE RED DOLLAR SYNDROME

Red dollars are a wonderful management currency. They can be created out of nowhere and used to achieve otherwise unachievable cost saving and profit improvement targets. Unfortunately, like the unicorn, red dollars do not exist. You cannot trade redbacks for greenbacks. And yet, they have a way of appearing in the works of fiction that sometimes pass as management accounts.

There are many ways of summoning red dollars into existence. I have seen one successful red dollar practitioner show 30 percent cost savings without reducing any costs. Against a 20 percent target, he was a hero with senior management, and a hero with his staff who suffered no cutbacks.

The principle ways of creating red dollars are "squeezing the balloon" and "scoreboarding":

Squeezing the Balloon

In squeezing the balloon, managers either externalize their costs, transfer their costs, or restate their costs. The red dollar savings flow, the targets are achieved, and the business sucks. Typical examples include:

■ Transfer the costs. This requires arguing about transfer charges and transfer prices. In one organization they talk about cost prices, which confuses everyone: is it a cost or is it a price? The transfer charging game is a particularly vicious and political one where all departments have been asked to reduce costs. Everyone wants to squeeze the balloon of costs so that the costs shrink in their area and grow in someone else's. The arguments for where costs should lie will be eloquent and rational. The way to kill the arguments is to swap the positions of department head halfway through the exercise and then watch them do intellectual somersaults as they try to justify their new, and contrary, positions.

■ Restate the costs. These are all the old accounting tricks. Capitalizing expenses, such as IT spending, has a great impact on reducing apparent costs without requiring any pain or tough decisions. Moving from leased to freehold property and not charging a notional rent has a similar effect of moving expenses onto the balance sheet.

■ Externalize the costs. This can create pink dollars: there is an element of reality to them, but there are no actual cost reductions. Examples would include: changing the toll-free number for staff and clients into a pay number; charging for internal services from the photocopy machine, coffee machine, and restaurant through to legal services. At best, cost externalization brings some new revenues into the business, at the price of irritating customers or staff. At worst, it leads to an avalanche of internal accounting between departments, which slows the business down and escalates, not reduces, costs.

Scoreboarding

This is a favorite of consultants. They will show that the process reengineering effort has saved the equivalent of 100 man-days of effort per month. These 100 man-days may be spread over 1,000 staff members, but the results will still be put on a scoreboard. The argument is that the productivity improvement has been achieved, allowing management to decide whether to take the cost savings or to reinvest the savings in other activities. Naturally, eliminating 10 percent of each person's time is impossible. So, the costs remain, even though the productivity improvement has been achieved. Both the consultants and the management conspire in scoreboarding, as both have an incentive to declare victory and move on.

COURTESY

To the cynical, this is a no cost, low effort way of winning friends and respect. It is also a way of living in a happier office. Courtesy pays. Being pleasant to support staff helps when you have a sudden crunch and you need a favor from them. Harassed production staff or technical support staff are more likely to put your work to the top of the pile, or to stay the extra hour if they know you and like you. Headhunters are more likely to be helpful if you are always responsive and helpful to them. It is the simple things that count. Outlined below are only the easy things that are common sense but are commonly not done:

Telephone Etiquette

- Always return telephone calls. Something good may come out of it. Even if it is a problem, at least you have dealt with it right away, and you look professional.
- When someone returns your call, thank them for returning the call.
- Answer the phone promptly: three rings at most.
- Never leave the phone on during meetings, unless you want to show the people you are meeting that they are extremely unimportant to you.

Support Staff

- Learn their names, and use their names. Say good morning.
- Say thank you.
- Take time to chat and find out a bit about them.
- Respect their personal lives: if you know that you need extra help, tell them in advance so that they can make arrangements.
- Treat them with respect. They are professionals in their own field and they are busy. Don't condescend: treat them as equals.

CULTURE, CRABS, AND THE DEATH OF THE TEA LADY

Cultural change programs do not work. Announce that you are going to change the culture of the organization, and watch the opposition grow. Telling people that you will change their culture is like telling them that you are going to mess with their heads because what they

have being doing and thinking in the past is all wrong. And, by definition, a cultural change program is an attack on the majority. So, even
if there is a minority cheerfully egging you on, there is sullen resistance from the majority.

Cultural change programs carry overtones of the cultural revolution, Mao, Pol Pot, and extreme dictatorship. Not the best start for a
creating a new, open, and empowering culture. Culture is best changed
crabwise: attacked sideways.

Values statements do not help. Values statements have meaning
only to those who have spent months carefully crafting and bitterly
arguing over the nuances of every word in the statement. To the rest
of the world, it is more meaningless management babble. People take
their cultural cues not from what is said, but from what is done. There
are four key levers:

Reward Systems

If call center staff are rewarded for productivity (number of calls handled), do not expect a service-intensive, customer-friendly culture to
emerge. They will be too busy getting through the calls for that.

Promotion Criteria

Forget about the written criteria. Most businesses have similar criteria
that list various skills, levels of responsibility, and achievement. But
what people really focus on are the unwritten rules. For instance, in
most consulting companies the rules for getting to be partner are:

- Sell loads of work: own clients who will generate revenues.
- Do something to show at least a notional contribution to recruiting,
  firm management, intellectual property development.
- Don't trample over the bodies of too many people on the way to
  the top.

This last rule is relaxed in one consulting company, which formally
releases a set percentage of its staff after force-ranking them. This positively encourages trampling and politics. In one life insurance company, the unwritten rules looked something like this:

- Become an expert in your chosen technical field.
- Never, never make a mistake: meet budgets, no nasty surprises,
  don't rock the boat, don't argue.
- Serve your time and wait your turn.

These promotion criteria are largely unrelated to the formal criteria, but absolutely drive the behavior of individuals.

Management Behavior

If the department head is a miserable, Machiavellian miser, it is unusual to find an open, enthusiastic team working within the department. People take their cues from what managers do, not what they say.

This can work positively for management. A new CEO took over in a very traditional, hierarchical company. In his first week, he started wandering around the office and talking to staff at their desks. It was as if the Pope had come from Mars to visit. There was shock and disbelief. At first people found it difficult to talk to him. Then at one desk, there was nowhere for him to sit. Instinctively, he turned a waste basket upside down, sat on it and talked to the clerk at her level. The story went round the building like wildfire. Suddenly, the CEO was not just human, he was approachable.

Symbols Matter

In one office in London, England, there was the tea lady ritual. Technically, her job was to deliver tea twice a day to managers. Culturally, her job was to reinforce the hierarchy and humiliate the staff. She did this very well. Twice a day she would stroll around each floor: if you were important she stopped and gave you a cup of tea. If you were not important, you got to watch as she walked by, and then you went to the coffee machine and bought your plastic cup of gunk.

The first step in the popular revolution was to shoot the tea lady (revolutions can be cruel) and put in free vending machines. From there the revolution went on to dismantle all the other symbols of hierarchy and status: the three levels of executive dining room, the reserved parking spaces, the separate executive bathrooms and elevators, and so on.

Communication

Many companies assume that communication is about broadcasting loud clear messages. This does not work. Management propaganda has all the integrity of *Pravda* in the Soviet era, and gains as much respect. Good communication is critical. The key principles are:

- Words and actions must agree. Don't pretend to want an entrepreneurial culture unless you can manage and accept risk and failure.

■ Communications are two-way: make sure you listen to what the organization says. And, act on it: if you listen and nothing happens, cynicism is simply reinforced.

■ Communication is personal: people respond better to personal communication than memos. They trust the grapevine more than official news. Work the grapevine. Find out who really moves and shakes in the world of the grapevine and feed them the messages.

■ Keep the message the same: repeat it through multiple channels time and again. Advertising is often a war of attrition; internal advertising is the same. The more you repeat the message, the more likely it is to be heard and understood.

CUSTOMER LOYALTY AND THE MOMENT OF TRUTH

Doing things right helps build customer loyalty. Doing things wrong does not necessarily destroy the relationship. It can enhance the customer relationship. When things go wrong, it is the moment of truth for the relationship.

The most successful ways of screwing up a customer relationship, as practised by a leading airline, include:

■ Do not empower your employees to sort out the problem on the spot.

■ Tell the customer he or she is wrong.

■ Put bureaucratic obstacles in the way of the customer.

■ Do not answer any letters of complaint that may follow.

■ When forced to respond, offer too little too late.

Everyone has their own war stories of service from hell, and enjoys recounting them. Typically, one service disaster will get recounted 10 times. The poorly handled moment of truth has not just lost a customer, but has created someone who is busily unselling your service.

Equally, everyone has their tales of service above and beyond the call of duty. It normally revolves around a service disaster that is turned into triumph. Shortly after the airline service disaster above, I flew with Virgin Atlantic and received an involuntary downgrade on a 14-hour flight. This was a disaster that they turned into triumph:

- Employees were empowered on the spot to sort things out: the seat was not there, but they did everything else they could to make the trip a success.
- They accepted responsibility, they sympathized. At stressful moments, a little sympathy goes a long way. Most customers realize that things occasionally get bungled, and are prepared to be reasonable.
- They did not wait for me to write a letter. Richard Branson, the owner of the airline, called directly. This is extreme, but effective.
- They made amends early and fully. A potentially irate customer was turned into a representative for the airline.

Empowering staff in the front line goes against the grain for old style businesses. It implies a loss of control. It may result in staff spending money when not strictly necessary. But it is also a way of losing customers fast. And that, ultimately, is a far greater cost.

CUSTOMERS FOR PROFITS

Loyal customers are profitable customers. Most businesses can understand product profitability. Few understand customer profitability. Businesses need to know how to drive both customer and product profitability.

Loyal customers spend more, accept higher prices in return for the convenience of not switching, buy a wider range of products, and cost less to serve than acquiring new customers. The math of customer profitability are simple: $NPV = (V \times M \times L) - CA$ where:

- NPV: Net Present Value of the customer. This reflects the lifetime value of the customer relationship. Credit card companies normally know this. They know how much it costs to acquire a customer from different sources (different print magazines, different mailing lists, member-get-member programs). This, combined with data on the application form, allows them to predict the lifetime value of the customer based on volume of transactions and length of relationship. This is not academic data. It tells the credit card company how much money they should invest in different member acquisition methods. And it tells them what sort of customers are worth promoting different services to.
- V = Volume of Transactions. Loyal customers not only spend

more, but are more likely to buy other goods and services from the same institution. This is a high value, high profit proposition. Even businesses that realize this, like banks, are often unable to track the total customer relationship. Their systems are all geared to measuring product profitability, not to a customer view of the world. At minimum this irritates customers as they are offered inappropriate services. It also means the bank finds it difficult to know what and how to cross-sell.

- ▪ M = Margins. Loyal customers do not always get the best prices. They will stay with you for convenience. Sixty-eight percent of savers do not shop around for the best savings rate. McKinsey, the consulting firm, estimates that the average US household loses $1,660 annually by mismanaging its financial affairs. Some of this is about not managing cash well. Some $950 comes from not finding the best prices for financial services. People are paying high rates for being lazy and loyal. In contrast, new customers tend to have to be attracted by attractive rates, and they cost more to serve in the first year of the relationship. Make it easy for customers, and their laziness will make them your loyal and profitable customer.

- ▪ L = Length of a relationship. The longer customers stay, the more likely they are to buy more products. One bank found that customers in their first year held an average of 1.2 products with the bank. After five years, this had grown to 3.6 products per customer. Clearly, the length of the relationship will also determine the discount rate applied to the projected revenues from the customer.

- ▪ CA = Cost of acquiring the customer. The cost of acquiring a new customer is typically about seven times as high as selling to an existing customer. Again, loyalty pays. This yardstick applies across a range of industries from consulting to banking to credit cards.

Customers Versus Accountants

The NPV of a customer is a nightmare from the traditional accounting perspective. None of the data fits into the neat little departmental boxes beloved of accountants. From a managerial point of view, customer profitability helps identify where to invest in customer acquisition, where to cross-sell, how to manage different types of customers. In other words, it is useful. At this point, make the accountants help. Make them serve the business and the customer, not the other way around.

CUSTOMER RESEARCH: LIES AND STATISTICS

Businesses must know their customers. And customer research is a good way of not finding the truth.

Customers Lie: Attitudes Versus Behavior

Customers do not mean to lie, but they do. Most customer research is based on attitudes, opinions, and post-rationalization. We conducted two pieces of research for a retailer. The first research asked customers why they bought their television. They gave post-rationalizations about price, features, performance, and quality. This showed the store should focus on price, features, performance, and quality.

The second piece of research focused on behavior, and caught people as they left stores either with or without buying. It showed that they wandered around a few shops and became increasingly confused about all the choices. Just after they had bought, they could not recall the different prices or features of different models. If they did not know this basic information, they could not have been making a completely rational decision.

In practice, the customers wanted to be told a story. They wanted to be reassured that they were making a smart choice and that they would not be embarrassed by finding their neighbors had made a better choice. This led the stores to provide an umbrella of price reassurance, without trying to be price leader all the time. More important were the in-store sales skills to provide customers with the reassurance that they wanted, which might focus on price, or on some special features or a warranty. Understanding behavior was more powerful than recording attitudes.

Similarly, in the UK savings market customers claim to make rational choices about comparing rates and terms. Looking at behavior shows that 68 percent of retail customers considered only one supplier in picking their savings account: this was normally their existing bank. Even small businesses fall into the same trap: over half do not shop around for the best savings or borrowing terms. This has profound implications in terms of pricing: existing customers can be penalized for their loyalty or laziness.

Even where attitudinal research is relevant, customers still lie. It is an exceptionally awful product or service that gets a "below average" rating. Customers are too nice to the researchers. When something is bad, they rate it average. But equally, they find it difficult to be enthusiastic: "exceptional" ratings are rare. So the research always tends to come back with ratings which give minor variations around the "above average" rating. The research department then has a field day analyzing the data for statistical significance, while missing the bigger picture completely.

Researching the Wrong Customer

Business to business research normally focuses on the immediate buyer. This carries two problems. Like the retail customer, buyers lie. Brokers in the life insurance industry invariably claim that the size of commission does not affect the choice of insurer that they recommend to customers. They lie through their teeth as any basic comparison of commissions and sales shows.

But often the immediate buyer is the wrong person to talk to. Typically the buyer will beef about price. His or her performance is measured on the costs achieved. But this may not be what the rest of the organization wants. Marketing may want short runs of product for test markets or to meet surges in demand. Paying a higher price for a small component that then allows them to increase sales is well worth it. Similarly, engineering, production, and even stock control may have specific product needs for which they would happily pay more. Talking to the buyer will not flush this out.

Effective Customer Research

Effective customer research is based on two principles. First, ask the right questions. Focus on behaviors and on the product in use, not on attitudes. Behaviors do not lie. Second, ask the right people: focus on the users of the product, not just the buyers. Look not just at the car buyer, but how the whole family uses the car.

You can pay a research agency a small fortune to find this out. You can also go and find out yourself. Customers are normally intrigued and delighted when a real manager from one of their suppliers sits with them to see how their product is used, and how it could be changed to help them even better. They have a tendency to produce insights that a numbers exercise can not produce.

CUSTOMER SERVICE: LIVING WITH REALITY

If you want to know how good your customer service is, use it yourself:

- Phone your own receptionist, going through the switchboard. Do not use the direct lines. (*See below.*)
- Phone the standard 800 number, not the VIP hotline.
- Be a mystery shopper at your stores or dealers.

If you and your staff have to suffer the same service levels that you inflict on your customers, the business will quickly find out how to improve service. Members of the aircrew pick up their bags before the passengers, and have priority clearance through customs and immigration. The howls of pain that would arise if they had to suffer the delays of their passengers would quickly put an end to airport lines. Car executives who have their new cars delivered never have to go though the pain of being ripped off on buying the new car and selling the old car, or of getting the car serviced and maintained. Intellectually they may see the problem, but they do not understand it.

And if government leaders had to suffer all the indignities of public transportation instead of chauffeured cars, health systems that do not work, and government agencies that are powerful, arrogant, and incompetent in equal proportion, there might be a chance of getting some improvement.

CUSTOMER SERVICE LINES AND CONTEMPT FOR THE CUSTOMER

Customer service lines are wonderful vehicles for showing how deeply you feel contempt for your customers. There are three golden rules for making sure the customers know how little you value them:

1. Understaff the phone bank. Plan staffing levels for average call rates, not for peak call rates. Most people, by definition, call at peak times so understaffing for peaks ensures that you can keep them all waiting. This conveys a simple message to your customers: "We value your time as less than the time of our underpaid staff, so we will keep you waiting and make you pay for the privilege of it (phone charges)." Of course, the person waiting may be a chief executive or vital customer: the customer service line should not discriminate. It should keep them all waiting.

   To rub salt into the wound, force the customers to listen to some advertising. Insert some messages about how much you value their

call: you value it so much that you can not be bothered to answer it promptly.
2. Make the customer do all the work. This has three benefits:
   - It reduces the costs of the call center.
   - It irritates the customer who will be deterred from using the customer service line again, further reducing costs.
   - It allows the business to claim high levels of customer service because it is putting the customer in control.

   It also reinforces your contempt for the customer. Make it complicated for the customer, with lots of screens with lots of options, which are intended to cover every eventuality. The message this sends is: "We do not want to waste money on helping you, we will do our best to stop you talking to anyone, and we can not be bothered to figure out a simple call screening method that would help you: you are on your own, tough luck."

   If the customer should breach the defenses of the automated system and speak to a human being, make the customer go through elaborate identification and security features, including full details of serial numbers of registration documents, which were probably lost years ago. This should see the customer off. This can also be creatively applied to outbound sales calls. British Telecom called its customers to sell them a new service. When the customers answered the phone, they had to identify themselves: this was based on the customer confirming the phone number that BT had just called and the customer had just answered. A sense of the surreal helps.
3. Underpay the staff. Don't give them proper training, just give them scripts that they have to follow so that they are no different from automatic voice response (AVR) systems. This means that it does not matter that you suffer high staff turnover rates, you can always replace the staff with an AVR system if necessary. It also ensures that customers do not get the help or support they need, and leads to a miserable life for the underpaid staff who have to deal with torrents of irate customers.

But the good news in all this is that this corporate function will be able to show that it has achieved its budget and productivity targets.

DELEGATION, EMPOWERMENT, AND DECEPTION

For the last 200 years delegation has been getting worse. Empowerment has become more or less nonexistent except in the speeches made by the big chiefs. Their speeches are deceptions.

The two great enemies of delegation and empowerment are communications and information. Two hundred years ago, the empire builders delegated and empowered without thinking about it. They had no alternative. Once the boat left Europe for India or the colonies it was gone. The next time the people on board would see the big chiefs who had sent them away, it would be years later. By then, they had either succeeded or failed.

If problems arose, they did not refer it to the head office. The boat would take six months to travel from India to England and back again. By then the riot, or whatever the problem was, would have faded into history. Even getting a message from one part of India to another and back again would take weeks. The man on the spot had to take control, had to use initiative.

The same pattern of delegation and empowerment was true of the Navy: Being out at sea meant being out of the immediate control of politicians. Admiral Nelson had to take control. And equally, he expected his captains to take the initiative. He had a simple command for his captains: "Any captain that lays his ship alongside that of the enemy can do no wrong." In other words, get on with it and attack. Don't ask for advice.

Nowadays, if we want to take a penny off the price of a detergent there will be committees, reviews, presentations, research groups, and analyses, and the whole panoply of corporate oversight and help will swing into force. And they call this delegation and empowerment. And once we have embarked on our course of action, we are under the microscope. There are weekly and monthly reports, progress updates, exception reporting, and budget reviews and revisions.

Management trust, delegation, and empowerment are inversely proportional to the frequency and volume of reporting required. By this measure we live in deeply mistrustful times, and the mistrust is getting deeper. Management falls into the trap of "because there is better communication and more information we should use it." And we use it because it gives us more control and reduces the risks implicit in real delegation and empowerment.

Demotivation and cynicism is not merely a product of the administrative burden that the deadweight of reporting represents. The cynicism also comes from knowing that the reporting is a vote of no confidence in those having to report, and that it lays them open to being second-guessed and overruled by the bosses. They are not being entrusted to get on with the business.

But there are other ways of getting control that can leave management more motivated and more focused on the marketplace than on internal reporting (*see page 45* on control).

DEMOCRACY AND DICTATORSHIP AT WORK

The revolution has already happened. Most of the old dictators have been swept away. Traditional command and control through a formal hierarchy is largely dead. There are still a few dinosaurs out there, but their time is up.

Dictatorship at work is a high control, low commitment way of managing people. It invites an "us and them" attitude in which managers hide behind status, rules, and hierarchy while workers organize to protect their rights from the dictators. As long as labor was in greater supply than capital, dictators could dictate.

As workers built more skills and became more mobile and more important to the enterprise, their value as individuals, not mere units of production, rose. The question is what to replace the dictatorship with.

The new age school of thought takes us down the full democratic, tree-hugging, world-saving route. Business is normally not about tree-hugging or saving the world. Democracy is not a viable alternative at work. Businesses are not democracies: they need clear and effective decision-making processes, linked to clear and effective responsibilities and accountabilities. Clarity and accountability do not come through groups, they come through individuals. There has to be a decision-making hierarchy. Not everyone can be involved in all the decisions all the time, and not everyone will like all the decisions.

For management the challenge is how to maintain control, enhance commitment, and make effective decisions without resorting to authority based solely on rank. The new non-dictatorial and non-democratic leadership model has to based on:

- Respect: the leader must be seen as capable.
- Mutual trust: there have to be common goals backed up by guidelines that help both the manager and the managed achieve the goals.
- Individual responsibility.
- Collective involvement.

DIVERSITY

Diversity is a dirty word in most organizations. Of course, for legal reasons and reasons of political correctness, organizations will try to get a smattering of different minority groups onto the payroll. Although there is some tolerance of minority groups, real diversity is avoided. Indeed, organizations pride themselves on their "one firm" approach, which means that you get the same approach, same skills, and same culture right around the world supported by global standards and management systems. So, regardless of your sex, race, or religion you either adapt to the one-firm way or you leave. This is not diversity.

The one-firm approach is linked to the preponderance of middle-aged white males in suits in all the top management positions. They set the culture, the standards, and the systems. And the culture and the values just happen to reflect the culture and values of white middle-aged males. This is not some white male conspiracy. Japanese companies are even more zealous in promoting a single, homogenous culture across the globe in their global businesses. The only non-Japanese in leading management positions in Japan are in companies that have been taken over by foreigners, such as Mazda and Nissan.

Intolerance of diversity is natural and unavoidable. Working on a global basis, management needs a common set of assumptions and beliefs if it is to operate effectively, make good decisions on a timely basis, and to communicate and understand each other properly. The Tower of Babel is not a good starting point for a global business. The only way an employee can manage this is to be aware of it at the recruiting stage. Find out what the rules of the game are, and if you don't fit in, don't join.

Warren Buffet wrote: "I find that when a manager with a great reputation joins a business with a lousy reputation, it is normally the reputation of the business that stays intact." It is the same with a culture. If you represent a different culture from the firm you join, rest assured that the culture of the firm will not change. Either you will change, or you will leave.

DRESS, SCHIZOPHRENIA, AND THE CASTE SYSTEM

Dress shows how we want to be seen in the world: who we are, which groups we belong to and, just as important, which groups we do not belong to. In the age of conformity, this made life pretty simple for both the individual and the institution. Everyone got to wear the corporate uniform, and no one had to think about identity very much. The only crisis came in deciding just how boring today's tie should be.

Dress codes now cause chaos. Institutions realize they want to be seen differently by different groups. The large-scale systems firm wants to be seen as big, trusty, and infinitely reliable by their risk-averse customers. Conservative suits and ties send the right message. But to employment recruits, the firm wants to be seen as hip, high-tech, and fun. Suits and ties are not quite the way to do this. The firm's schizophrenia has been revealed by dress codes. It cannot be all things to all people at all times without large-scale deceit.

The dress crisis goes into the heart of the institution itself. In place of one uniform, there are hundreds of uniforms that define a person's position in the business with the precision of the caste system:

- Each function has its own style: finance and accounting want to look conservative and trustworthy, creative types try to look creative, IT types try to look hip.
- Each level of management has its own style: custom-made for top management, designer labels for aspiring middle management, off the rack for junior management, and dead casual for support staff.

■ Each country has its own style, from the overwhelming conformity of the Japanese to the tyranny of the buff chinos for Americans; each nationality dresses its culture.

Connoisseurs of dress can tell exactly which country a person is from, their department and level just from the dress worn. This matters because it says that people feel a sense of community not with the organization, but with their function or peer group or country. Years of corporate disloyalty to staff through downsizing, restructuring, and reengineering is being repaid by a comprehensive expression of disloyalty to the organization. If people feel that their identity is primarily as an IT professional, not as an employee of MegaBucks, it is no surprise that they feel relaxed about hawking their skills to the employer with the best package.

Trying to turn the tide back and go to the 1960s or Japanese standards of dress conformity is pushing against history. The battle has been fought and comprehensively lost. The greater battle for trying to rebuild a sense of community and loyalty, a psychological contract based on mutual commitment has hardly begun.

DUE DILIGENCE

This is a process in which the following happens:

■ A lot of very highly paid advisors sit in a room amidst the increasing chaos of half-eaten pizzas, smelly socks, fuzzy milk, and fuzzy thinking.
■ The advisors charge outrageous fees, regardless of whether the outcome of the bid is successful or not.
■ The advisors seek to justify in every way possible that the client's gut instinct to launch a takeover bid was correct, in spite of overwhelming evidence to the contrary.
■ The thrill of the chase overwhelms management and advisors alike, throwing objectivity out of the window. Winning is all, even if the cost is out of hand.

Generally, the only antidote is a used envelope. On the back of it write out clearly why you believe the takeover is right, and what the top price is that you should pay. Do this before you talk to the advisors. Keep the envelope with you at all times. Then you know when you should walk away.

EASY DOES IT

Make it easy. For your customers, for your staff, for yourself. Put idleness to your advantage.

Make It Easy for Your Customers

Customers are busy. They have lives to lead. It may be climbing mountains or sitting in front of the TV watching football. But it is almost certainly more enjoyable and important to them than worrying about your product and service. And they do not want to spend their lives figuring out how to use your service. Equally, they do not have the time, inclination, or expertise to do a full assessment of your offering versus all of those in the marketplace. This is true of retail products. Even businesses do only limited beauty parades and comparison shopping.

This is wonderful news for business. It means that price is not always the most important thing. Make it easy for the customer to pick you and use you, and the customer will stay. Make it easy to pick you: branding (retail markets) and reputation (business to business markets) count. Make the decision an easy one.

Make it easy for them to use your service. Look at e-business Web sites to see how not to do it. Some Web sites have been hijacked by the techies. They are so keen to show off their technical prowess that the site is fit only for rocket scientists or those with the patience of a saint. Or the product people have hijacked it. They are so keen to show all the bells and whistles of their great service that it is unusable to all bar the initiated. The simple sites are intuitive, invite people to use them, and make it easy. The simple sites win. The sophisticated sites lose. If you make the complex easy, people will reward you with loyalty and pay higher prices.

Make It Easy for Your Staff

This is not about idleness, it is about effectiveness. There are three ways to make it easy for staff:

- Focus. Keep it simple. Know the priorities, know what you will not do. This makes life easier for the staff, and makes for better results.
- Delegation. Don't put the staff in a position where they are always second-guessing you, checking with you, and reiterating work. Delegate. Put the pressure on them to get it right first time. Avoid rework.
- Expectations. Be clear about what is and is not expected. It is not enough to have focus, the staff need to understand the focus and what it means to them personally.

Make It Easy for Yourself

If you have made it easy for your staff, you have probably made it easy for yourself. You should have staff doing what they should be doing, leaving you to focus on what you need to focus on. The wrinkle is that the focus and expectations setting also needs upwards management: the boss needs to have the same expectations as you and your team. The easy life is the good life.

E-BUSINESS: THE MASTER AND THE SERVANT

E-business contains one big truism and one big lie. The truism is that the Internet will transform business. Already it has been adopted faster than any other disruptive technology such as the telephone, television, radio, or car. And yet business is still only starting to learn how to harness the potential of the Internet. How it will develop we can only guess.

The big lie is to see the Internet as the master, not the servant, of business. In the headlong rush of entrepreneurs and venture capitalists into the Internet this basic mistake was being made repeatedly. The assumption was that the new technology would blow away all the boring old management disciplines such as offering customers a distinctive benefit or controlling costs. This was putting technology before business. Like putting the cart before the horse, it does not work. The fortunes will continue to be made by those who marry new economy insight with old economy disciplines.

EMOTIONAL CYCLE OF CHANGE AND THE VALLEY OF DEATH

Rational managers are not meant to have emotions. Smart managers recognize there are emotions, and use them to their advantage. As consultants, one of the strongest sales weapons we had was an understanding of the emotional cycle of change. This helped us lead clients through change, and helped us know when and how to sell the next multimillion dollar change effort.

The emotional cycle of change is like a big dipper. The highs are very high, the lows are very low. The downward rush is always faster than the upwards haul. The emotional cycle has five stages, which repeat themselves constantly throughout the change program.

This example looks at just one cycle. It is one major consulting firm's sales cycle. In eight weeks they will take the client from a modest start to signing up for a multimillion dollar change program. They achieve this by explicitly managing the emotional, as well as political and rational, aspects of change. It is manipulative, so it works. Managers should apply this to themselves:

1. Week zero. Euphoria. Everyone has got past denying there is a problem and spreading the blame. They have agreed on a solution: call in the consultants. The problem is now transferred to them. Something is happening and people start to relax. By the end of week one the consultants will have demonstrated a fast start, the client will now feel confident that they have made a smart choice and the confidence grows.
2. Week two. The death spiral. The consultants are now bringing back strong, validated data to show that the business is in far worse shape than management at first believed. Consultants know where to look to find the skeletons. Rationally, management sees the argument. The consultants are whispering in private to management that yet worse is to come. The sense of nervousness of management is growing.
3. Week four. The valley of death. This is where the consultants will say: "This is the worst we have ever seen." This valley of death exercise is conducted in private with each senior manager. The object is to show that:
   - the situation is truly awful: denial or inaction would be fatal, a solution must be found;

- management owns the problem, and the solution: they cannot blame anyone else;
- the situation is urgent and personal: this is not a rational debate about business survival, this is a question of personal survival. Until managers get into this valley of death, they cannot move on. They will still be denying, spreading the blame, or lacking urgency. And they have to go through this valley of death personally. It is not a happy group exercise. The consultant's challenge is to get everyone to march through the valley of death individually but at the same time.

4. Week six. The cautious recovery. The consultants are no longer painting a picture of the apocalypse. Instead, they are offering a lifeline, some potential solutions that management can buy into. The deeper the valley of death has been, the more ambitious (expensive) the solution is likely to be. Management is grateful for the lifeline. The consultants are crafting an agenda that they can deliver and that will satisfy all the different management constituencies. This is now a political exercise.

5. Week eight: return to euphoria. After the hell of the last two months, management has peered into the precipice of doom and found a way of leaping over it. There is a solution. The solution depends on the friendly consultants who have found a way out of the valley of death. The multimillion dollar investment (not expense) of the consultants promises great returns and the business is ready to move on. Inevitably, this is followed by buyer's regret in a couple of weeks as the enormity of the task in front of them, and the expense, becomes apparent. But by then, it is too late to go back. Management is committed and the emotional cycle of change starts again as they go back down the death spiral.

ENTHUSIASM

"All creatures of the universe: rejoice! On pain of death," Emperor Min to the creatures of the universe in *Flash Gordon*. Being told to be enthusiastic is the best way to destroy enthusiasm. But unless people have some sense of enthusiasm and enjoyment, they are not going to have that extra commitment that will make the business succeed. People are not good at what they do not enjoy. People only excel at what they enjoy.

There is one thing that will not help you create a sense of enthusiasm: taking staff away to corporate events, team building exercises, and forced fun parties are a waste of time. Some of the staff will like the event, but the moment they return to a miserable office, the misery and old habits kick straight back in. The rest of the staff probably don't want to go abseiling or building rafts, and hate every moment of it but know that they are not allowed to say so. Practically, there are three things a manager can do to build a sense of enthusiasm:

- Be enthusiastic yourself. You either have it, or you don't. But staff take their cues from management. If you are a miserable, political bastard, do not be surprised if the staff seem like miserable, political bastards. Cultures are self-reinforcing. Bad ones get worse, good ones get better. If you have no enthusiasm for what you do, you are probably doing the wrong thing.
- Show that you know your staff and care for them. A survey of how staff rated management showed that if staff believed that a manager cared for them personally, then all the other attributes of the manager (intelligence, insight, effectiveness, results, etc) were seen positively. Managers who did not care for staff were rated badly on all other management criteria as well. If you ever want a good 360-degree feedback, showing you care is the way to get it. This does not mean being false-nice: it means being honest and taking the time and trouble to listen to and talk with each staff member.
- Give staff a sense of direction and purpose. Human nature hates ambiguity and risk. You can take that away by painting a clear picture of where you are trying to go, and of what it means to them in terms of opportunities. You may need them to climb Everest, but that is better than leaving them meandering, lost in the foothills.

ENTREPRENEURS, BUSINESS, AND THE PACT WITH THE DEVIL

Businesses like to think they are entrepreneurial. They lie, and fool only themselves. The entrepreneurial approach is as palatable to businesses as salt to a slug.

Ambiguity, Risk, and Speed

Corporations tolerate risk but hate ambiguity. Planned risk is part of any investment or new market initiative. But there are no mechanisms for dealing with ambiguity.

The entrepreneur will seek to minimize risk: his house is probably on the line. But ambiguity is tolerable: it creates opportunities to do things differently and create some new competitive space. So where there are two or three different ways of attacking a market, the entrepreneur will probably try a couple of ways, see which works, and then scale up fast. The corporate executive will want to research everything in detail, document and prove the best case before teams of managers, and then proceed. By which time, the entrepreneurs have already moved.

Hustle

In the corporate world everyone takes vacations. When employees take vacations fall sick, retire, resign, or die, the business moves on. The entrepreneur quickly discovers that unless he hustles, nothing happens. And the hustle has to be hustle on all fronts: finding customers, recruiting talent, managing people, sorting out the finances. There are no large company departments to take all of these problems away.

Corporate Life Support Systems and the Pact with the Devil

Anyone who has escaped from the corporate to the entrepreneurial world is shocked:

- Flunkies do not come round with fresh flowers for the office.
- You have to do your own photocopying at a local print shop.
- The air-conditioning system means opening the window. Getting more money is not a matter of politics and a new budget system: it means crawling on your knees to hard-nosed banks and venture capitalists.
- Managing cash flow is not a budget item: it means either paying the rent or not.
- Traveling economy is possible without dying.
- There are no committees to block you, but none to support you and share the blame. You are responsible for your own decisions.

This is the pact with the devil that employees sign up to with their employer. The employer puts in place all sorts of corporate systems that both support and suppress the individual. As long as you go along with the corporate systems, life is fine. Buck the system, and it will strike back. This does not make big company employees into natural entrepreneurs. It does not make it easy for big companies to accommodate the true entrepreneur. They are different beasts.

The solution for corporate executives is not to pretend to be entrepreneurial. It quickly leads to corporate confusion and schizophrenia. Entrepreneurialism has to exist outside the safe confines of the corporate world. Fostering entrepreneurialism means creating a unit outside all the normal controls of the business, preferably far away geographically, with a powerful political sponsor who shoots any corporate managers that tries to help.

ENTROPY AND EXCELLENCE

Excellence is the holy grail of management. It will never be found, and it is not necessary. The daily reality of most management is dealing with the fog of war and the constant forces of entropy that create chaos out of order. For most management, competence and survival is a success. That's the bad news. The good news is that the competition is struggling just as hard with the fog of war and the forces of entropy. This means that competitive advantage is not based on some abstract notion of absolute excellence. Competitive advantage simply requires being less incompetent than the competition.

In some areas of some industries the levels of competence are genuinely high: the technical expertise required in producing microchips, the marketing skills of Procter & Gamble, or the trading skills of some investment banks are outstanding. But even these organizations will recognize that they fall far short of excellence in all that they do. The trading skills of P&G are awful: they lost hundreds of millions by trying to be too clever. And investment banks have no idea about marketing.

The search for excellence is pointless and wasteful. The challenge is to focus on doing the basics right, and to keep on improving, preferably slightly faster than the competition.

EXCESS CAPACITY

Excess capacity is not a sin. It may well represent a smart investment. Think of all the times you have been stuck in checkout lines, or waiting in line at the airport, or waiting on the phone for the 800 number to answer. You, as the customer, are being forced to pay for the service provider's lack of capacity. You may get slightly lower prices in return for service that sucks.

Think of all the initiatives you would like to start, the research that needs to be done, the markets that need to be tested and opened, but you can't for lack of capacity. The organization may be extremely lean and efficient, but at the cost of underinvesting in its future.

Any system that operates with no excess capacity, that strives for 100 percent efficiency is inherently unstable. It cannot cope with any unexpected demand, nor respond to any unexpected problems. An office where all the staff are already working 50 to 60 hours a week just to maintain the status quo is not a happy place, and probably does not have a good future.

Excess capacity in the office is rarely measured in individuals who are doing nothing at all. It is more likely that six or ten or twelve people each have a quarter or half their time that could be redeployed effectively. The art is to know where that slack exists and then focus it. Keep a list of all the initiatives you would like to start, and then you can marry the excess supply to the demand. As and when a business shock comes along, you can then redeploy that excess capacity away from the discretionary efforts and on to the full-time work. You have a business that can deal with peaks and troughs, and can pursue the discretionary efforts that are the investment in the future.

EXCUSES

Never use or accept excuses. If there is a problem, explain clearly why the problem occurred. If you know why it happened, you should also have the solution. Bring both the problem and the solution to the table. Then you look positive, proactive, and in control.

Weak and defensive managers simply turn up with their excuse. Worse, they try to hide or shift responsibility. When found out they appear untrustworthy, defensive, reactive, and not in control.

Equally, do not accept excuses. Prevention is far better than cure. Set your team up to succeed, and help them win, then no excuses are necessary. If excuses start appearing, then it is as much your fault as the fault of the people making excuses. First, get the team to come back with solutions, not excuses. Then figure out what you need to do to prevent a reoccurrence of the problem and the excuse reaction.

EXPATRIATES

Expatriates are rarely worth the trouble for either the corporation or the individual. I should know: I was one. From the corporate point of view, the expatriate in theory does a lot. He or she helps transfer skills, helps build the one-firm firm globally, helps maintain global standards, and provides insight to global management about regional opportunities and performance. An expatriate posting is also a way of stretching and developing individuals. There is, however, an alternative reality:

- Expatriates are extremely expensive compared to local hires.
- Expatriates take time to get up to speed: they underperform relative to their capabilities while they learn the local language and local business.
- They do not represent a vote of confidence in local management: morale can be damaged and it becomes harder to recruit good locals if they see the path to the top obstructed by foreigners.
- Expatriates are likely to leave once they have finished their tour of duty: the skills so expensively nurtured will be lost.

From the expatriate's point of view, things do not look much better:

- Culture shock is real: about 40 percent of the people we sent to Japan washed out inside two months. This was a typical experience.
- Reintegration into the home business is difficult. No position can be held open for three years. And no one will be overly keen to give up their chance of promotion to someone who has not been around.
- Culture shock on the return is real. Having got used to running a business and being a big shot far away, it is difficult to readjust to being stuck in the matrix of middle management back in the home office. Many expatriates leave the company at this point.

There is always going to be the need for some expatriates. From the corporate point of view, they should be minimized. From the individual point of view, be very wary of accepting an expatriate position. And never believe any of the promises of what will happen when you return.

EYES OF MANAGEMENT

Different managers can look at the same thing and see completely different things. This is a source of huge strength when all the different angles are brought together to create a common picture. It is also a source of endless conflict when the different points of view are in competition with each other.

Try walking into a grocery store and do the "eyes of management" test. See how different people will see exactly the same thing. A good grocery store is a beautifully choreographed show, which the consumer is scarcely aware of. Looking through the eyes of the different players illustrates how radically different perspectives have to come together. For example:

- The manufacturer's salesperson sees just his or her own products and how they are displayed relative to the competition, whether the promotional messages and the prices are correct, and whether each brand has the correct number of facings for its market share. This then leads to a discussion with the buyer about how to position the products better.
- Shelf-fillers see the gaps in the shelves and the sell-by dates on the products that need to be rotated.
- The store manager is seeing detail, detail, detail: looking for stockouts, display errors, checkout lines, staff deployment and behavior, pilferage, maintenance issues, compliance with head office guidelines on displays and promotions, as well as the general administration of the store.
- Security is looking at customers and staff and for the typical patterns of pilferage.
- Maintenance see broken light bulbs, dirt, faulty wiring and fixtures that are, hopefully, invisible to others.
- The area manager is seeing the detail of the store manager, but is also looking at how the store manager is interacting with the staff, what is going wrong, where the store manager needs support or coaching.
- The marketing manager starts looking in the car park: how many people there are, what sorts of people they are (singles, families, age, level of affluence) and what the local environment is (competition, transportation, other complementary stores). Implicitly he or she is looking at the potential of the store, which can then be

checked against the reality of what is happening in the store: how customers are moving around the store, where they are stopping and buying and where they just pass through.

Through this, the customer wanders barely aware of the extraordinary performance being choreographed around the shopping cart. It is not possible for the customer to see everything that all the managers and staff see. The strength of the organization is in the choreography of the show. Managerially, the challenge is to move from the cacophony of management to the choreography of management: see and coordinate all the different perspectives of all the different players.

FINANCIAL ACCOUNTING: THE ROAD TO IRRELEVANCE

Financial accounting was never perfect. A system that was born hundreds of years ago is looking as relevant to today's business as the quill pens that were used in the first ledgers. There were always some basic problems:

- Financial accounting looks backward, not forward. This is fine for keeping score, but not for scoring goals.
- Accounting conventions leave enough room for interpretation that there is huge potential to mislead. Profit figures massaged year after year by exceptional items, write-offs, depreciation of goodwill, different treatment of stocks, inventory, and even different ways of recognizing sales give plenty of room to maneuver. No wonder analysts and fund managers trash companies that miss earnings targets by a penny. If they miss even after all the expectation setting and numbers massaging, then something fairly profound must be wrong.
- Financial accounting is only a starting point for understanding corporate performance. Market share, sales, growth, productivity, new products are probably better forward indicators of performance than backward-looking financial data.

The twenty-first century is making the problems worse. The financial accounting profession is still fighting the battles of the last century. They are trying to harmonize irrelevant standards. The challenge for the profession is not standardization, it is relevance.

At the heart of the problem are intangible assets. When Pacioli invented double-entry bookkeeping, it was based on the presumption that the book entries represented real, tangible assets that had a clear market, cash value. This 500-year-old assumption is still at the heart of accounting. But a look at the shape of twenty-first century business shows that this assumption is wrong. The assets of today's businesses are not physical or tradable assets:

▓ Nike: the value of the business is in the brand. Production is outsourced. There is not that much in the way of physical assets beyond a lot of old posters. Heroic, but unconvincing, efforts are being made to value brands. From the accounting point of view, there is no reliable way of putting the brand on the balance sheet: is advertising an expense or a capital investment building the value of the brand?

▓ Investment banks: the assets are walking out of the door each evening. The assets are the skills of the staff. One hundred years ago, accounting did not have to worry about skills: capitalists provided the capital, managers managed, and workers worked. Workers were not skilled, and were easily replaced.

▓ Dot-coms: the value of the business is not physical assets. It is based on the value of the intellectual property, the business idea of the dot-com.

▓ Pharmaceutical companies: the value of the business is in patents supported by a strong distribution network. The physical assets are largely irrelevant, except for their cash mountains. Financial accounting does not reflect the value of those assets, nor how investment in those assets should be treated.

The shift from physical to intangible assets is also linked to a parallel shift from costs being largely variable to largely fixed. When Adam Smith observed the pin-makers in Gloucester, the cost of each pin was related to two main variable costs: raw materials and labor. There was virtually no overhead. The pin-makers did not have advertisers, training departments, strategy or HR functions, computer systems, telephone networks, corporate headquarters, accounting staff, or any of the other overhead that represent today's corporate life support system. This explosion of overhead and semi-fixed cost is a nightmare for traditional financial accounting systems:

▓ Costs and profits are becomingly increasingly dependent on potentially arbitrary overhead allocation decisions. Financial accounting, based on departmental budgets, does not give management a rational basis on which to make allocation decisions.

■ The balance sheet is becoming increasingly disconnected from the value of the business and the true, intangible, assets that underpin it.

■ The profit figure is open to distortion: a good starting point for looking at an annual report is not the profit and loss but the notes to see how the figures will have been massaged.

About the only figure that has much integrity left is the cash flow statement: even that can be distorted on an annual basis by timing sales and expenses smartly. Over a three- to five-year period, it is hard to have a cash flow statement that lies. But five years is history, not an actionable time frame for management or investors. Management accounting is starting to come to grips with the challenges of the twenty-first century. Financial accounting is stuck in the wrong century.

FINANCIAL ACCOUNTING: ROADS TO RICHES AND RUIN.

If you marry an outdated accounting system which is open to abuse with poor corporate governance and, in the words of Alan Greenspan, "infectious greed," you have a recipe for disaster. The dot-com bubble provided a perfect breeding ground for the abuse of the financial accounting system. To make money from bubble surfing, everyone had to believe that the laws of economics, accounting and competition had been suspended so that ever greater wealth could be conjured out of thin air. To keep the bubble afloat, stock analysts needed a flow of good news. Companies and their auditors were all too happy to provide the material to keep up the hype of the analysts.

The new economy brought new financial accounting tricks. Special purpose vehicles at Enron helped disguise liabilties and hyped-up profits. Telcos "increased" sales by selling unused capacity to each other. Neither side gained any net extra revenues, but both sides could report growing sales and hide unused capacity. Portfolio investments became a great way of finding exceptional profits. As long as the market was rising, any portfolio investments provided a ready source of capital gains. None of these were sustainable.

For managers, keeping the bubble afloat with financial accounting was the road to riches. One hundred forty-four senior managers at Enron received $744 million from the company in the year before it went bust. Twenty-five managers from just six companies that went bust as the bubble burst managed to make $2.6 billion between them. On average, they made over $100 million each in the year before they let their companies go bust. For the shareholders of Global Crossing, Enron, Exodus Communications, McleodUSA, XO Communications and Metromedia Fibe Network, this was the road to ruin, not riches.

In the aftermath of Enron and the dot-com bubble, accounting standards will be tightened. But the regulators are simply sticking their finger in the dyke and hoping the dam will not burst. The next boom will bring a new wave of accounting scandals. As long as we have an arcane and complex financial accounting systems with its origins based on medieval assumptions, the system will be open to abuse.

FLAT ORGANIZATIONS, FLAT RESULTS

The flat organization can be a very high performing organization. At its best it is a high commitment, high energy, flexible business that works closely together. Seeing this, some traditional organizations have tried to flatten themselves. In the process they have flattened their results. They lack the culture, legacy, or capability to perform as a flat organization. They should be true to what they are, and not pretend to be what they can not be. Despite claims to the contrary, elephants do not learn to dance except as a comic routine in old-fashioned circuses. Here's how one very successful but traditional organization tried to flatten the organization and succeeded in flattening its performance:

■ Massive centralization and bureaucracy. The new organization still needed to integrate and coordinate its efforts. This used to be achieved through the hierarchy. In place of the formal hierarchical control, lots of staff jobs appeared to coordinate training policies, recruiting policies, standards, quality, communications, financial controls, and companywide initiatives. Once in, the staffers are impossible to shift.

■ Exponential growth of internal communications and focus. Decisions that used to require two or three people would suddenly require 10 or 20 people. The number of points of contact and communication grew exponentially with the introduction of each new dimension of the matrix. The flat organization had a five-dimensional matrix. Normal human beings can not think in more than three dimensions (or four, if time is a dimension). This meant decisions would now involve industry groups, geographical groups, functional groups, product/service groups, and skills-based groups. Each had competing agendas and overlapping responsibilities.

▪ Politics rose and accountability declined. The matrix allowed people and performance to hide. It enabled individuals to associate themselves with initiatives if they looked like being successful and to disassociate themselves if it looked like being unsuccessful.

▪ Managers stopped talking to each other. The complexity of communication became so great that at first a few managers found it easiest to call large meetings of all the interested parties together, rather than talk to other managers one to one. It was the easiest way of squaring up all the different agendas. Where previously one manager would call another directly and discuss the issue or arrange to meet, the secretaries took over to coordinate multiple diaries.

▪ Internal meetings and conferences proliferated. Everyone belonged to all five sides of the matrix. To assert their authority and influence, managers of each dimension would summon their underlings to meetings, training events, and increasingly lavish offsite events designed to woo the underlings.

Naturally, the business was so busy coordinating itself, it lost sight of the customer.

A flat organization is as much a cultural statement as an organizational statement. Put a flat organization chart onto a hierarchical organization and the nightmare starts. The traditional hierarchical manager takes the flat organization chart too seriously, and spends the whole time looking at what it means in terms of accountability, responsibility, power, and authority. They make the mistake of believing the chart. The result is not a lean, flexible, and market-focused business but a bureaucratic, political muddle.

FORECASTING AND EXPERTS

Everyone gets their forecasts wrong. Experts are wrong with greater eloquence and authority than the rest of us. Here's the expert view on:

- Telephones: "An amazing invention, but who would want to use one?"—U.S. president Rutherford Hayes, 1876.
- Electric lighting: "Good enough for our transatlantic friends . . . but unworthy of practical or scientific men"—British Parliamentary Select Committee, 1878.
- Record players: "The phonograph is of no commercial value"—Thomas Alva Edison.
- Computers: "There is no reason for any individual to have a computer in their home"—Ken Olson, President of DEC, 1977.
- Computers (again): "I think there is a world market for about five computers"—IBM founder Thomas J. Watson, 1947.
- Radio: "I have anticipated its complete disappearance – confident that the unfortunate people who must now subdue themselves to 'listening in' will soon find a better pastime for their leisure"—H.G. Wells, 1928.
- Atomic power: "Anyone who expects a source of power from the transformation of these atoms is talking moonshine"—Nobel prize-winning physicist Lord Rutherford after he had split the atom in 1911.
- The stock market: "Stock prices have reached what looks like a permanently high plateau"—Irving Fisher, professor of economics at Yale University, September 1929, just before the Wall Street crash.

Of course, corporate forecasts are never so foolish. Are they?

FREQUENT FLYERS

Frequent flying is a disaster for business. Just because frequent flying is possible, it does not mean managers should fly frequently. Flying may be tedious, uncomfortable, tiring, cause jet lag and destroy productivity, but it is a powerful status symbol. The more you fly, the more important you must be. And if you travel business or first class, then you must be even more important to the business. Complaining about jet lag, poor service, and delayed flights is simply a way of articulating your status to people who do not see you travel and do not realize the status it brings with it.

Because flying is still a status symbol, the rot starts at the top. Some of the most frequent, and certainly most expensive travelers, are senior managers. Flying reinforces their status: while they turn left at the aircraft door to go business or first, the underlings enjoy the humiliation of turning right into the cramped seats at the back. The apartheid of status is rigorously laid out by corporate travel policies and enforced by the airlines as you step on the aircraft.

Senior managers are articulate about why they need to spend up to $10,000 to rent a bed for six hours while they cross the Atlantic. It's all about their productivity. Which is another way of saying that the productivity of their staff traveling economy does not matter so much to them. The airlines reinforce the frequent flyer abuse through their loyalty programs. The loyalty programs mean:

- People make more business trips than necessary.
- They pay full fare when they could find a discount with a cheaper airline.
- They fly at awkward times to gain loyalty points with their chosen airline.

Travel policies and procedures do not stop this abuse. Travel policies may dictate class of travel, but do nothing to stop the extent of travel or choice of airline. Stopping this abuse by trying to claim ownership of the air miles earned on corporate expense, invites a long emotional battle with staff that is not worth fighting. One solution would be to name and shame the worst culprits. Publish a table with the number of miles flown per manager, the cost per mile, and the total cost. If senior management set a good example, junior managers would be reluctant to be seen to be outspending and outflying their bosses.

Unfortunately, this is a table that most senior managers would quietly like to lead, with the junior managers trying to emulate them. Consultancies have an effective, if dishonest answer. They implicitly treat travel as a perk of the job, and simply charge their clients for the expense. It is a cost-free perk to the consultants, and an expensive one for their clients.

GLORY AND LIES: THE ANNUAL REPORT

The company annual report has one main objective: to glorify top management. The glorification starts with lots of pictures and comments by the Big Shots. This is where the lies start. To show that they are worthy of their glory, the annual report has to show how well the business has done, regardless of the actual results.

Below is the patent lie detector test for annual reports. Any annual report scoring over 75 percent gets a gold level award. You will then be entitled to send a scored copy of this test to the chairperson of the company with a raspberry or whatever reward you think is most appropriate for the gold standard lies you have detected. There are three categories of lies:

1. Category one lies: We are a happy, politically correct company. Evidence is mainly in the pictures:
   - Pictures of the only senior women or minority executives or non-executives to disguise the glass ceiling that operates in the company.
   - Pictures of smiling employees with disabilities, women, and minority frontline workers who are on low/minimum wages and struggling to survive while doing dirty, dull, or dangerous jobs.
   - Pictures of charities that have benefited from the company's need to appear politically correct.
   - Statements showing that the firm cares for the environment (the most polluting companies claim this the most vigorously).
   - Pictures of happy, local employees in exotic destinations: also on low wages—avoids pictures from exotic but politically incorrect countries (dictatorships, kleptocracies).
2. Category two lies: management is doing a great job. Annual reports will either provide excuses in bad years or will claim management

excellence in good years. Any company that admits management failings in bad years or luck in good years is probably worth investing in: they have a strong grip on reality, if not on deceit. Evidence: mainly in the chairperson's and CEO's statements:

- In bad years, score points for each excuse: market downturn, government action or inaction, supplier and input costs, currency effects, weather and calamities, and other more creative excuses. In other words, all the bad stuff is attributed to external factors, not management.

- In good years, score a point for each claim to fame: new product successes, new strategic direction, cost-cutting programs, quality programs, new systems implementation, new advertising, new alliances, and any other actions, which on further examination are common to this company and all its competitors. All the good stuff is attributed to management, not to external factors.

- Give double points to any company that gives both excuses and a list of claims to fame, which are no different to those of its competitors.

3. Category three lies: the numbers are not so bad. This is where the financial director earns his or her money. The goal is to make sure that the numbers are in line with analysts' expectations, regardless of the underlying performance of the business. The evidence is in the profit and loss account, the balance sheet and the cash flow statement. The notes are where the forensic evidence can be found to nail the lies. These lies could fill several books. The highlights are:

- Smoothing the profit and loss downward: higher than normal write-offs and exceptional items, special pension contributions, provisions for restructuring, and bad debts.

- Smoothing the profit and loss upward: lower than normal write-offs and exceptional items, pension holidays, write-backs, gains on sale of assets, capitalization of expense items (IT investments).

- Massaging the balance sheet to make the ratios look good: off balance sheet financing and obligations, stocks valuations and write-offs, property revaluations.

- Massaging the cash flow statement: fix the timing of major payments or income streams to fall just outside the accounting period.

If the financial director can not make the numbers come in line with expectations, then either he or she is incompetent or the results are truly awful. Either way, the overreaction of the investment analysts and the share price plunge will be well justified.

GRASS IS GREENER ON THE OTHER SIDE OF THE FENCE

The Risks and Opportunities of Moving On

Everyone likes to believe the grass is greener on the other side of the fence, even successful people. Business people may dream of the power of politicians, who may dream of the glamor of actors, who may dream of the glory of sportsmen, who may dream of the artistry of poets, who may crave the genius of scientists. There is always someone else who seems to be better off. A good starting point is to recognize that no one has it all; even those who appear to have it all still crave something that is beyond the reach of money or power.

The only consensus I ever heard was as a hippie: everyone agreed that Pokhara in Nepal was the other side of the fence: truly the grass there was the greenest and the best, they said. This does not help business people in the throes of deciding their careers.

Moving jobs is fun. You learn new skills. But it is inherently risky. In the thrill of the chase, both the hunter and the hunted tend to overpromise. The hunter will tend to overplay the strengths of the company and the importance of the role on offer. The hunted will tend to overplay his or her achievements and track record. So, the first thing that happens is disappointment versus the expectations that have been raised. Then reality strikes for the new hire:

- No support network. In large organizations, this is built up over years, helps people to navigate their way around, and is essential for making things happen. Because it happens over years, it seems natural. Without it in the new organization, the new hire is desperately exposed until he or she can build a new network, at speed.
- Unclear rules of the game. Every organization has unwritten rules about how to make things happen, what is good and bad behavior, what to wear and how to work. Unconsciously, the new hire is stepping on landmines left, right, and center. The politics are totally obscure.
- Scepticism. People will want to see you prove yourself, fast. Especially if there were internal candidates for your job. But proving

yourself fast in a new environment where you do not know the politics and rules of the game and have no network is harder than proving yourself in the old organization.

▦ Disillusionment. The grass is not greener on the other side. Many companies in the same industry end up with similar sorts of skills, people and styles. They may be new, but not necessarily better. And, even if the culture is different, this leads to the discovery that the strengths and weaknesses are simply different from before. At least this makes the source of frustration different.

Given the credulity of recruiters, and their tendency to overvalue outside experience relative to internal experience, it should be possible to promote yourself out of your current firm. Two years later you can always get another promotion and raise by rejoining the old firm with your new experience.

GUARANTEES: PROMISES AND LIES

Businesses like the idea of offering guarantees. It shows that the business has faith in its product and can attract customers. But many businesses wimp out when it comes to offering or fulfilling the guarantee. This is when the caution of the bean counters and the lawyers overwhelms the logic of the marketplace. Wimping out of guarantees is typically driven by three concerns:

▦ Some customers will cheat. At college an old scam was to buy a suit from Brooks Brothers, wear it to an interview, and then return it to the store and get a cash refund. The students effectively cashed a check and rented a smart suit for free. In return, Brooks Brothers acquired many faithful future customers. And the cheats, students aside, are a small and affordable minority.

▦ Acts of God. We cannot guarantee overnight delivery if disaster strikes. This is true. Part of the solution is to stop disaster striking. If delivery people on the ground have their van break down, empower them to do whatever it takes to make the delivery. The guarantee works not just on the customer, it works on the business by forcing them to find solutions that will improve performance and ensure that customers do not have to call upon the guarantee.

▦ Costs of the guarantee. These are driven by poor performance and some customer cheating. The challenge for the business is that the costs of the guarantee are immediately apparent; the benefits flow only later through improved performance, customer loyalty, and word of mouth referrals. This is where management shows its loyalty: to the bean counters or to the market.

The wimp's response to the problems of the service guarantee is to offer a meaningless guarantee. The typical ways of making a guarantee worthless are:

- Make it highly conditional. Put onerous maintenance requirements on customers in order for them to keep the guarantee alive.
- Make it difficult to claim. Oblige customers to send in a registration form within seven days of purchase, and then require full proof of purchase and the original packaging to be sent at their expense when submitting a claim. This should eliminate 99 percent of claims.
- Make the value of the guarantee low. Consultants often offer a one-month discontinuation clause as a guarantee. This is worthless.

The effect of these non-guarantees is that customers are not encouraged to claim. The business does not hear what is going wrong, it does not receive signals showing how and where it needs to raise performance, it destroys customer loyalty, and leads to disaffected customers unselling its reputation in the marketplace. A low claims cost is achieved at a terrible price to the business. In contrast, the effective service guarantee has several key elements:

- It is relevant. Delivery by noon next day, guaranteed, is relevant for people shifting important packages. The power of this guarantee meant that one firm in New York had managers using FedEx to send packages from one floor of its office building to another. All the packages went from New York to Memphis and back to New York again at great cost, simply because the guarantee was reassurance the package would arrive there, versus the uncertainties of the internal mail system.
- It is unconditional. Domino's pizza promised to deliver the pizza in 30 minutes, or the pizza was free. The guarantee was unconditional: no excuses for bad weather, traffic, breakdowns. And, importantly, the customer did not have to do anything to claim. They simply could take the pizza and not pay. The sting in the tail of this

is that the guarantee was withdrawn when a delivery driver rushed too fast, knocked a pedestrian over, and Domino's pizza was sued for $78 million.

■ It is easy to understand and easy to claim, as in the Domino's pizza case.

■ It is credible: lose 40 pounds next week or your money back, speak a foreign language like a native in two weeks or your money back—these sound too good to be true. And they are.

HEADHUNTERS

You know who you trust and who performs well. Build your network. You will need it whether you are buying (looking for managers) or selling (looking for new opportunities). The headhunting job is not magic. Even if the people you know and trust do not have the skills you need, they will probably know other people who do have the skills. Push the network out.

You Are Your Best Headhunter

The first time I approached a CEO with a proposal that he should leave his business, my heart was in my mouth. I was not a headhunter: I wanted him to join my new venture. I quickly discovered that CEOs, despite appearances to the contrary, are human. They are intrigued and flattered to be approached. And you can treat them as your peer: you are not asking, but you may be giving them something. You can afford to be bold.

This works in reverse: your network is probably the best opportunity for identifying opportunities that will work. Because you know each other, the chances are that expectations on both sides are accurate. Accurate expectations and high trust are a good start for a good business relationship. You can not achieve this so easily through headhunters.

Treat External Headhunters Well

You never know when you may need them. Always return their calls, help them with their searches. Do not offer yourself up for a job unless there is real interest: don't waste time. Chasing inappropriate jobs destroys your credibility. If they think you are the right person, they will chase you.

Even if you have no intention of leaving, it is worth getting to know the headhunters. Many, even from the big firms, are deeply unprofessional: they do not even return phone calls. Others are outstanding: they show deep insight, are careful about what they offer and manage the relationship professionally. When you want to brief a headhunter, it helps if you have seen life from the candidate's end instead of relying on the headhunter's pitch. You will know who does a good job.

Headhunters can not understand your business fully. Educate them. Stick with them so they learn what you need. See candidates, and be clear with the headhunters why they fit or why they do not. They will learn fast.

HEAD OFFICE

Head Office Help

"I'm from the head office and I am here to help." The head office is either a beast out of control, or it is a vital part of corporate success. This partly depends on where you are: people in the head office have a different view of their value from the people in the trenches. It also depends on what the head office does. It has four distinct roles, which tend to get confused. Each role needs to be managed separately:

Senior Management Role

Senior managers need to decide what they are going to manage. They cannot do everything. For instance, in one global insurer senior management controls four things:

- Allocation of resources across businesses. This is the classic conglomerate style of financial control, and the conglomerate does not need to go much further in defining the role of senior management.
- Development and selection of senior management. Putting the right people in the right places is at least as important as putting the right financial resources in the right places. Holding this role centrally ensures the development of a leadership team that understands each other.
- Brand strategy. Show the business with one consistent face to the customer across the world.
- Technology strategy. In insurance, IT is the factory. Costs can spiral out of control if every country does its own thing, and co-ordination becomes impossible.

Pure financial conglomerates would not control branding and IT strategy. More integrated firms would seek to control product development, promotions, all management HR, and operations. The role of head office management has to fit the style and strategy of the business.

Control Infrastructure

Senior managers may not need to manage everything, but increasingly they want to control everything. This is where the mandated activities lie: they will tend to include things like audit, financial control, and planning. Their use is non-optional. The danger is that the control infrastructure gets out of control. The goal of gaining control can never be fully achieved from the head office point of view. There is always another report that will yield some more nuggets of information. And there is always another special analysis that will shed new light on what is going on. To prove their value to the corporate entity, control staff have to produce more and more, which they can only do by putting more and more pressure on the businesses for more information and by imposing new authorization and review procedures.

Senior management may believe that it is genuinely empowering and delegating to line management. In practice, what it gives away with one hand, it takes back through the hands of the control staff. Managers end up less empowered and with less delegation than they would in a traditional hierarchy.

Support Services

The head office typically provides a range of centralized services to support the business. This can go to extremes. One retailer was like a medieval walled city: everything that it needed to sustain life was to be found within the walls of corporate headquarters, including their own printing presses. Typically, these are services that can be subjected to a make or buy test: businesses outside the head office should be able to take the service from the head office or subcontract it out. Typical support service activities include: payroll and employee benefit administration, treasury services, public relations, legal counsel, marketing services, and internal communications.

Conflict appears when these services are forced onto the businesses by the head office: the supplier then becomes effectively a monopoly supplier of unwanted services, and the quality of service normally reflects this position.

Mandated Services

These are the corporate initiatives that senior management hopes will transform the organization. It is the home of the Chief Knowledge Officer, The Lifetime Learning Office, The Quality Bureau, and the Head of Reengineering. It is fad country, a useful place to park executives who have no other home. It is also the home of the consultants.

These mandated services are clearly dangerous. First, they take up time and effort. Second, by living in the head office, they are not best positioned to get the enthusiastic support of the businesses. Third, once they are in place they feel the need to start justifying themselves. This causes extra effort all round, and conflict between the priorities of the head office and the priorities of the business. So fourth, the businesses end up being even more disempowered by the help of the mandated services people.

When the head office beast gets out of control, the reaction of senior management is often to launch a study. There is then a furious argument about what the best sort of study is: should it be an SLA (Service Level Analysis) leading to service contracts, or should it be an OVA (Overhead Value Analysis) leading to cost reductions? The answer is that it should be neither. The first job of senior management is to decide what the role of the head office should be and take it from there.

The Head Office: Beauty and the Beast

Part of the head office should be beautiful. This is the bit reserved for clients and important visitors. The rest of it should be beastly, small, and remote. No overflow offices are allowed.

Keeping it small will make it physically difficult for the corporate functionaries to grow large empires. With small empires, they will be forced to do only the things that are most important and helpful to the business. Corporate managers are excellent at justifying their existence, and will grow over time, unless space stops them. Every time one manager asks for more space, let him or her have it. On condition they find it within the existing space: either they have to displace another manager or crowd up like the sardines in a can.

Keep it remote from the businesses. Discourage line managers from wanting to go to the head office. There is a tendency to treat the head office either as the devil in disguise, or as corporate Valhalla for those who graduate from the line. Neither is true. The head office serves some necessary roles.

Finally, make the head office beastly: at least do not make it so palatial that senior managers want to spend all their time there talking to each other. The head office is removed from reality, and reporting numbers is not a good way of knowing what's really going on. Encourage management to get on the road and be with the business and with customers. Innovation tends to grow the further away you move from the head office.

HERD INSTINCTS

Managers are herd animals. Sticking with the pack is the low risk route to survival. Leaving the pack tends to accelerate careers: they either succeed fast or they fail fast. Just as managers are herd animals, so businesses display herd instincts. They all tend to follow the same fads at the same time. But what may be safe management behavior can be suicidal business behavior.

The Management Herds: Investment Analysts and the Herd Instinct

Analysts, fund managers, and economists show signs of big group think. Fund managers are evaluated in terms of performance against a benchmark. So it makes sense to stick closely to the benchmark. There is a chance of a small overperformance against the benchmark that can be trumpeted loudly. Any small underperformance can be ignored until another quarter's results come in. This is the dull, safe route to success. Taking a contrary position to the rest of the market could be successful. But if it is unsuccessful, it is a career-limiting move. Investors will shift their funds, and the manager will lose his or her job.

Similarly, analysts or economists who stick out against the consensus are taking big risks. The consensus forecast is likely to be right, especially for analysts where corporate management increasingly goes to great lengths to ensure that expectations are set the right way for research analysts. If the analyst sticks out against the crowd and is wrong, he or she looks like a fool. If the consensus is followed and the consensus is wrong, then there is little blame. Everyone else was equally wrong, and most of the blame can probably be pointed at corporate management as they watch their share price plunge. Sticking with the crowd is a no-lose position. Except for anyone who is looking for real insight.

Corporate Herd Instincts: The Gadarene Swine and Industry Extinction

Corporations, like managers, are herd creatures. But this leads to disaster. Where all the corporations in an industry adopt the same strategy, they have a zero sum game. If every competitor reengineers to reduce costs and prices by 25 percent, then at the end of it no one is better off. If everyone decides to enter the same business sector at the same time, the result is huge excess capacity and losses for all players.

Following the herd may be right for managers. But taking risks and taking different approaches to the market is essential for corporate and industry health.

Wherever everyone is doing the same thing, it is probably wrong. The wise do not receive the received wisdom of the industry and the markets.

For example, everyone believed that dot-coms were creating a new economic paradigm which justified ever higher market valuations. As a result a wall of money flooded into anything resembling a dot-com business. This had two problems. First, over-investment is as hazardous as under-investment: the Japanese are still trying to recover from massive over-investment in the 1980s. Over-investment invariably means too much investment in poor plans, with the subsequent need for write- offs. Second, dot-coms were only going to make ever rising profits if the laws of competition ceased. In a capitalist country like the United States, capitalism and competition are unlikely to stop any time soon. In other words, any productivity and efficiency gains were likely to get "competed away" in favor of the consumer, and shareholders would only succeed if they backed a few winning horses. This is exactly what happened.

Exactly the same happened in the telecom industry. Everyone believed their own hype about ever increasing demand. So there was an orgy of investment in fiber and wireless capacity, which has led to an equally predictable orgy of write-offs and bankruptcies as capacity increases far outstripped demand increases.

Failure to take risk and stand out from the crowd is more dangerous for corporations than avoiding risk and following the received wisdom.

HONEST FEEDBACK

This is up there with military intelligence and the paperless office as one of the great oxymorons of our time. Everyone has been there, asking for or being asked for honest feedback. CEOs are particularly prone to this, because they will never get honest feedback from anyone in their organization. No one likes giving honest feedback, least of all to people who have displayed enough trust in us to ask for it. We do not want to hurt their feelings.

But there is a way of giving honest feedback that works. There are three linked principles:

- Depersonalize the feedback.
- Abstract the feedback.
- Tell a story.

Example one: A slightly underperforming staff member asks about his or her prospects. Telling someone they are slightly, but not seriously, underperforming is devastating to morale, and unnecessary. Depersonalize and abstract the discussion by talking about the challenges faced, and the skills that need to be developed by people at that stage of a career. Highlight the ones that are most important to the person's situation. Relate this to some real life examples of similar people in his or her situation and talk through what they did to tackle the challenges. Ensure that you have specific examples of actions and behaviors that you can identify in the staff member so that the story is relevant and credible. Discuss it. This then creates a positive program of action for the individual to take forward, rather than a demotivating message that the person is slightly behind.

If, some months later, the challenges are starting to look insurmountable, that is the time to start asking about how confident he or she feels in taking on the challenges. You can then mutually decide if this is the right business for the person.

Example two: A CEO asks for feedback on how he or she is doing. There are plenty of ways of canvassing for anonymous points of view from his or her team, but the chances are that you already know what they think. And the CEO probably does not want to be embarrassed by the canvassing process. So you need to respond honestly, but positively. This is a risky exercise in which trust is either rapidly built or destroyed.

Again, abstract the problem by telling a story about the challenges that other CEOs in his or her position have typically faced, and what they did about it. Depersonalizing the feedback makes it a lot less threatening. And it makes it easy to discuss: if there is disagreement about some of the feedback, it can easily be dropped from the story. Clearly, doing this needs experience. It is no use trying to invent some stories on the spot. They have to be real and relevant.

All of this is separate from the official bureaucracy of performance appraisals. These are important to keep HR happy, for legal reasons if it comes to dismissal and to support decision making around promotions and compensation. But in terms of honest feedback and career counseling, the standard box-checking exercise that ranks everyone on a good/bad scale is hardly useful.

HUMOR AND THE SENSE OF HUMOR TEST

Passing the sense of humor test should be mandatory for managers. This test occurs on days when one unbelievable disaster follows another. At one moment the world looks like it is about to cave in. This is called the sense of humor test. If you can still step back and see the whole bizarre nightmare in perspective, you have passed the test. If you start losing your cool, you have failed. Failing the test leads to behavior that upsets everyone else, makes things worse, and sends the day into a death spiral. Enough perspective and a fine sense of the bizarre can help defuse the tension. There is a fighting chance of stepping back from the brink.

Next time the outrageous happens remember to tell yourself, "I think this is a sense of humor test." Just saying it increases your chances of regaining perspective and passing. Of course, once you have said it, you can also decide to fail the test and to go down with all guns blazing.

Despite plenty of evidence to the contrary, managers believe that management is Not Funny. Senior management think it is Not Funny At All. Trainees may get away with going out in the evening, drinking beer, getting drunk at the bar, and complaining about the management. Senior managers are meant to go out in the evening, drink wine at the restaurant, pretend not to be drunk, and have weighty conversations about the state of the nation.

Lack of humor is not to do with reality, but with culture. Senior managers like to be seen to be serious, and to be dealing with weighty issues with appropriate gravitas. Slapstick is out, although the occasional dry witticism that reflects conventional wisdom is safe. It can show you are intellectually smart if the witticism is clever enough.

Lack of humor is a shame. The bizarre world of management deserves respect, perspective, and humor if it is to be valued properly.

HUSTLE: CONTROLLING YOUR DESTINY

Entrepreneurs, politicians, and sole traders understand the art of the hustle. It is about making something happen that would not have happened without you and your hustle. And it is about making it happen when you have very little by way of personal resource or power. CEOs rarely have to hustle to get their way: they have power and resource to smooth their way.

Some corporate managers understand hustle. They are the ones who always seem to make things happen. Others get lulled by the security of the corporate life support systems. Because everything can be done for them, they let everything be done for them. They even let their agendas get set for them by others. This is fatal.

The best book you need never buy is called *Control Your Destiny or Someone Else Will*. It is about Jack Welch's first 10 years at the helm of GE. The substance is good, but the title is the message.

For individual managers, the level of hustle is a good indicator of how far they are in control of their destiny. Here is a simple test:

- Do you make more calls than you receive?
- Do you send more individual e-mails than you receive?
- Do you call more meetings than you are called to?
- Do you spend more time on initiatives you have started and lead, versus ones other people have started and lead?
- Are you taking more solutions than problems to other people?
- Are you taking more ideas than reports to other people?

The hustler is taking control of his or her destiny: he or she is proactive more than reactive. Hustlers answer yes to all the above questions. The bad hustler just irritates people with endless low value interventions. The good hustler will always have something of interest for the person he or she is reaching. And hustlers are persistent. They will take time and effort to build the alliances, to acquire the resources they need to succeed. They do not give up.

Hustlers, like relationship managers, fall into four categories depending on the frequency and value of their contact:

	High frequency	**Low frequency**
High value	Superstar High respect and impact	Sleeping giant High respect, low impact
Low value	Pain in the arse Low respect, negative impact	Disaster hustler No respect, no impact

INFORMATION INFLATION: BACK TO THE FUTURE

In the medieval period, each word was precious. It might be painstakingly illuminated by a monk using quill on parchment. There were few books, and those that were around were treasured. Information was valued and nurtured. For many, words were beyond them: pictures on church walls were used to unravel the mysteries of the faith.

With the printing press, and then the photocopier and finally e-mail and the computer, we have gone from information deficit to information overload. And the pace of overload is increasing all the time. Looking back at 1960s advertising for detergents, each advertisement seemed like a soap opera in its own right. It would last 60 or even 90 seconds, while the virtues of the detergent were explored in excruciating detail. By the 1980s, advertisements were down to 30-, perhaps 40-second slots. Now 30 seconds seems like a luxury, 20 seconds is normal and 10 seconds is becoming more common.

Information overload has serious consequences.The value of information deflates as rapidly as the volume inflates. Finding good information is harder, like finding a needle in a haystack. Attention spans are reducing: we listen to a message only briefly before moving onto the next message. Information is trusted to the extent that we trust the information provider.

We are heading back to the medieval period in the way we use words and pictures. Now we want fewer words. Ideally, we do not want words, we want a picture that will sum up the message. Visual literacy is taking over from verbal literacy. All this matters to managers. It means:

- Write short, not long. Use visuals.
- Build credibility into the message through the messenger. As an

individual, that's you. As a business, it is your brand. The message supports the brand and vice versa.

■ Be consistent in the message: in the world of information an overloaded message takes a long time to get through, and two messages simply confuses everyone. So, pick your message with care. This is true of brands, internal corporate communications, or how you present yourself to the business. Senior management will not know everything about you other than perhaps one claim to fame or infamy. Make sure you know what it is you want to be remembered for.

IT CONSULTANTS: THE BUILDER'S BRICK

IT consultants and builders are the same. You can never find a good one when you want one; the work always costs more and lasts longer than you expected, and the workers cause huge disruption when they are in. Of course, one lot have bellies over their jeans, and others have partners in custom-made suits. Next time the IT consultants come selling, imagine them with their beer barrel bellies and site clothing. It makes it easier to tolerate the builder's speech that they will then give you.

Score them on the speech. When they pass 5 out of 10, quietly get up and give each of them a brick. Do not explain why. One week later, send them a photocopy of this page, complete with your scoring. Here are the builder's comments to look for:

■ They trash the previous work. "Whoever did that plastering should be shot" versus "COBOL? Hardly anyone has that nowadays."
■ The work will be bigger than you thought. "That's not a bit of damp, buddy, you'll need to put in a whole new damp course" versus "Of course you'll have to replace all those systems as well."
■ The work is not just big, it's tricky. "Flat roofs are always tricky" versus "You can't buy a package for that: we have to build something special."
■ So of course it will be expensive. "It's going to cost you" versus "This will be a big investment."
■ And it will take a long time. "It'll take a long time" versus "It'll take a long time."
■ But they can't say how long. "Until we've seen what's under the floorboards" versus "Until we've done a full specification."

■ And they can not guarantee the price.

■ They will promise a worthless guarantee. "We can always fix it up later if you need" versus "You can give us just one month's notice (once you are totally dependent on us)."

■ They will try to broaden the job. "We could do your front drive at the same time" versus "This needs to be linked to a proper change program/strategy."

■ But this is your lucky day: they have just the people for the job. "Mick's a great plasterer, he'll be free as of Tuesday" versus "Of course you know how difficult it is to assemble a team with the right skills, but we should be able to do it for next month, if you give the go-ahead now."

There are other uses for the brick. Do not be tempted.

IT: INTERMEDIATE TECHNOLOGY

For the last 30 years, information technology has been intermediate technology. It has always been promising to do more tomorrow than it can today, and it always does. Moore's Law has held true: processing capacity has doubled and costs have halved roughly every 18 months. This has been a disaster for management, and a gold mine for the IT industry.

The pace of change is what makes IT crippling for business. At least in the last industrial revolution the technology was relatively stable. Railway lines have not had to suffer changes in designs, routes, and specifications every three years. And the changes that had to be made could be done fast. When the Great Western line was converted from broad to standard gauge, 213 miles of track were replaced in one weekend by 4,000 workers. Most businesses would happily hire 4,000 workers for a weekend if that were all it took to change their technology infrastructure.

Rapid obsolescence of technology has given management three broad options:

■ Ignore the technology upgrades, stick with current systems, and watch the competition sail by as they find ways of serving customers better at lower cost through technology.

■ Become upgrade junkies; add little bits of new systems everywhere to keep up to date. The result is a back office that looks like a technology museum: systems and languages from all eras and all parts of the world. Most banks do not even know what systems they have, and do not have the manuals or expertise to know how to fix faults. One bank had 1,290 systems, few of which talked to each other properly. This was the Tower of Babel in the form of a bowl of spaghetti.

▪ Scrap all the existing systems at vast expense and effort to get a clean sheet again. Incur all the data migration and run-off difficulties, and then realize that by the time the three-year program is complete, the technology is already out of date.

Managers are doomed with technology. Whatever they do, it will be expensive and once they have completed the job, they just have to start again. The obvious solution is to get into the IT industry, which has been a licence to print money. Barely competent managers have been able to make fortunes by riding this wave.

The alternative is to hand the technology infrastructure over to one of the technology firms. They are better placed to keep on upgrading all the required skills, know the right technology solutions, and deliver the results better than an in-house operation.

INNOVATION: WINNING WITHOUT FIGHTING

The best battles are won without fighting. The bloody battles for a couple of market share points have to be fought. But even better is to occupy territory that no one else has thought about. It is about outflanking the competition. There are two sorts of innovation:

The Better Mousetrap

This is the world of the inventor. It belongs to James Dyson (bagless vacuum cleaners), Trevor Bayliss (wind-up radios), and 3M (Post-it notes). All these products and people created new markets and built businesses on the back of them. The challenge is to institutionalize this sort of innovation. The evidence is that this sort of innovation is not naturally institutionalized. Corporations have to look to another form of innovation.

Creating New Markets

In each of the cases below, an incumbent could have occupied the new market space. In each case, the companies left it to an outsider, which then became a formidable competitor in its own right.

The photocopier used to be a central function based on a leased machine with high performance and high maintenance. Canon made the photocopier a cheaper, purchased machine with acceptable performance that could be used across the business in each department locally. It was a totally new way of attacking the market. Xerox was slow to follow because of fear of cannibalizing its own market.

CNN created the first dedicated news channel. Because of the scale of costs of creating a similar network, and the brand image advantage CNN has, competition has found it tough to follow. The traditional U.S. networks and BBC would have been better placed to be first to build a 24-hour news channel.

FedEx created the overnight parcel delivery service. UPS could have owned it; they followed up a late and poor second.

Apple created the personal computer market; Microsoft dominated the operating systems market; Dell reinvented the PC market with a direct-to-the-buyer model. All the might of IBM, DEC, and Fujitsu was spent fighting the wrong battles, battles for market share among themselves.

Naturally, no one in any of the losing organizations was fired for missing the big opportunity. Plenty were probably fired for missing their budget target, sales target, or share target in what was the wrong battle. Meanwhile, the strategy consultants were all earning their fees advising their clients on how to fight the wrong battles.

The job of senior management is to make sure that the business fights the right battles. This requires taking the blinkers off and thinking outside the box. People who think outside the box are likely to be new, younger employees; rebels in the organization; customers; advertising agencies. Go away for a weekend with them and senior management and brainstorm. It does not matter that 99 percent of what you get will be garbage. The real battle is the battle for ideas. Win that battle, and the competitive war is transformed.

INVESTING TO LOSE

Resource allocation, the investment of money, time, and people, is central to the management task. Franklin Roosevelt remarked that he was really just a traffic cop: directing people to go in, hopefully, the right direction.

As managers we are also taught to be prudent. This means that we want to make sure every investment dollar is spent wisely. We should not overspend. So we look at investment proposals and see how we can minimize the investment cost. Lower investment has the wonderful ability to raise the ROI.

A $100 investment yielding a marginal 10 percent, can be transformed into a yield of 12.5 percent if we hold the investment at $80. We have saved the business $20, and raised the ROI. We may also have ensured that we have invested just enough to lose the whole lot: $80 lost for no return. But, by then, everyone will have forgotten how the decision was made and by whom.

The alternative approach is to give the team everything they ask for. Suddenly, there are no excuses. They have all the resources they need to do the job and to win. And they have the motivation of knowing that they have been backed to the hilt, rather than being nickled and dimed. They will be totally committed to success. And if the proposal is so marginal that the investment needs to be cut back to achieve the desired ROI, it probably should not be approved at all. Invest to win. Prudent investing is investing to lose.

"-ISTS"

The "ists" are still out there. The ageists, racists, and sexists. From a competitive point of view, this is great news. The ists will help the competition fail. It's not just the risk of litigation that will hurt. They are losing out in the war for talent. And they are failing to freshen up the gene pool of their business. They are creating a uniform, inward-looking group think.

Today the test is not about hiring across genders, ages, races, and faiths. The person doing the hiring still feels in a position of power and is not threatened by the diversity: if it does not work, they can always move or fire the person. The challenge is about promoting and then working for people of a different age, race, gender, or faith. This is where most businesses fail. The gene pool can be diverse at the bottom of the business, but conformity strikes at the top.

In the U.S., women comprise about half the workforce. Just 5 percent of the senior managers of Fortune 1000 companies are women. But 72 percent of corporate boards have a female member. This shows that tokenism and the glass ceiling are alive and well in corporate America. Hiring a woman non-executive director makes for a worthy picture in the annual report and absolves management from taking real diversity seriously. The challenge is not hiring for diversity, or having diversity in the annual report. The challenge is to promote for diversity.

Working for people younger than yourself or from a different race or sex can be great. Some of them may be brilliant, others may be turkeys. But they are human, and they do offer a different view of the world. It's a great way to learn, and gives the confidence to promote across the gene pool when your turn comes at the top.

JAPAN: LEARNING TO EAT SUSHI AND CONQUER THE WORLD

During the 1980s and early 1990s, forests were destroyed to print books on the secrets of Japanese success. Everyone was keen to follow the Japanese example and learn how to conquer the world. There were three problems with these books:

- Most of the authors had not actually worked in Japan. They relied on second-hand material and recycled cases from the same companies. It looked great to outsiders and would generate book sales and speaking engagements. People who had worked in Japan could see most of it was nonsense. Western business was not going to succeed by implementing second-hand recycled nonsense.
- The Japanese miracle was a mirage. Like any economy, Japan has significant areas of relative advantage and significant areas of relative disadvantage. Japan had not discovered the philosopher's stone, the universal recipe for business success. A walk into any Japanese retail store would be enough to dispel notions of universal excellence and world-conquering power. Again, Western business was not going to succeed by copying a mirage.
- Whatever else the Japanese are good or bad at, they are world class at being Japanese. No one else is going to be more Japanese than the Japanese. The West will never appreciate sushi or sumo as much as they do, or learn to bow quite the way they do. And yet the premise of most books was that we had to copy the Japanese.

Copying the competition is the most certain way of losing. It is a game of catch-up in which the others will always be ahead. The only way to compete is by finding ways in which we can be different and better.

Ultimately, this is what happened: the United States discovered it had more flexible working patterns, better capital allocation methods, and better use of new technology. It is winning by being different, not by copying the Japanese.

But the same mistake is being made again. Now everyone is learning how to be American, and how to be a dot-com. Now the bubble has burst and the search will be on for new heroes to copy. In the meantime, we should dare to be different.

JOB DESCRIPTIONS VERSUS THE PSYCHOLOGICAL CONTRACT

Job descriptions are primarily job justifiers for underemployed HR staff. If an organization has boxes full of job descriptions, it is probably suffering severe bureaucratic tendencies.

Job descriptions answer questions such as "What is my role?" and "What is my status?" Roles and status do not build a business and do not represent achievement. And they are not a basis for judging performance.

The job description is not useful to the business or the employee. What is more useful to both is the psychological contract that the individual has with management. This psychological contract may not be written down, but the expectations are real. The expectations tend to revolve around five questions:

- What am I expected to achieve?
- What resources will I have?
- What skills do I need to develop?
- How will I be measured and rewarded?
- What will you do to support me?

The psychological contract is more demanding on both sides than the job description. Acrimony arises not so much when the job description is broken, but more when the psychological contract is broken. Because this is a two-way contract it is different from traditional MBO (Management By Objectives), which is a one-sided commitment. Managing the expectations on both sides of this psychological contract is essential to a successful relationship and business.

KILLING IDEAS

Some managers are brilliant at killing ideas. These same people will complain about the lack of innovation and new thinking in the business. It is human nature to react with hostility to new ideas. New ideas represent a threat to the status quo:

- They involve risk, they may not work.
- They are a challenge to the way we have done things before, implying criticism of us.
- Even if the idea succeeds, it will take extra work and will put extra performance expectations on us.
- We did not come up with the idea, we are not in control.

Naturally, the hostility is not normally overt. It normally comes in the form of helpful questions. We have all been in meetings where an idea surfaces. First one person shoots a heat-seeking missile, normally characterized by a "Yes, but . . ." or "I think it's a good idea but. . . ." Remember, everything before the "but" is B.S. The real message comes afterwards:

- "It's great, *but* has it ever been done before?" If yes, then it's old hat and not worth doing; if no, then it is too risky to do. Fight your way out of that one.
- "I like that, *but* of course funding it would require cancelling this year's advertising."
- "Yes, *but* would the unions/regulators/trade accept it?"

Once one person comes up with a killer missile, everyone else in the meeting joins in. The more deadly the missile, the more it shows the commentator is smart. It is easy pickings for everyone, except the person who suggested the idea. By the end of the meeting, the meeting has achieved three things:

- It has killed a potentially good idea.
- It has thoroughly demoralized the person with the idea.
- It has taught everyone in the meeting that having good ideas is a career-limiting move.

These are not healthy outcomes. Three things can be done to save ideas:

- Pre-sell ideas before the meeting, so that by the time of the meeting there is a core of support for the idea and the major concerns have been identified and preempted.
- As chairperson, force people to evaluate the benefits of the idea before they comment on any concerns. Thinking positively is unnatural for most people, and is harder work than coming up with criticisms. This makes putting benefits first a good discipline in its own right. Recognizing the benefits of an idea first also puts the criticisms into perspective. If the benefits of the idea are huge, it may be worthwhile overcoming some huge concerns. If the focus is only on the concerns, then the idea will be stillborn.
- As chairperson, make people express their criticisms positively and in an action-oriented way. The easiest way to do this is to insist that concerns be prefaced with two words: "How to. . . ." These two words at the start of a sentence are at first unnatural. But they put the concern into an action framework, which invites other people to think up possible solutions to the concern.

KNOWLEDGE MANAGEMENT

Knowledge management should be important. But it has become a fad trying to hit the wrong target the wrong way.

The Knowledge Management Fad

It is always possible to spot a management fad. When someone appears on the executive committee with an unfamiliar title, the title is normally the clue to the fad. It started with the appointment of Chief Quality Officers, and has moved through to Heads of Reengineering,

Innovation, and then Knowledge. The appointment of a Chief Fad Officer achieves several goals:

▪ It demonstrates to investors that the business is up to date with the latest management thinking and practice.

▪ It provides a useful and harmless role for a displaced executive, who can later be gently eased out of the business when the next fad comes along.

▪ It gives the impression of doing something while not actually interfering with the organization: we must be a knowledge-based company because we have a knowledge officer on the executive committee. This puts the fad into a nice safe box, away from the business.

Knowledge Management Is Hitting the Wrong Target

Knowledge management in Western countries assumes that knowledge is explicit. It assumes that any knowledge worth having can be documented, and then reapplied based on the documentation. This has the potential to lead to vast swathes of bureaucracy, which achieves little.

In Japan and other Asian countries, people recognize that much of the most useful knowledge is tacit. It is more about how people do things more than what they do. It is much harder to document, and cannot be replicated remotely by simply reading the manual. It assumes learning comes more from the apprenticeship model than from formal academic learning.

Intuitively, most Western managers understand the value of tacit knowledge. When we want to use a new computer, or learn how another salesperson is so successful, we do not reach for the textbooks. We ask someone.

The Wrong Target Is Being Hit the Wrong Way

Because there is excess focus on explicit knowledge, there is excessive documentation. Knowledge teams produce self-directed learning discs and manuals. There is often a motivational problem with self-directed learning: people either don't do it or they skimp and cheat. And they are right to skimp and cheat, because it is not teaching what they want, which is the tacit knowledge.

The nadir of knowledge management is when it is reduced to bringing in consultants to build some big knowledge-management software at great expense, both in financial cost and the cost of management time.

The alternative is to build and strengthen the internal networks of people talking to each other. Staff and managers value most learning from successful peers: it is demonstrably practical and tailored to the needs of the business. And normally successful peers have enough vanity to want to share their expertise and to be recognized as an expert in the business. Everyone wins, with relatively little effort, and the results are direct.

LANGUAGE

Language is our most powerful weapon. It is more abused than used well. Language can manipulate. Three of the most common forms of language manipulation are worth looking for:

The Inverted Qualifiers

The three most famous inverted qualifiers are *just, only,* and *but.* Here are some examples of but:

> "I like this proposal *but* . . ."
> "Your presentation was good *but* . . ."
> "You could go to that conference *but* . . ."

Basically, everything before the "but" is B.S. Ignore it. The speaker does not mean it, the speaker only means what is said after the "but." The way to deal with the but speakers is to repeat back to them exactly what they said after the but and ask them if that is what they meant. Then tell them everything before the but is B.S. You may not win friends, but they will stop using but and start saying what they mean. Here are some examples of "just" and "only":

> "Could you *just* type this proposal?"
> "It's *only* a small document, problem, error."

"Just" and "only" are sure-fire indicators of someone feeling very defensive about something: they have done something wrong or they are asking for something unreasonable. At this point your B.S. detector should start working overtime to find out how serious the just or only really is.

Power Words

Documents are often scattered with power words such as urgent, important, significant, and strategic. Power words are meant to lend weight and importance to a document, but they don't. They are too often unqualified personal judgments by the writer. If something is important or urgent, the substance of the document should make that clear with relevant facts and arguments, not with qualitative judgments that invite the alert reader to disagree. Once you have invited the reader to disagree with one judgment, you have invited the reader to disagree with everything. Power words backfire. The unalert reader will fall into the trap of taking the judgments at face value.

I and We

Some people make a management religion out of using "we" instead of "I." We is certainly more inclusive and less adversarial or hierarchical than I. Examples include:

"I want you to . . ." versus "We need to. . . ."
"I got that sale . . ." versus "We got that sale. . . ."
"I haven't got the time . . ." versus "We need to find another time. . . ."

Generally, "we" is much more positive and constructive. But it is also totally presumptuous in some situations. It assumes a level of intimacy and agreement that may not exist, for instance, on meeting a new client for the first time.

LAWYERS AND THE REVOLUTION

When the revolution comes, it will not be all bad news for managers. Of course, we can expect to join our colleagues in being put up against the wall and shot. At least we should have the pleasure of seeing the lawyers shot before us. In the meantime, we have to deal with them.

The world is getting ever more litigious and rights-aware. Trust is a good way to do business when things are going well. But it provides no cover when things go wrong. And by then, it is too late to bring in the lawyers.

Bring them in early: prevention is better than cure. But pick your lawyers with care. Lawyers who are business focused are worth their weight in gold. They will focus on what you can do, not on what you cannot do. Avoid the ones who insist on swamping the entire business with legalese. They may minimize all the legal risk, but at the cost of freezing the business in a legal swamp where no one dares to move without taking three lawyers in tow.

The simple test of a lawyer is the language they speak. If they start mumbling on about obscure cases and subsections of 200-year-old acts, drop them. If they start talking about your business and how it can be supported, they are at least in the right game.

LEADERSHIP

Most people think of the CEO as the leadership. All the academic writing about leadership focuses on the role of the leader. This is totally misleading. Every manager should act as a leader.

Kissinger defined leadership as the art of "taking people where they would not have gone by themselves." In other words, it is about stretching the organization and enabling it to achieve those stretchy targets. This form of leadership can be achieved at all levels of the organization. It can be as simple as getting a trainee to make his or her first successful sales call.

Most managers wind up being somewhere between administrators and leaders. Here is a simple test to see what sort of management you have got:

Criterion	Administrators	Leaders
Basis of authority	Organization chart	Credibility, trust
Key resource	Budget	People
Basis of promotion	No mistakes	Beats stretchy goals
Focus of attention	Inputs, costs	Outputs, results
Communication	Top down	360 degrees
Style	Compliance, control	Empowerment
Attitude to change	Risk	Opportunity
Outlook	Detail	Big picture

Ideally, managers have both administrative competence and leadership capability. This is rare. Generally, it is easier for a leader to find an administratively competent manager to make up for his or her deficiencies than it is to find a genuine leader to support an administrator.

Leaders and the Led

Everyone grumbles about management, if management is understood to be anyone more senior than yourself. To listen to the grumbles, you might believe people hate being led. People love being led. Being led is essentially lazy and low risk. To the extent that people dislike excess work or risk, leaders perform a great function for them. Followers let the leader take all the strain and risk of deciding where to go and what to do. Then the leader can be blamed when things go wrong.

If flat organizations are to have meaning, it requires that partnerships are formed both vertically and horizontally across the organization. The days of the all-knowing and omnipotent leader are long gone, even if they ever existed except in people's minds. But this partnership requires that followers do not passively follow: they push back, advocate new directions, and take responsibility themselves. In other words, everyone in a flat organization should be a leader. Being led is lazy, passive, and unproductive. But it is also an attractive recipe for an easy life.

Leadership Heaven and Hell

Leaders from hell can be just as successful as leaders from heaven. This is bad news for employees who have a leader from hell. And it is bad news for all the academics and consultants who try to prescribe what a good leader should and should not do.

For the management survivalist, the point is not to judge the leader, let alone try to change the leader. The point is to learn from the leaders what it is that they do: why they succeed and what behaviors they value and display. This will tell you all about the rules of the game that you need to succeed. Then you can either play by the rules of the game, or get out.

We all have memories of leaders from hell and leaders from heaven. Judging them reflects partly on the leader, and greatly on the person doing the judging. With this is mind, here are personal profiles of two real leaders: one from hell and one from heaven:

Leadership Criterion	Leader from Hell	Leader from Heaven
Style	Command and control: "Do as I tell you"	Inspirational: "Let's go for it"
Basis of authority	Rank	Trust, respect

Performance	Don't make a mistake	Overperform
Expectations	Risk intolerant	Risk tolerant
Focus of control	Process: meetings and papers on time, neat	Outcomes and results
Attention to detail	High	Low
Insight/big picture focus	Low	High
Communications	Boss: "I/you" Secretive	Peer: "We" Open
Political skills	High	High
Technical skills	Fair	High
Social skills	Low	High

From the business point of view, the leader from hell is as successful as the leader from heaven. In a large, traditional hierarchy that is risk-averse and process-focused, the leader from hell represents a perfect fit with the culture and needs of the organization. The leader from heaven would be an unmitigated disaster in such a business.

From the personal point of view, some people will prefer the leader from hell to the leader from heaven. In practice, the leader from heaven has much higher expectations and is a much more demanding taskmaster than the leader from hell. The leader from hell simply expects compliance and no mistakes: you can leave your brain at the front door and still succeed. The leader from heaven expects outperformance. Outperformance is tougher than compliance.

LEARNING, MISTAKES, AND THE B.S. DETECTOR

"He who never made a mistake never made a discovery"—Samuel Smiles (1812–1904), *Self-Help*. The strongest learning we make is from our own mistakes. Just like a child learning that fires are dangerous, so managers slowly learn what is dangerous and what is not. The more painful the lesson, the more it is embedded in how we work.

Over time, these defenses build up, and we acquire highly tuned B.S. detectors that can smell a problem at a mile. The longer we stay in an industry or a company, the more highly tuned the B.S. detectors become. We know all the euphemisms and jargon that everyone uses to disguise what they really mean. We see beyond their form of words to the real meaning. New kids on the block do not stand a chance. The B.S. detector is vital to management survival.

But as soon as a manager leaves for another company, another role, the B.S. detector is close to useless. It needs to be retuned, at speed. We tend to take our B.S. detectors for granted. When we change jobs, we find out too late the risks of it not being fully tuned.

LIES

Forget the morality problem. The effectiveness problem is the killer. Most corporate lies get nailed, eventually. It took 30 years to rumble the tobacco companies, but normally it is faster. Most individuals' lies get nailed, because most of us are no good at lying. The occasional bit of résumé inflation is sustainable. Other lies have a tendency of becoming increasingly complicated, and eventually unravel. Unless you are an expert liar, it's not worth it. The reputation risk is too great, and it lasts forever.

About 5 percent of managers appear to be pathological liars. And the good ones are very good at it. They get a lot of practice. They succeed because most of us are too trusting. Moral outrage is not a defence. Vigilance is.

LUCK

Napoleon preferred lucky generals. He was right. Lucky people have a habit of consistently being lucky. Which means that it is not really luck. Look behind luck, and there are normally three characteristics: practice, persistence, and preparation.

Practice

Arnold Palmer said: "The harder I practice, the luckier I get." This is true: the 50/50 chance of putting a hole becomes a 60/40, and the 60/40 chance becomes a likely 70/30 chance. Management is the same. There are always close calls. The more practice and the more experience managers have, the more likely they are to make the right call.

Persistence

Many successes come after serial failure. The chilling words of the IRA after they failed to blow up Prime Minister Thatcher in Brighton summed it up: "This time we were unlucky. Remember, we only need to get lucky once." The difference between failure and success is often as simple as giving up.

Preparation

Lucky people prepare. When the opportunity comes along, it is there for everyone to see. But only some of the people are looking. In retrospect, most opportunities are so obvious we end up saying: "We could have done that." Except that we could not, because we were not looking in the right direction. Often it needs an industry insider who can look at the business with fresh eyes. Examples include selling books over the Internet (Amazon) and portable personal music (Sony Walkman). The slings and arrows of outrageous fortune do sometimes make a difference. But for the most part, lucky managers are as consistently lucky as Napoleon's generals.

MANAGEMENT: WHO IS IN CHARGE?

In one large bank I found one consistent answer: management is my boss and above. So in the customer service bull pen the first line supervisor was management. But equally, very senior managers referred to the level above them as management. Only the executive committee recognized that they were management. Sadly, the belief that management refers only to the people above is widespread. Even partners at one large consulting firm fell into this trap.

"Management is above me" is a symptom of a sick organization. On one hand, it shows a denial of responsibility by the people claiming that management is above them. On the other hand, it is a reflection of disempowerment throughout the ranks of management. It reduces middle management to their traditional role of mere ciphers communicating orders from the top of a hierarchy to the bottom. Anyone who has responsibility for any people or resources should think of themselves as managers and should act accordingly.

MANAGEMENT ACCOUNTING: DEATH AND REINCARNATION

Management accounting as we knew it and hated it, is dying. It is being reincarnated as something that could be useful. It is worth making sure you have the twenty-first-century version of management accounting, not the twentieth-century version. Twenty-first-century management accounting should differ in six critical areas from the twentieth-century version:

From Functional Costs to Cross-Function Costs

Cost control used to reflect the traditional hierarchy. Each "silo" had its own budget. This had the huge virtue of simplicity. It was good for budget control purposes, but was lousy at cost management. Most costs are driven by business activities that cut across functions. The process of acquiring and setting up a new banking customer drives costs in marketing, sales, or relationship management, credit analysis, documentation, and products. Account acquisition drives the volume of activity, and hence the costs, in each of these departments. Controlling budget costs while not controlling the activity is a case of looking in the wrong direction.

From Allocated Costs to Cost Drivers

Departmental costs were relevant in an age when most costs were direct and variable costs. The more they become indirect and fixed or semivariable, the more there is the problem of cost allocation. At worst, this becomes a political dogfight. At minimum, it makes it harder to understand true customer and product profitability. Understanding the drivers of costs across the business improves the chances of not just allocating costs fairly, but enabling management to focus on actions to manage the costs.

From Historic Costs to Forecast Costs

Twentieth-century management accounting kept a financial scorecard of how well you were doing against forecast, and could produce endless variation analyses and year-on-year analyses to help keep score. But it was essentially after-the-event accounting. By looking at activity costs that cut across functions, it is possible to forecast costs based on forecast demand. It is easier to control costs by looking ahead than looking backwards.

From Counting Beans to Making Decisions

Traditional cost accounting was backward-looking, so that remedial action was nearly always reactive. With forecasts of costs and volumes management can look ahead and manage costs proactively. Critically, managers can do it with the cooperation of other departments who will drive or influence their own costs.

From Cost Control to Profit Management

Cost management is not necessarily good profit management. The most vulnerable items in a cost-cutting drive are the discretionary items. Advertising, promotion, and research are soft targets for the cost cutter. These may also be the things that will most help drive up profitability.

A proper understanding of what drives costs also allows management to see which products and which customers are making profit. Traditional cost accounting methods tend to underestimate the costs of acquiring and serving small value customers, small deliveries, and customized products. Activity-based costing identifies these costs, and allows management to make informed decisions about segment and product pricing and service strategies to optimize profits, not just costs.

From Centralized to Decentralized Cost Management

The traditional cost accounting function was a specialized staff function. They did all the analysis and produced the scorecards for management to look at. The new cost accounting is much more managerially focused: it is about proactively managing for profit across the business. This means that all managers need to be able to speak the language of management accounting, understand it, and act on it. It is not simply a question of knowing whether the brackets in the right-hand column are a good thing or a bad thing.

Naturally, new management accounting is not a free lunch. It has several preconditions if it is to succeed:

- Accounting literacy across the business.
- An understanding of how costs are driven in the business. This is not a static, one-time-only exercise. The nature of the cost drivers changes in response to management action. This makes cost management a dynamic, not a static process.
- Systems that allow the information to be gathered the right way.
- Managers who want to make it happen and to use it.

This is still a revolution in progress. It is still more art than science, and feels cumbersome to implement. Switching off the traditional systems is premature. But it is time to start testing the new approach, adapting it to local conditions, and creating the capability to exploit it in the future.

MANAGEMENT BY WALKING AWAY

The grandfather of modern management books, *In Search of Excellence*, advocated MBWA: Management By Wandering Around. The idea is that this would keep you in touch with how things are going on. An equally valid version of MBWA is Management By Walking Away.

Part of the art of management is knowing where you genuinely add value, and where others can do the job as well as you. The key principle is that all jobs should be done by the most junior person possible. This maximizes the leverage for senior management and maximizes the development of the junior management. It is also more motivational to be fully entrusted with work than to have to be checking every five minutes with the boss.

If you think that someone is 60 percent, or even 50 percent up to the job, give it to them. Stretch them. They may have to work all day and all night because they are slow and making mistakes. But they will learn and grow as a result. And if they make a commitment to deliver a certain result by a certain time, trust them. This can get hairy, but if you try to take away all the risk then you probably end up doing the job yourself. High trust is consistent with a high performance culture where you expect people to deliver on their commitments.

Management by walking away is different from abandoning the team. You may walk away, but you make sure that you are always available to help and counsel whenever they want it. The difference is that instead of intruding on their work, you let them ask for help when they want it. Your intervention will be valued more highly if they ask for it than if you inflict it unilaterally.

MANAGEMENT INFORMATION SYSTEMS

The years BC (Before desktop Computers) was the golden age of MIS. At least you could see the rubbish. At one insurance company the weekly MIS data was printed out from a mainframe, put onto a fork lift, and carted up to the executive floor. The data weighed in at 45 pounds. No one read it or understood it.

In the years AD (After Desktops), MIS data has gotten even worse. We have evolved from reams of rubbish to gigabytes of garbage. This is worse because the technology allows the amount of data to explode. Because no one can see how much garbage there is, there is no incentive to clean it up.

Getting the MIS Information You Need

We all know that computer systems are meant to produce information that is timely, relevant, and accurate. Just like firms are meant to grow profitably. We know what is meant to happen, but not how to make it happen. Here are the key principles of getting the information you need:

■ You won't get there by starting from here. You probably need to start over with your database: create a zero base.

■ The data you gather should represent a balanced view of performance including financial, market, organizational, and innovation data.

■ Drive the process top–down.

■ Throw away the old system. This forces the pace of change.

Taming the MIS Beast: A Case Study

The insurance company eventually got tired of chopping down trees and printing useless information on them before taking them past executives on the way to the incinerator. This was not productive work. And management needed information to run the business. Step one was for the CEO to sit down and write on one piece of paper the information he needed on a weekly basis to run the business. He reviewed it with his executive committee and then finalized it. It caused shock. The information concerned all sorts of stuff that did not even exist on the computer. Broadly, it fell into four categories:

■ Financial data. This was the relatively easy bit for the MIS people. It is by its nature backwards-looking, a scorecard of how we have done in the past. But it is useful. Inevitably, the structure of the information required was different from what the system could produce.

■ Market data. This looks at how the business is performing in real time. But it was not only about traditional sales measures, but also about service quality, complaints, and terminations. These represented warning lights over future performance, and had not been seen at CEO level before.

■ Organization data. Partly this was about traditional departmental cost and performance data, and partly HR data on headcount and turnover.

■ Innovation. This stunned MIS. This information was crucial to understand the future potential performance of the business. It included information on progress of key projects and an innovation index: the proportion of sales coming from new products, new channels, and new customers.

Step two was to invite each executive committee member to create their own one-page summaries, which covered their own areas of responsibility. The only constraint was that the information they requested had to be consistent with the information that the CEO requested.

Step three was to roll the process down through the organization. At each level, there were vast gaps between what people needed, and what they had. What they needed was much less in volume but much more in value than what they were used to.

Step four was for the executive to start using the new information. This involved throwing away the old system. Immediately, there was a crisis. Large parts of the data simply did not exist. The rest had to be collected or collated manually. This crisis forced the pace of change in producing the new system. And as soon as other managers saw senior management using the new system, they were eager to use the same system.

MARS BARS, UTILITY, AND THE SALESPERSON

Many kids like Mars Bars. Give them one and they will eat it with pleasure, if not with thanks. Give them another, and if they are really hungry they might eat that as well. Give them a third Mars Bar, and only the greedy are still chomping away. By the fourth or fifth Mars Bars even the most dedicated fan is beginning to groan. The sixth Mars Bar will be avoided like the plague.

The perceived utility, or value, of each Mars Bar decreases the more you give. If you want kids to value the Mars Bar, keep them hungry. Even better, make the kids earn their Mars Bar, then they will set great store by it. Let them have a Mars Bar just once in a while. Ingratiating yourself by letting them have six at a time is not productive.

Salespeople and managers too often forget the Mars Bar lesson. They try to buy support by giving too much away too early. They don't make the other person hungry for it, and don't make them work for it. Don't chase them, make them chase you. You can then give away far less, and they will be far more grateful to you for it.

MEETINGS: THE GOOD, THE BAD, AND THE UGLY

Meetings are a great way of wasting time while giving the appearance of great activity. We have all spent more hours than we can count in useless meetings. No one is taught what makes a good meeting, or how to run a good meeting. If they were, office productivity would soar, and the office bill for coffee and pastries would plummet. Inevitably, the rules of effective meeting management represent little more than common sense, which is routinely ignored whenever a meeting is called.

The model below applies to the typical, run-of-the-mill internal company meeting. It does not apply to brainstorming sessions or to large group meetings or to formal board meetings where there are other constraints and special requirements.

The Purpose of the Meeting

A test of a good meeting is to ask the following three questions:

■ What will be different as a result of this meeting? This is normally the result of making some decisions. Referring an issue to a committee or asking for more information is not a decision and does not make the business different.
■ What did I learn from the meeting? The learning should be significant, relevant, and useful.
■ What do I do next? There have to be clear next steps coming out of the meeting.

If there are no good answers to these questions, then either it was a lousy meeting, or you should not have been there. In planning a meeting, it is worth thinking about how each of the participants will be able to answer these questions at the end of the meeting. If they will not have good answers, they probably should not be there. Ultimately be clear about what you will get out of the meeting, whether you are chairing it or attending it.

Attendance at Meetings

Everyone wants to go to meetings. Junior staff want to go to get exposure to senior staff. Senior staff want the junior staff there, because they have probably done the donkey work and the senior staff feel exposed without their help. Every department wants to send someone so that they are represented. Jamborees do not make for good meetings.

Generally, once attendance rises above between six and eight people, it becomes difficult to sustain a significant discussion among the whole group. Either a core group comes to dominate the meeting, or the meeting degenerates into a sequence of bilateral discussions between the chairperson and individual attendees. Either way, many people have become spectators and are not contributing. Meetings are not meant to be a spectator sport. A few simple rules on attendance at meetings:

- Avoid meetings with more than six or eight people, unless the purpose is to broadcast a message.
- Only people with a role to play by bringing expertise, resources, or authority should be there.
- There should be no duplication of roles: two people are not required to represent one point of view, unless they are representing quite different perspectives on it.

Meeting Preparation

This is easily skipped, with unfortunate consequences. The key preparation is about setting expectations with other attendees. Expectations setting includes:

- The role each person is expected to play.
- Homework required.
- Preview of critical issues. It is better to talk to a potential adversary before the meeting to understand and manage the concerns in private, than to invite a brawl in public. Build the consensus beforehand, a process institutionalized in Japan as "nemawashi."

Clearly, logistical preparation is required. Beyond the obvious points of location, facilities, and perhaps catering, there are the less obvious decisions about room layout. The traditional long table with a chairperson at its head is about the least effective format for a discussion, and makes looking at a presentation at one end of the table nearly impossible. Room layout is constrained only by your needs and your imagination. Hollow squares are common. One attractive option is to get rid of chairs and tables completely. A standing meeting is guaranteed to be faster and more focused than a meeting with deep comfortable chairs and lots of coffee and cookies. Standing meetings are not outlandish: the President uses them with his Cabinet. A good way of keeping long-winded politicians from using too much gas.

Meeting Logic

Agenda items that get the most discussion are those that come close to the start of the meeting, when everyone is still fresh and energetic;

where everyone is an expert; and where no one will be offended by the outcome or by the discussion. In other words the debate is risk-free for the participants.

This creates great opportunities for manipulation. One of my favorite executive committee meetings met at 11 A.M. The first item was a discussion about giving the staff a glass of champagne at lunchtime to celebrate the recent merger and the official launch of the new brand and the new business. This hit the jackpot in terms of generating discussion. Everyone was fresh and wanted to be seen by the CEO to be contributing.

Everyone was an expert; some argued that giving champagne would set the wrong example, make disciplinary action over drinking at work impossible. Others argued that it would be atrocious to celebrate with a glass of water, management would look mean and morale would plummet. For 90 minutes there was mortal combat over the glass of champagne. No one present could be offended by the discussion or the outcome: a glass of champagne did not represent the risk of stepping on anyone's turf. Opinions could fly, risk-free.

At about 12:30, coming up to the 1 P.M. lunch break and still with three agenda items to go, a request from the IT director was put to the committee to extend a systems integration program across the two businesses. This was vital to the business: millions of dollars of investment were at stake, it effectively doomed one set of platforms and one set of employees, and had significant impact on the product development and servicing capability of the business. Inevitably, it went through on the nod, because everyone was exhausted from the champagne battle, and had their eyes on more agenda items before lunch. Only the IT director really understood what was at stake: finance, marketing, and personnel were completely out of their depth. And the IT director had the sense to square the CEO beforehand. Any challenge would have been risky: it would have been directly questioning the IT director's expertise. Set the agenda to get the level of discussion and the results you need.

MERGERS AND ACQUISITIONS

Theory and Practice

All the academic literature shows that most acquisitions fail. M&A activity gets larger every year. Either business people are stupid, or the academics are missing something.

The academics can show that the main benefits of an acquisition flow to the shareholders of the acquired company. Countless studies show that typically an acquirer will have to pay a premium of about 40 percent above the open market price to secure control of a target company. The target company shareholders lock in a quick 40 percent gain. The acquirer's stock typically underperforms relative to the market following the acquisition. The result is that fewer than half of acquisitions succeed from the acquiring shareholders' perspective. This analysis may be rational and logical, but the logic is incomplete.

Acquisitions are about management, however, not just about shareholders. From the management perspective about 50 percent of managers win. The successful acquirer wins the power and the glory, and the acquired lose. The dead don't laugh. Management and shareholder perceptions of victory are not the same.

This is more than vanity. By acquiring another company, the acquirer earns the right to stay in the contest. The company can not only derive some short-term financial benefits and cost savings; it gives itself more room to maneuver strategically. It gives itself the chance of winning long term. The acquired company has lost, cannot play, cannot win. Game over. Naturally, not all acquirers go on to win: that is the nature of competition. But from the management perspective, it makes more sense to be predator than prey.

Mergers Versus Acquisitions: The FUD Factor

Managers hate the FUD factor: Fear, Uncertainty, Doubt. When the FUD factor rises, morale and performance plummet. Resistance, politicking, and internal rivalry rise.

Acquisitions bring the FUD factor to boiling point. And rightly too: the target company management and staff have good reason to fear for their jobs. Even if the acquisition is about growth, not scale economies, there is the uncertainty of what the new management will look like, what they will expect, and how they will manage.

However, a well-managed acquisition will drive through the FUD factor fast. The decisions on who survives, and in what role, will be made quickly. Those who have to go, will go soon. There will be pain. Well managed, the pain will be short if sharp. The FUD factor will be blown away, and managers can get on with managing the business, instead of jockeying for position and survival.

This means that the post-merger integration should be thought out in advance so that the acquirer can strike fast. Normally acquirers are so wrapped up in the thrill of the chase, that when they win there is a hiatus that leads to the crisis: they do not know how to integrate the acquired business.

Mergers bring the pain to boiling point, and keep it there for a long time until the entire management and the business is well stewed. The more equal the merger, the worse it is. In the desperate struggle to be fair to both sides, management ducks all the difficult decisions. This is one case I lived through, where management was desperate to be fair, rational, and even-handed. Here's how they approached the key decisions:

■ Who will be in charge? We will both share responsibilities.
■ Where will we cut back? We will set up some task forces to look at the question objectively and they will report back in six months.
■ Which systems will we use? We'll think about it.
■ Which offices will we close down? Let's keep both running until the other decisions have been sorted out.
■ How will decisions be made? To be fair, we will make sure that all key decisions involve managers from both sides so that we can reach the best solution for the business as a whole.

Naturally, this was a mandate for politics and internal rivalry on a grand scale. The business turned in on itself. Everyone realized the real competition was not in the marketplace: it was the other management team. And this was going to be a fight to the death. There were never going to be two CEOs, two marketing directors, two finance directors. The more management tried to fudge the issues, the worse became the FUD factor.

The business was set back two years in the marketplace and never really recovered. Instead of a clear direction there was waffling and evasion, which confused everyone and suboptimized the business.

Having been acquired and having lived through a merger, the acquisition is less painful and more effective than the merger. Clear decision making is good management. Compromise is not.

THE MIDAS TOUCH

King Midas wished that everything he touched would turn to gold. The gods granted his wish. He was delighted. He embraced his wife. She turned to gold. Shocked, he turned to pick up a drink. The wooden goblet turned to gold, and then the wine inside turned to gold. He could eat and drink nothing. This is said to be the origin of the old Greek curse: "May all your wishes come true."

Corporate wishes are expressed not in prayers to the gods, but in reward and measurement systems for the staff. And some reward and measurement systems have the true Midas touch:

- Customer service reps measured on the number of calls handled. Result: unsatisfactory customer service and longer waiting time as throughput is maximized.
- Bank relationship managers sold on size of loan book generated. Result: low-quality loan books and expensive write-offs.
- Hospitals measured on the length of time between a patient seeing a specialist and having an operation. Result: patients kept off the waiting list by delaying their appointment with the specialist.
- Capital markets dealers measured on profits. Result: dealers take huge risks with the firm's capital, even resorting to deceit to bypass risk control measures. The bigger the risk, the bigger the potential gain or loss. When it goes wrong, the business can lose nearly a billion dollars and go bust thanks to one trader (Barings, Singapore).

MULTINATIONALS AND MULTILOCALS

It is fashionable for multinationals to present themselves as multilocal. They want to be seen as good citizens of the community and responsive to local needs. They do not want to be seen as fast food or carbonated drink imperialists squashing out the local culture.

The logic of the multinational says that any localization has to be window dressing to pacify the local constituencies. It helps to appear local to the national government when it comes to bargaining over regulations or investment incentives for building new factories or for tax reviews.

Otherwise, the logic of the multinational forces it to be global. The management presumption has to be in favor of the global approach over the local approach, despite the complaints of local management. Operationally, the multinational succeeds by working globally, not locally:

- Production costs can be minimized by global sourcing.
- Marketing costs are minimized with one global campaign.

- Stock costs are minimized by having a single package design globally, so that stock can be used internationally. This also drives longer production runs, fewer changeovers.
- Overhead costs are minimized: ultimately brand groups can go global, administration can be consolidated, and only one set of research and development is required. This can go to extremes. I have seen rice cookers being developed and tested in Groningen, the Netherlands. They don't cook much rice there compared to Asia. The idea of globalization was right, the execution was not.
- Learning is optimized: by having one customer service phone bank in Dublin for all its European corporate customers, a bank not only smoothes capacity utilization, but also learns more about the patterns of corporate needs across Europe. A fragmented approach would not lead to this kind of learning.
- Where customers are global, either structurally (business to business) or in taste (consumer), the business has to move to a global response.

Managerially, multinationals have to take a global perspective. Decisions on resource allocation, production, products, and branding have to be global if the global economies of scale are to be achieved. Decision making is easier when there is a cohesive group of managers that understand and trust each other. At minimum, that requires a common management language. This is driving even some French multinationals to adopt English as the corporate language. But it also drives top management to be homogenous. The executive committees of American multinationals tend to be American, and Japanese multinationals have Japanese executives. Multinationalism does not reach the executive suite.

Of course, there are pressures to adapt to local needs. But if the local needs are truly unique, a local company will probably best exploit them. A multinational will never be as local and as responsive as a good local company. A McDonald's will never produce a soufflé quite the way a fine French chef does: it does not need to compete on such local fare. The pressure within the multinational has to be to drive management, operations, and ultimately the market and its customers to a standard global model. As with auto manufacturers that use global chassis, engines, and parts, the end result may be tailored to local needs, but the economics, management, and standards are global.

MYTHS OF MANAGEMENT

There are three myths at the heart of management. For those that recognize them and can deal with them, they are useful.

We Know Where We Are

This is a big myth. Of course, it is a mortal sin for managers to admit that they do not know where they are. And in the course of trying to find out exactly where we are, we gather more and more detailed information ever more frequently on every aspect of our business. But no one is ever satisfied: we can never know enough. Knowing where we are is about being in control. But we can never gain the level of control or information we want. We will never know exactly what is going on in other functions, other parts of the business. We certainly do not understand what the political and emotional agendas are of all our colleagues. We usually do not know until too late what our competition is up to. We are always surprised by random events in the outside world: storms, strikes, new technologies like the Internet blow up out of nowhere.

As managers we should recognize that the search for perfect knowledge is self-defeating: it consumes so much time we will never do anything except find and file information.

The solution is not to worry. Focus on the few things that are important, that we can control and make a difference in. The tighter the focus, the more chance we have of being in control and making a difference. This is true for individuals and for institutions.

We Know Where We Are Going

There is a simple test for this one: dig out the five-year plan from five years ago and see how accurate it is. The world is awash with examples of how forecasts go wrong. In any takeover, there is at least one party for whom the takeover was not part of the five-year plan. Look at economic and financial forecasts and compare them with reality. *Fortune* magazine highlighted 10 attractive technology stocks (September 18, 2000). Within a month, five of them had fallen by more than 50 percent, two had fallen by 80 percent. The unexpected happens.

Since we are not in control of the whole world, we are not entirely in control of our own destiny. Again, the solution is not to try to control everything. It is impossible. The solution is to fix on a few goals and to focus on the key actions that are likely to get there. Be fixated about the goals, but flexible on the means.

Even if the reality is that the future will not turn out as we intended, it is worth sustaining the myth that we know where we are going. People need a sense of leadership, direction, and focus. Giving them focus is not just about motivation: it is about getting results in the areas we believe are important. If we are wrong, we can always start again.

We Know How to Get There

If we don't really know where we are or where we are going, we are not in a strong position to claim we know how to get there. But the myth that management is fully in control demands that we be clear about how we are going to get there.

Again, this myth is worth sustaining to the extent that it gives the organization a sense of direction and momentum. Where the myth becomes dangerous is when managers leap onto the latest management fad as a way of demonstrating that they have a plan to get to wherever they think they are going. The eagerness of management to jump onto fads is indicative of its uncertainty about how to go forward. But fads are often solutions to problems that are not relevant.

So What Do We Do About It?

For the health of the business, these three myths should be sustained. It would be a career-limiting move to tell the stockholders at the general meeting: we don't know where we are, we don't know where we are going, and we don't know how to get there. People like the sense of security that a direction gives them, even if it is a false sense of security.

The real danger is when managers start believing the myths themselves. Then they try controlling too much, build inflexibility into their plans for the future, and are easy prey for the quack doctors selling the latest fad. A healthy scepticism about these myths encourages managers to focus only on what they control and change and to be flexible about adapting for the future; and weans them off dependency on fads.

NEGOTIATE TO WIN

The best way to win in any negotiation is to negotiate for a win–win. Make sure the other side can walk away with a win and give it to them.

The traditional win–lose negotiation causes conflict. In a sales pitch it normally ends up focusing on price and ignores other things that may be of value to both sides.

The win–win negotiation requires an understanding of what the other side values. It may be something you give at low cost. Let them have it. In return, you will probably be able to get what you need.

These negotiations happen all the time in the office. A technology person asks some advice on a business plan: no sweat. I need some technology help, I get it back. This sort of negotiation is as natural as breathing air. We do it, because we can see it is in our interests to help each other.

The same is true of alliances that are more formal. In setting up alliances, it is crucial to know what the other person stands to gain. If they see no gain, they will put no effort in. In one alliance in Japan, we had some strong technology; they had the distribution muscle in what is an otherwise difficult market to enter. We both had something that we could easily give, at very low out-of-pocket expense in return for something that both sides saw as very valuable. There were many areas of contention: governance, economics, focus, timing, staffing, success measures. Language barriers, cultural differences, time zones, and internal organizational barriers did not help. But with both sides having a clear view of the win–win, we were able to proceed.

NEW ECONOMY BLUES

The perfect future is a world where we can get anything, any time, any way we want. This is consumer heaven. It is also management hell. For managers, creating the perfect future means doing everything, all the time in every way. The freedom to consume is mirrored by the prison of work. The electronic tags of e-mail and voice mail mean that we never escape.

Technology is not freeing managers, it is enslaving them. It simply raises expectations. What would have been a one-page typed memo, is now expected to be a 20-page presentation with graphics and spreadsheets full of sensitivity analyses. The content may or may not be better, but the style is in a different league.

Ultimately, it is up to management to master technology before technology masters management. Technology mastery is not about being a technical wizard. It is about knowing how to use technology to be more effective. This in turn requires knowing when not to use technology.

Wanting all the information all the time leads to the tyranny of technology. Learning to focus on what is important is effective management. It makes technology the servant, not the master.

OFFICES: FORM FOLLOWS FUNCTION

You can tell a business from its building. Learn to read the signals. The interior of the office is a statement of what the business is like. The exterior of the building is a strong statement about how the business wants to be seen. Many are functional, simple offices in business parks. But a clearer statement is possible:

- Traditional banks built like marble palaces give customers a sense of the bank's strength and stability.
- Local government offices with cheap flooring and decoration reassure tax payers that their money is not being frittered away.
- Central government offices with magnificent buildings project the power of the state.
- Modern architectural landmark buildings for IT consulting firms show them to be at the leading edge.
- Anonymous, discreet-but-rich offices for strategy consulting firms.

The principle of form follows function applies to the inside as well as the outside of the building. There are two competing forces at work. The first is the simple functional requirements of the building. An investment bank will require a huge, high-tech open area with good air conditioning and room for cabling to support a trading floor. A media design company requires more intimate space.

Consulting companies increasingly arrange the interior space so that consultants have no permanent desks. They want to keep the consultants out of the office and at the client site, where they can earn fees. So the interior has plenty of hot desk space, personal filing areas, and informal meeting spaces.

Internal space is not just about function in the utilitarian sense. The other key function it serves is about status. You can tell how hierarchical a firm is from the number of private offices it has, and whether there are separate elevators, floors, and dining rooms for different levels of executives. In contrast, a firm that needs to promote internal communication will have plenty of open space. In between is the compromise of cubicle land. Cubicles are meant to create the best of open plan communication with personal space. They tend to achieve the worst combination: poor communication and little privacy.

Use of space is not just a design issue; it is a management issue that helps to drive costs, behavior, attitudes, communication, and morale.

Status and Executive Apartheid

Burn the private offices and the executive floor. If the executives are desperate to cling to their offices, burn them anyway. Let the executives fry or flee.

For most offices, form follows function. For executives, function is about status, not utility. The executives are the ones who most need to stay in touch with everything that is going on, and they are the ones who put up the greatest barriers to a free flow of information. The separate executive floor is a good way of creating and enforcing the corporate apartheid system: executives only, riffraff stay away. In one business, the executive floor was known as death row. You only went there to be hired or fired. This was not a business with easy communication, high trust, or openness.

Individual private offices ensure that communication is minimized and formality is maximized. The quick chat is made more difficult. The riffraff are not allowed onto the executive floor without an appointment, so there is no chance of seeing if the boss is available for a quick word. Even among the executive team, the separate offices mean that each executive is not aware of what the others are doing, unless they meet. There is no point in having an open door policy if no one is allowed to see the door or to get onto the same floor as the door without an appointment booked through a secretary who tenaciously guards the day planner.

There is an alternative. It is called back to the future. I have worked as a partner in two firms. The difference illustrates the impact of different executive arrangements.

The Very Old-Fashioned Future Perfect Partnership

This partnership had a Victorian approach to the partners' office: all the partners shared one room. Their status and net worth could have justified magnificent personal suites. But sharing an office worked:

O

- Formal meetings were not required: we all knew what was happening with the business. If anyone needed help, or there were decisions to make about a client, all it took was a shout across the room.
- We knew how all the staff were performing. You got to know after a while that every time X came into the room, a good conversation would seem to happen. Every time Y came into the room, it would be tense and difficult. You would not listen to the conversation, but the impact was obvious.
- There were no secrets. This helps build trust among the partners.
- Open plan for the partners made for open communication throughout the firm: there would be a steady trickle of people coming in and out of the room. It was not a big deal to see the partners. The partners were literally on top of the business.
- There was no place to hide. If you were being idle or had nothing to do, it was obvious. If you were not contributing, it was obvious. Peer group pressure is a powerful motivator.
- There was a constant buzz. This was energizing. Some people claim only to be able to think in a private space. You get used to the open space fast.

The Traditional Hierarchy

The second partnership was a traditional command and control hierarchy, with the troops kept at arm's length. The loyalty and commitment of the troops was correspondingly an arm's length affair.

All the partners clung tenaciously to their private offices. They had poor communication among themselves. Nearly all decisions had to be arranged through formal meetings, which would flow up and down the hierarchy of partners. Cooperation was formal and poor.

Most people at all levels had much greater affection for the first firm than for the second; there was a sense of family in the first versus a desire to build a career and make money in the second. And this showed in the quality of people and service.

ONE-WAY OPTIONS

Options serve neither management nor shareholders. When the tide rises, both the cream and the debris rise to the top. A rising stock market rewards good and poor management alike. Clearly, some managers do better than others. Those in fundamental growth industries like software, telecommunications, financial services, and pharmaceuticals have done very well. Managers in steel, food manufacturing, and old economy industries will have had to struggle to keep up, however good they are. Managers are not being rewarded for performance. They are being rewarded for working in a growth industry during an economic boom.

Equally, managers should not be punished when the economy hits a recession. The recession, when it comes, will not have been caused by the option holder.

The response of boards in these situations is the wrong response. They reprice the options. So, the options essentially become a one-way bet for management. If the share price rises, they win. If it drops, they get the options repriced and they get to play again until the stock market lifts them out of trouble. This is not an incentive to outperform.

If directors and management are serious about rewarding performance, they have to focus on outperformance. There are two ways, use of economic performance measures or share performance measures. In the first, you incentivize management to achieve profitability in excess of the required rate of return on the capital employed in the business. This can lead to game playing. Reducing the apparent capital employed through write-offs is an easier way of improving profitability than actually improving performance.

In the second, you reward management based on outperformance of the share price relative not just to the stock market but to its immediate competitors and peer group in the market. This enables management to be rewarded even in a falling market, provided the stock price does not fall as fast as the peer group. Whether the market rises or falls, managers have to earn their results, rather than get lucky.

ORGANIZATION CHARTS

Boxes Are for the Dead

Draw them up and throw them away. Big organizations need to draw organization charts. Drawing up the chart is a way of forcing management to make basic decisions about what roles people will have, where accountabilities will lie, and how decision-making processes will work. Some organizations pride themselves on never having drawn up an organization chart. They are the ones that have the least internal clarity about how things get done. The result is confusion and politics on a grand scale.

Once the discipline of drawing up and communicating the organization chart is complete, throw it away—unless you are a traditional command and control hierarchy, in which case publish it widely so everyone can see which box they lie in. Otherwise, don't let people hide in their little boxes. They will have plenty of time to hide in a box when they are dead.

Organization charts ossify the organization vertically and horizontally. The horizontal divisions of the chart convert the organization into layers, like pancakes layered on a plate. The pancake at the top is the most important. Don't let managers hide in their pancake. It simply reinforces the traditional control versus commitment hierarchy.

The vertical divisions of the chart split the organization up into deep silos. Again, this is consistent with a command and control hierarchy. But if lateral communication and cooperation is important, don't let formal structures get in its way. Silo mentality is a great way of avoiding responsibility and shifting blame.

Silo mentality allows for passing the buck. When sales dropped at an electrical goods manufacturer, the sales force immediately blamed marketing for putting together the wrong promotions. Marketing blamed product development for not bringing the right products to market. Product development inevitably blamed R&D who in turn blamed finance for cutting their budgets. Finance pointed back to the sales organization for underselling, which meant the budgets had to be cut.

The silos spent months making sure that the blame did not fall into their silo, when they should have cooperated across the silos to reach a solution. The only winners were the competition.

Upside Down Thinking

Upside down organization charts are very trendy. A 50-year-old manager showing an upside down organization chart looks as trendy as a 50-year old going out clubbing.

The upside organization chart preaches wisdom that the front line workers are the most important. The chart means to show that the boss at the bottom of the pyramid is simply supporting the people above him or her.

What is said by the boss and what is understood by the listeners is quite different. The audience does not see the upside down pyramid. They see a spinning top out of control, where the boss likes to believe that everything depends on and revolves around him alone. No one is taken in by the claim that the front line troops are the most important and the boss simply supports them. The decisions all still flow from the boss, while all the salary and status flow to the boss.

The upside down chart is misleading, dishonest, patronizing, and not credible. And it is not even original any more. But it makes for a speech the boss feels good about, and makes him or her feel trendy. So, expect to see a lot more upside down organization charts.

OVERPAY PEOPLE

If people really are your most important asset, then it makes sense to overpay them relative to the market. Paying over the odds has several positive consequences:

- You stand a chance of recruiting the best people. In sales, top quartile performers are often four to five times as productive as bottom quartile. Overpayment is a good investment.
- You stand a reasonable chance of keeping attrition down. The cost of attrition is not just the recruiting cost, but the far greater cost of bringing new people up to speed together with the risk that they may not work out.
- Overpayment sets high expectations of performance. People tend to achieve what is expected: low expectations get low performance, high expectations create the potential for high performance.

Low pay may ensure lower costs, but it also ensures lower performance and lower morale. Employing more low paid staff is not a substitute for quality.

There are bad and good ways of overpaying. Overpaying should be linked to performance. And it should be linked to a culture of high performance and putting people first. Overpayment is not just for the management big shots. At least as important are the receptionists, the people who staff the 800 number, and front line service people who represent the business to the customer. They should all be excellent.

PARETO PRINCIPLE

Originally, this was an assertion by the Italian economist Vilfredo Pareto that about 80 percent of the wealth in any country was held by 20 percent of the population. This has found its way into management thinking in the theory that 20 percent of the effort produces 80 percent of the result. This is inaccurate. For management, the 20/80 principle is often much more like 5/95. Everyone knows this, but does not apply it.

These examples are worth testing in your own business to see how well the 20/80 stacks up. The real challenge is for management to then act on the results:

1. Customer profitability. Twenty percent of the customers typically produce over 100 percent of the profit contribution. This is fairly consistently true when activity-based costing is used to measure the true cost to serve different customers. Most businesses do not differentiate customer service and pricing in line with profitability and the cost to serve.

2. Product profitability. Perhaps 20–30 percent of the products produce over 100 percent of the profits. This is a powerful message that is being applied by Unilever and P&G as they refocus their businesses on the most successful global brands.

3. Effort and results. Ninety-five percent of management effort is used to maintain the business or to justify work that will move the business forward; 95 percent of the work is spinning wheels, 5 percent results in moving forward.

4. Ten percent of the management produce 90 percent of the value. Names, please.

5. Ten percent of the people cause 90 percent of the problems. Names, please.

6. Ten percent of salespeople's time is spent selling to customers, 90 percent is spent on administration, souped up service, and some sales call preparation. This is tried and tested as a ratio. In business-to-business selling the ratio can be nearer 5/95. It represents a great opportunity for performance improvement.

7. Ninety-five percent of the probability of a project's success is determined before it starts, 95 percent of the effort happens after it starts. Projects, like battles, tend to be won and lost before they start: the right problem with the right team and the right resources is set up to win against a project on the wrong problem with the wrong sponsor and the wrong team.

8. Ten percent of the specifications drive 90 percent of the cost of the new IT program.

9. Managers spend 90 percent of budget reviews testing 10 percent of the budget: they test not the most important parts, but the bits that are easiest for everyone to understand; are most discretionary; and are least volatile politically.

10. Five percent of this book will give you 95 percent of the value. But for each person, it will be a different 5 percent. Good luck!

PARKINSON'S LAW

Few management insights stand the test of time. Parkinson's Law* is one of them. It will be as true during the twenty-first century as it was during the twentieth:

1. "Work expands so as to fill the time available."
2. "Officials make work for each other."
3. "An official wants to multiply subordinates."

Rules one and three are self-evident in the daily work of managers. Rule two is the killer for the twenty-first century. As organizations become flatter, so the number of officials tends to grow.

Previously, a factory manager could probably decide if the washrooms needed to be refurbished and would get the work done. Now the corporate life support systems swing into action to help him. The health and safety people offer all advice on the standards that need to be applied; the purchasing people produce a list of preferred suppli-

*Parkinson, C.N. *Parkinson's Law*. Houghton Mifflin, 1957.

ers; the lawyers check the contracts; the accountants check the estimates and control the payments; the HR people make sure that the staff understands what is happening and get the newsletter to communicate the refurbishment; and of course the whole management chain gets involved in the procurement process, giving approvals, with staff checking the submissions and other staff checking progress with yet more checkers checking that the checkers are doing the checking the right way. Then the designers, consultants, architects, surveyors, cleaning contractors, and builders get involved. The result is a jamboree for all. The refurbishment should have cost $1,500, but just managing it will have cost $15,000.

The flat organization does not make it worthwhile challenging this management feeding frenzy. From the factory manager's point of view it takes longer to fight the system than it does to go along with it. And none of the zoo of managers needs to challenge their own existence. Finally, each one of them can demonstrate that they, individually, are adding value to the process.

There is no one in the system who has an incentive to stop it spinning out of control. Even top managers have other battles to fight, rather than grappling with the internecine warfare of the internal bureaucracy. The beast is out of control until it causes a crisis. Then it is chopped back ruthlessly. Like pruning, this simply allows it to flower yet more vigorously the next time around.

PERFECT PREDATORS

Some consultants were on safari, and they decided to design the perfect predator. Each took responsibility for one limb. The result combined the best of all the animals. The perfect predator had the legs of a cheetah, the neck of a giraffe, the head of an elephant, the hide of a rhino, the teeth of an alligator, and the wings of an eagle. The animal collapsed under the weight of its own improbability.

When they returned to work, they decided to create the perfect company. Each contributed his or her greatest strength. This was the business that came out:

- It would be a high commitment workplace, for as long as management wanted the staff.
- It would have detailed, world-class reporting and control systems and highly empowered management.

- It would have great strategic intent to beat the world and be ruthlessly reengineered to minimize costs.
- It would be a flat organization with a clear decision-making hierarchy.
- It would have the lowest prices and highest service in the marketplace.
- It would be global and local.
- It would serve its shareholders, customers, staff, and the community outstandingly.

This business did not turn out to be a world-beater. It was just the same as all the other businesses in the marketplace. And it too, eventually collapsed under the weight of its own improbability.

The perfect predator is not a mix of all the best bits of best practices from elsewhere. It is not a mix of every fad to have wafted through academia and boardrooms in the last 10 years. The perfect predator, like the lion or the crocodile or the eagle, is perfectly adapted to its own environment and has made the trade-offs required to become perfect. Luckily for business, as the environment changes there are endless opportunities to achieve perfection by not being the same as everyone else.

PLANNING HEAVEN AND HELL

Good planning can move a business forward quickly. Bad planning is a bureaucratic hell that sucks up management time and achieves nothing. Every business has its own unique planning system, normally guarded by managers for whom the planning cycle is their meal ticket for life. Attack the process at your peril: the planners will defend their system with eloquence.

Planning should not be a dry technical process. It should be about mobilizing, aligning, and committing management to a course of action. That will not happen with plans dictated by staff.

You probably know intuitively if your planning process comes from heaven or from hell. Here's how you can substantiate your instinct.

Planning Hell

- Driven by staff, not management. Once staff start leading with their numbers and judgments of the business, it wastes an inordinate amount of time and effort to change what they are writing.

▣ Historic trend-line mindset: extrapolate the past into the future. This is a surefire way to guarantee incrementalist thinking. It does not encourage ambition, and it ignores the changing obstacles and opportunities for each business.

▣ Single-point planning. This normally dissolves into the debate about what the target for next year should be. Some testing for sensitivities under different scenarios is more useful, as well as differentiating between base and stretch objectives.

▣ Bottom right-hand box bias. Everyone knows what the answer in the bottom right-hand box of the spreadsheet should be, so they fix and fudge all the assumptions to get there. If the box is meant to show $10 million profit or 15 percent ROE, it will always manage to come in just above the number. Do not test the number. Test the assumptions behind it.

▣ Politically driven. Power and selective facts are used to drive targets up or down.

▣ Complicated: search for endless detail and spurious accuracy. This is normally linked to control by the staff. Arguing over secretaries' salary assumptions is not going to make for a plan that builds the enterprise successfully.

▣ Long-winded. Management has other things to do than go through endless iterations of a plan.

Planning Heaven

▣ Driven by business management. The planning process simply articulates the commitments that managers make to each other. Intermediation by bureaucrats does not help the process of commitment.

▣ Market-based assumptions about what will happen. This is better than plans that are based on looking backward (historical trends) and inward (extrapolate costs and results forwards).

▣ Sensitivity testing against different scenarios, which is a natural consequence of being outward- and future-focused.

▣ Balanced goals: get away from the tyranny of simply trying to fix on the profit target. The plan should reflect progress for the business in four areas:

1. Financial progress: profit, capital effectiveness, revenues.
2. Market progress: share, service, quality, satisfaction.
3. Organization: new skills, capabilities, focus.
4. Innovation: this is about working smarter rather than just trying

to work harder to get more results. Long term, this is the only way progress will be sustained.

Ultimately the planning process should help mobilize and align management. Budget proposers should feel a sense of ownership over the plan, rather than accepting it as something that has been handed down to them by bureaucrats and management. And senior management should have a better understanding of the challenges and opportunities that each business or department face.

POLITICAL CORRECTNESS

Political correctness and the quality movement suffer the same disease: the process has overtaken the substance. The objective of political correctness is not to be politically correct, but to be seen to be politically correct. And the political correctness fundamentalists are management's greatest allies in this respect. By insisting on awkward language (coffee with milk, not white coffee; abolition of Christmas, etc.), they are hugely helpful to politically incorrect management:

- They give the old guard some easy targets to attack.
- Compliance is easy. Saying a phrase is simple, and if said with a sneer and rolling eyeballs, it is a good way of inviting sympathy.
- It forces management to do nothing about the substance of political correctness. In the Fortune 1000 companies, just 5 percent of senior managers are female and only 3 percent are nonwhite. The club of middle-aged white males is still firmly entrenched. The only way the minorities get into the boardroom is to take notes, clean, and to serve coffee.

The challenge is that PC is about control, not commitment, at a national level. The more it is about control, the more people resist the control. The best form of resistance is overt compliance (process compliance) but covert resistance (apathy, leading to the club being maintained). The commitment model demands strong role models, as in the US army, which has actively promoted minorities, including the former chief of staff, with success.

POWER GAMES

You suffer them as a junior manager. It's only fair you should enjoy them when you become a senior manager. Pass the misery on from one generation of management to the next. If you haven't made it yet, use this checklist to score all the Big Shots. Give the winner a power Oscar at the next big conference. A statue of Napoleon should do the trick.

Meeting Power

- Always be the last to arrive: keep them waiting.
- Never read documents ahead of the meeting. Read them in the meeting. This shows you are very busy, and very smart because you can absorb 100-page documents in five minutes while chairing a meeting.
- When people come to meet you, keep them waiting outside your door. Ideally, the door should be open and they should see you are doing e-mail. This shows the visitors how unimportant they are, and gives you the chance to complain about the 200 e-mails you receive every day. This shows you are important.
- Interrupt the meeting to take a call or to step outside and talk to someone. Tell everyone they can carry on: it shows that their agenda item is unimportant and leaves them trying to guess your point of view.

Travel Power

- Whatever your travel arrangements are, change them at the last minute. Show you are busy and maximize disruption for staff.
- Travel with junior bag carriers: changing travel plans should mess them up. And when you board the plane you turn left, they turn right. Let them know their place.
- Never pay for the taxi. Either put it on account (weak) or make a junior pay and make the junior sit in the front seat (strong).

Office Power

- Make sure you have the plum office. A separate executive floor, with separate reception, a separate elevator, and ideally separate security protects you from the riffraff and spells power.
- You should have the most up-to-date computer. Never use it, except for e-mail.
- Doctor photographs to show you with various presidents or prime ministers, and leave them where they can be seen. Alternatively, a picture of a grand country house or vintage car will help.

Communication Power

■ Always make your secretary receive and make phone calls for you; then keep the other person waiting on the line for a while.

■ Internal newsletters are there to carry your picture on as many pages as possible. You should either be seen awarding prizes, doing a royal visit to a factory, or making speeches about the future.

■ Only communicate to other managers through your staff. You are too busy to deal with them directly. And it makes it harder for them to argue with you.

■ Write either with an antique fountain pen (tradition, expensive) or with a red ballpoint (good for commenting on papers: makes recipients of your comments feel like they are back at school).

Conference Power

■ Public conferences: turn up only for your speech and then leave immediately afterwards. Shows you are busy.

■ In-house conferences: make the big speech. In coffee breaks only ever talk to people at your level or above. Do not talk to underlings.

■ Give underlings the impression that you are deciding their fate, even if you are only arranging the afternoon golf match.

Eating Power

■ Have a special diet. It should be very awkward to meet, force people to offer some sympathy about your allergy, but not be too cranky (like vegan). A gluten-free diet is perfect.

■ Be the big host. Always go to an exclusive place, where you will see some celebrity that you can talk about later (use Christian names, implying that you regularly meet him or her). This is the one occasion when you do pick up the bill so that everyone knows how generous you are.

■ Maintain the private dining room for entertaining guests. Eating in the office is good: shows you are busy. But the sandwiches must be on proper china, be high quality, well presented and come with the bowl of fresh fruit (uneaten) every day.

Pastime Power

■ Pastimes should show you have money and mix in the right circles: opera, riding, the country club are good.

■ Active sports where you can claim some talent are good: it irritates everyone else who has not got the time to be superfit and it's one up against your more sedentary peer group. Skiing in exotic locations is good: combines the illusion of health with conspicuous consumption.

- Bad pastimes: softball or baseball (common); nerdy past times (stamp collecting, bird watching).
- Charities are good: shows compassion, implies wealth, and helps you meet other power people.

Dress Power

- Custom-made is expensive, discreet and good.
- Designer is trashy.
- Cufflinks are a must.
- If forced to wear a casual oufit, make sure it is expensive, new, and very crisply turned out. This shows that you maintain high standards and keeps some distance between you and the junior staff.

PRESENTATIONS

We are victims of presentations. And most of us also guilty when it comes to giving deadly dull presentations. Here's what to look for:

Purpose

Presenters often seem to think their purpose is to get through their slide set, or to show they are smart or to make their point. Most presenters think of the presentation from the wrong point of view: their own.

Effective presenters think of the presentation from the point of view of the audience. The purpose of a presentation should be to persuade and inform a target audience of something that is important and relevant to them. If you have a focused audience that's fine; if your audience is diverse, focus on that part of it that is most important to you.

Style

Audiences remember very little content. Try to remember the substance of the last three presentations you heard. At most, you will remember a couple of headlines, and maybe a few choice phrases that were used. But you will have a memory of whether the presenter seemed any good. That is a reflection of the presenter's style.

Remember the three Es: energy, excitement, and enthusiasm. If you display these, you are probably enjoying the presentation, and you have a chance of getting the audience to enjoy it. There is little worse than trying to concentrate on a dull presenter with a monotone voice. A little trick like standing slightly on the toes of your feet help keeps the energy levels up and keeps your body looking alert.

Keep the audience on its toes. Presenters often talk while looking at their slides or at the rear wall. The audience is disengaged. Each sentence should be addressed to an individual. Look them in the eye. If they were doodling or their minds were wandering off, the effect is electrifying: they will absolutely pay attention if they know you are making eye contact with them. This works as well in a large audience as it does in small audiences.

Substance

There is a fourth E to remember: expertise. It is hard to have or convey excitement about a subject where you are not expert and you live in fear of the tough question. No expertise, no credibility.

Presentation Aids

The ideal is to have dumb aids and a smart presenter. The more common approach is to have expert aids with a dumb presenter. The expert aids come in the form of detailed slides with lots of writing on them, which the presenter proceeds to read. The audience can read it faster than the presenter, and everyone gets frustrated. Worse is when the slides are shown on computer; techies particularly like this because it shows they can use technology. But what it means in practice is that they lose all flexibility in terms of the pace, priority, and adaptability of the presentation. They will refuse questions so that they can get through to the end of their slides. This keeps them happy and irritates everyone else.

The smartest aids are the simplest. A blank sheet of paper and an overhead projector—or even a chalkboard—is a good start. On this you can then draw a diagram or write the key words that make your point. This is not casual or spontaneous: you will have prepared what you will draw as carefully as the techie prepared his slides. The difference in effect is huge:

■ The act of drawing something transforms your presentation into a live performance: people are always curious to see what is being drawn and how it will turn out. You draw the audience into what you are doing.

■ As you draw, you can adapt your diagram to the comments that are being made. This gives you flexibility, draws the audience further in as you discuss their comments, and enlists their support as they see that the presenter apparently concurs with their ideas.

■ It allows you to adapt the pace and content of the presentation to the audience; you are not tied rigidly to a set number of slides.

Clearly, you will need some structure and some pre-prepared aids. But again, these should be simple, and it should be possible to write on them to illustrate or emphasize different points.

Presentation Flow

The old adage of tell them what you are going to tell them, tell them, and then tell them what you have told them remains true. This is for two reasons. People like to know where they are going, and why they should listen. There is little worse than sitting in the middle of a rambling presentation not knowing where it is going, when it is going to end, or what the purpose of it is. So, make this clear up front. And give everyone a clear reason why they should want to listen. Tell them what the purpose of the presentation is. People will judge whether they are going to enjoy your presentation in the first minute.

In addition, people do not hear messages clearly. Just because you have said something, it does not mean anyone has heard it, let alone understood or accepted it. A key message needs to be said at least three times before people realize it is important. It should be said at least three different ways.

PRICING

Chaos and Confusion

Controlled pricing chaos is profitable. Uncontrolled pricing chaos destroys profitability.

Controlled Chaos

Controlled pricing chaos takes advantage of consumers who lack the time or inclination to understand pricing choices completely. In reality, no one has the time to price-shop all that they buy. Instead, consumers want reassurance that they are getting good value, and that they are not getting ripped off.

The reassurance comes in two forms. The first form of reassurance is the brand. No one who goes grocery shopping price-shops every item in the basket before deciding which retailer to use. Usually, they choose one retailer, and then rely on that brand to let them fill the grocery basket at reasonable cost. Even after the shopping is completed, customers are unable to recall individual product prices accurately, and have little notion of whether shopping would have been cheaper elsewhere. But the sting in the tail is that if the customer does sense that they have been overcharged, the trust in the brand is lost, the loyalty and the customer go.

The second form of reassurance comes from pricing chaos. Customers want to know that they have got a good deal, that they are not stupid buyers and that they have not been ripped off. Pricing chaos helps provide this reassurance, while giving the business the chance to price profitably. Essentially pricing chaos and segmentation go together.

Here are two examples. First, telephones. It should be possible to compare prices on the humble phone call. In practice, it is not. There are several thousand rates. By mixing line rental, call charges, volume discounts, free minutes, differential rates for different times of day to different types of phone at different destinations, price comparisons between carriers become an arcane art.

Calls from the U.S. to Japan cost anything from a nickel a minute to over a dollar a minute. This allows carriers to make a profit. Industry pricing has disguised the essential commodity nature of the product. But it also allows the customer to believe that they are getting a good deal: they can always find some package that suits their particular usage patterns. The customer can always create a good story, or post-rationalization, as to why their deal is the best: because they don't pay any line rental; or they get a lot of free minutes every month; or calls are cheap at peak periods or at off peak periods. Chaos allows consumers to create in their mind the story that reassures them they have done the right thing.

Second, electrical goods retailing. Everyone wants to believe they have gotten the best bargain on the new computer. The evidence of how people shop is that the belief of getting the good deal is more important than the reality. After a little shopping around consumers get totally confused about all the different makes and models, the different options in terms of delivery, installation, service, guarantees. After a while, they give up. They want a salesperson to give them some decent guidance, and to reassure them that they have made a good decision. This allows the manufacturer to price for profit, and it allows the consumer to be given some rationale for why they have made a good decision.

Uncontrolled Chaos

This is familiar in business-to-business selling. There is the price list, on which profit assumptions are made. But then, one FMCG (Fast Moving Consumer Goods) firm offered its retailers the following:

- Prompt payment discounts.
- New store stock allowances.
- Featuring and advertising allowances.
- Occasional promotional allowances.
- Returned goods allowances.
- Coupon handling rebates.
- Volume discounts.

By the time the list price had cascaded through all these discounts and allowances, the achieved price could be 25 percent lower than the list price. Given the net margin was about 8 percent, this was a recipe for disaster. Control over the discounts and allowances was split between finance, sales, and marketing. And the information systems could not track clearly the achieved price and profitability by product and customer. Essentially, profit was being eroded in an uncontrolled way for unknown benefit.

Pricing for Profit

Profit is a function of margin and volume. The perils of overpricing and losing volume are acutely seen and felt. The perils of underpricing are just as acute. Raising margins from 8 percent to 10 percent has the same effect as a 25 percent volume increase. The way pricing is set is central to profitability, and is often poor. The pricing questions that are asked are often the wrong questions. Asking the wrong question is a good way of getting the wrong answer. The wrong questions focus on margins. The right questions focus on value. Typically, there are two sorts of margin-driven question. First, cost plus calculation. The aim is to sustain margins by setting a target margin. Second, the historic price plus calculation. This is a minor variation on the cost plus equation. It takes last year's prices and tries to adjust them up by inflation or better.

The margin-driven approach has internal logic. And it is extremely easy to apply. There are simple, visible metrics that drive the pricing decision. It is a relatively simple process. It keeps the accountants happy: it is a rational way of keeping the financial ratios whole. As a way of setting pricing tactics day to day it is fine.

But in many industries it is fatally flawed as a logic. It ignores the customers' point of view, until the customers start voting with their feet and deserting the business. That is the only signal that the business gets that it is overpricing. It gets no signal that it is underpricing. As an incrementalist approach it does nothing to attack some of the broader risks and opportunities of the business. The day-to-day pricing tactics need to be set within the context of a clear customer and competitor-focused pricing strategy.

Pricing and value questions are externally focused, and harder but more profitable and sustainable to answer than internally focused margin discussions. The ideal pricing strategy is customer focused. It asks: what value are we adding to the customer? The answer is normally messy. Different customers give different answers, and it is difficult to pin a price on both the tangible and intangible value of the offering. The effective pricing strategy has four major elements:

- It clearly focuses on value, not just price. Value is about product performance versus price and expectations. So the pricing decision is part of the broader product and positioning question. It will also force the discussion about how value and price can be differentiated to different customer segments.
- The market logic and financial logic should marry. The market logic should force difficult questions about how to achieve superior product and cost performance. The financial demands for profitability should force the awkward questions about how to go to market effectively.
- The pricing discussion should be based on aggression, not incrementalism. There are two forms of aggression. The Japan Inc. version typically looked at rapid volume and share growth supported by pricing down the learning curve: lowering prices in expectation of future scale cost reductions, which are achieved by lower prices.

The alternative is to look at aggressive price increases to maximize profitability.

■ Pricing will look at competitive logic. Aggressive pricing upward can send strong signals to the competition and can help industry pricing and profitability rise. Downward pricing either destroys industry profitability and is self-defeating, or simply leaves one winner in place.

Pricing Strategy in Action: The Launch of Ariel Automatic

Detergents are seen by many as close to being a commodity. Even the industry began to fall into the trap of treating them as a commodity. The pricing strategies of the leading brands all called for prices within 3 percent of the market leader. This was the classic incrementalist approach to pricing that was generating unacceptable profit. Competitively, there was no escape.

Then P&G decided to launch a new flagship detergent in Britain: Ariel Automatic. Everything was set, and on the day of the launch the salespeople gathered to see the dry ice, dancing girls, and detergent. They were disappointed. The launch was pulled at the last moment by the head office in Cincinnati, much to the consternation of the managers in England.

Upper management had second thoughts about the pricing strategy, which had been to stay within 3 percent of the market leader. Given the trade would accept lower margins on the market leader, this meant that the price to the public would be about the same as the competitor's market leader. The economics sucked. One week later, the salespeople got to see the dry ice, dancing girls, and detergent. But the real eye-opener was the price: A full 7 percent above that of the market leader. This was busting the commodity mindset big time.

The new pricing strategy meant:

■ The economics of Ariel Automatic were transformed, enabling it to double the advertising spent and get the message across that it was a truly better product. The high price justified the advertising and vice versa.
■ The economics of the industry were transformed: competition got a signal that it was safe to price up occasionally, not always to price down. Ariel Automatic gave the industry pricing cover.
■ A high price/high value position denied the market leader the traditional response to a new entrant. Normally it would lead a short

sharp price war. The biggest brand with the most trade power and lowest costs would always win. A price war would be financially painful against the higher margin Ariel Automatic. It would also reinforce in the customer's mind the perceived quality gap between the brands.

■ Strategically, Ariel Automatic outflanked the market leader. The market leader was caught between the low price products on one hand and the high price products on the other. It could not fight on both fronts and had to concede share somewhere. Pricing had created different market segments.

Other examples demonstrate the potential of pricing for value. In none of these cases would a cost plus logic reach the pricing or profit potential that value pricing achieves:

■ Mineral water has minimal product costs, but can retail for $3 a liter. The value is in the convenience, perceived taste and health benefit, and status.

■ Airlines charge anything from $300 to $10,000 to cross the Atlantic on the same plane at the same time. The difference is space, a low cost investment in some food and wine, and status.

■ Consulting firms will hire a new graduate for $50,000 and charge the graduate out at $250,000. The value is not in the individual consultant, but in the solution that the consultant promises to bring to the client's business.

Pricing, Profits and Prison

Making a 10 percent price rise stick is a lot more pleasant than trying to find another 10 percent off the cost base. And it has more instant gratification than hoping to double sales volume, which would have the same effect if margins are at 10 percent currently in a variable cost business.

The problem, of course, is making the pricing stick without being crushed in the stampede of customers heading for the exit to your nearest competitor. Some industries are consistently better at making price rise stick than others. There are, broadly, six ways of making a price rise stick. Some of them are legal.

Create a Cartel

Strictly illegal, unless you are OPEC, in which case it is strictly politics. Some industries still operate effective cartels. In one industry I found that no one spoke of competition. They only referred to their co-producers. Presumably, they used different language to the anti-trust authorities.

There all sorts of way of signaling intentions across competition without the cartel having to meet in shady motels or Viennese palaces. One cartel contracting for government services used the phases of the moon. Depending on the phase, three competitors would put in very high bids, one would put in a good bid and win. They were caught. In an auction for telecommunication licenses, different competitors used the last three digits of each bid to signal which licence they most wanted. There was no actual collusion or agreement, and the authorities were left frustrated.

The problems with a cartel is that it is illegal. Prison does not get to be more fun the older you get. It is hard to maintain cartel discipline. OPEC has had occasional success and years of failure. It invites new entrants into a market that they see as being profitable and inefficient.

Use Pricing Signals

It helps if all the competitors have explicit pricing strategies. Unilever and P&G have explicit pricing strategies, and over the years have evolved rules of the game without ever colluding. Price lists inevitably leak from the trade to the competition. Far from damaging commercial confidence, this is helpful. It is a way of checking that pricing strategies remain in place. When one of the price leaders raises prices, all the other brands can follow. When one brand cuts prices, the competition can see whether it is a temporary price reduction for a promotion (retaliation not normally necessary) or whether it is a permanent reduction (retaliation absolutely necessary). By reading and respecting the pricing signals, the two competitors can still slug out their brand wars without destroying the pricing structure of the industry. Competition remains, but it is not focused on price. Price discipline is enforced by the retailers' own brands at the bottom end of the market.

Create Pricing Chaos

In fragmented, competitive markets, pricing signals and disciplines cannot be maintained. If the product is also a commodity, like a telephone call, potentially prices are driven down to the marginal costs of the weakest competitor. This is not a recipe for profit.

The response of the telephone companies has been to create pricing chaos. There are well over a thousand pricing tariffs in Britain alone, all of which are changing frequently. No one can keep track of all the tariffs, know which is best and keep switching to the best one. The result is that the intensity of pricing competition is reduced, especially as there are switching costs in terms of effort from the telephone user's point of view.

Segment the Market

Flying across the Atlantic can cost anything from $300 to $10,000 on the same plane. There are some people who will happily pay the $10,000 (provided the company picks up the tab). For others, the choice will be made on the basis of $2 difference between the two cheapest flights. In between there is a range of trade-offs in terms of convenience, comfort, flexibility. Effective yield management optimizes the revenue from these segments.

Focus on Non-Price Competition

In the retail market, this is the purpose of brands. They promise the customer non-price value, in the form of product performance, values, or lifestyle.

The professional services market is profitable because it is based on non-price competition. For instance, in a takeover the predator and the prey do not choose their advisors on the basis of who is cheapest, but on who will maximize their chances of success.

Other business to business markets are more susceptible to price competition, especially where there is a price-driven purchasing department mediating the purchase. As long as the suppliers are unable to deliver value beyond price, they are likely to be locked into a price war. Unless they have a cartel.

The Radical Alternative: Declare an All-Out Price War

Price wars tend towards death or glory. The glory version is akin to the entry of Japan, Inc. into autos and consumer electronics in the 1980s. By pricing ahead of the learning curve they undercut competition, which allowed them to build scale, go further down the learning curve, reduce prices further and enjoy a virtuous circle: low prices to more volume to lower costs to lower prices. Meanwhile competitors were forced into the death spiral of smaller volumes, higher unit costs, and higher prices. Eventually, the Japanese turned to non-price competition, which has enabled them to sustain scale and profitability.

The price war can backfire. It can attract justified or unjustified anti-trust and government action, like the imposition of anti-dumping duties on imported steel. It also drives profitability out of the market and makes it difficult for any of the competitors to thrive, as in the global glass industry. It structurally builds low profitability into the industry until the industry is restructured and enough capacity is taken out of the market.

PROFESSIONALS AND PYRAMIDS

Professional service firms are pyramid structures. They are also pyramid selling schemes. The partners take all the financial gain while junior staff do all the work. As with all pyramid selling schemes, this only works as long as the pyramid keeps growing. As soon as the pyramid stops growing, disaster strikes.

It is possible to argue about the morality of this. It is more profitable to argue about the career implications of this. In essence it means that a small partnership has a better chance of sustaining fast growth and creating more partnership opportunities than a large partnership. Do the math.

Let's say two consulting firms maintain a ratio of 15 staff members for each partner. Average time to partner takes eight years. Both firms grow at 20 percent per year. Firm A has 100 people. Firm B has 60,000 people.

In both firms, the chances of becoming partner, provided they promote 100 percent from within, are about 3.5 to one. If the time to partner is extended to 10 years the chances become 2.5 to one, but no one wants to wait that long. So the pressure is on to promote people faster. That can only be done if people are also weeded out faster, or if the growth rate is faster.

Small firm A only has to grow to 429 staff to sustain a 20 percent annual growth rate. Big firm B will have to grow to be a mega-firm with over 250,000 staff to achieve 20 percent annual growth for eight years. That is not a partnership, it is a bureaucracy. It is not based on having the best talent, but having the best machine with average talent. And it also faces a big challenge in growing to 250,000 staff. The chances are its growth will be slow, while the small firm can grow fast.

Different growth rates affect the potential to become partner dramatically. If the growth rate slows, in the conditions described above, to 15 percent annually only one in five new recruits can expect to make partner. Smaller firm B, if it grows at 25 percent annually, can expect to make 1 in 2.5 recruits into partner.

Arguably, if recruits cannot do the math and cannot figure out the risks, then they deserve to land up in the wrong firm. The trade-off is between business risk (the smaller partnership could fail) and promotion risk (the larger partnership will not fail so badly, but its growth prospects are not so great either). Even the math may not help. The temptation for the partners to sell out before you get there is just too great.

PROFESSORS AND THE ONE-NIGHT STAND

Good business school professors are great for a one-night stand. They are very smart and entertaining, and they normally have one great insight and one great speech in them. After one night you have got the insight and got the speech from them, and they have done the job of energizing and enthusing the team with a new perspective.

The temptation is to then ask them back again for some more of the magic. Don't ask them back. You will simply see the same trick again, or a pedestrian imitation of someone else's trick. The magic will be gone and you will be disappointed. (A few world-class professors stretch to two tricks, one stretches to three.)

Remember that their magic is essentially a solution looking for a problem. It is the same solution, the same insight that they bring to every company. If you have their problem, great. If not, they are still worthwhile for the entertainment value and the different perspective. Just don't expect to get your problem solved.

Also, the stories and the cases they give you in immense detail are not true. They are not trying to recount history. They are trying to make a point. Nowadays, professors have got smart about this. Working with one professor in Europe, I was astounded by the range and depth of cases he was able to draw on from Asia. Working with him in Asia, he told all the same stories but with all his cases drawn on European companies. I knew they were detailed works of fiction, but the audience had no chance of catching him.

PROJECT MANAGEMENT

The Four Horsemen of the Apocalypse

There are four ways to destroy a project. Savvy consultants and managers know this instinctively and respond accordingly.

The Wrong Problem

The best way to focus on the wrong problem is to focus on the latest fad or solution, and to decide to implement it. Many consulting firms will happily aid and abet you. They need to sell something to keep the revenues flowing and they probably have teams that can do the fad. The partner gets no reward for not selling, or selling something that you need and they cannot deliver.

You may have the right problem if you can clearly see some significant benefits from fixing it. Size the prize: the prize does not have to be all financial. If the solution being offered does not yield a big prize, it may well be that it is a solution to a problem that does not really exist.

It does not matter how well you do everything else, if you have the wrong problem, you have the wrong result.

The Wrong Team

Worthwhile projects are normally tough projects. This means it needs great people working on it. So the right people are probably the ones you can least afford. This gets down to priorities. But if the project does not merit the best people, then it probably is not a very significant project. Go back to the problem, size the prize again, and figure out where it is on the list of corporate priorities.

Sure-fire losing teams are ones that come from staff functions, or from just one department. The project needs to be embedded in the line and owned by the people who will be responsible for producing the results. This is not the consultants, nor the staff, nor one department alone. It will be cross-functional, and line led.

The Wrong Client

The client is the godfather/godmother or sponsor of the project. He or she will be powerful. The sponsor will have resources and the power to work across the business. Critically, the individual will also have enough time to be a sponsor and to make things happen when they need to.

A sponsor from a staff function, too low in the organization, with no direct stake in the outcome of the project and too busy to sponsor the project, would be a good way of killing the effort.

The Wrong Process

Provided you have the right problem and the right team, you will probably find the right process (quality, reengineering, change management, etc). Select the wrong process and the team will go charging down the wrong road. It will be very difficult to recover.

These four horsemen of the apocalypse will strike before the project has even started. Effectively, by the time the project has started, it is already destined for success or failure. Like most battles, it is won or lost before it starts. This means that overinvesting in the right project setup pays huge dividends later on.

The actual management of the project represents 90 percent of the effort, but influences perhaps 30 percent of the outcome. And most project management can be done by managers, without consultants.

The DIY Guide to Project Management

Project management is how consultants earn their fortunes. It is fundamentally simple. This enables the consultants to employ lots of junior staff on project management. From the consultant's perspective, the ideal project management assignment is executed on behalf of the chief executive, with the consultant project-managing a lot of client teams who deliver the actual results. This gives the consultant power, no real responsibility, and the perfect hunting licence to go through the organization and find more selling opportunities.

Project management is something that management should do to themselves. Tear away all the consulting babble about risk logs, problem logs, work force charters, training, and empowerment. It is a smokescreen. Management can do all that the consultants do. This is what the consultants really do, and what management should do:

1. They empower the project and themselves, but not the management.
   a. Empowerment comes from getting sponsorship at the right level of the organization. Once a CEO has sponsored a project, he or she is not going to let it fail and the organization will respond to the priority the CEO gives it.
   b. Empowerment comes from getting a large budget and significant company resources devoted to it. With a large budget, all the pressure is on the CEO to show that the budget is not being wasted; the CEO has to make it succeed.
   c. By putting themselves between the CEO and the rest of management, the consultants empower themselves and disempower management.

d. Managers clearly have the capacity to do this all themselves: they can get the sponsorship at the right level of management, they can get the right level of resource and budget commitment, if the project is worthy of sufficient priority. By doing it themselves, they increase the level of accountability and empowerment within the management team.

2. Consultants set up and organize work teams to work on different parts of the project. There are three elements to this:

a. Resource allocation. They will inevitably ask for the best people, on the basis that since the project is so important, it should have the best people on it. This is true. It is also true that the best people are capable of managing themselves. Resource allocation is essentially about priorities (what should people work on), risk (dare we reduce the focus on our daily business) and politics (no one wants to give up their best people or forsake some other priorities). This is a management task.

b. Work stream design. This is about dividing the work into manageable chunks, and assigning responsibility for each chunk of work. The typical result is a work stream charter that will have the following four elements:

- Objective: measurable, relevant and achievable.
- Time frame for delivery and key milestones.
- Team membership: a team leader responsible for delivery, a senior manager as sponsor responsible for overseeing quality and giving political power to the team, and team members who between them have the skills and power to achieve the objective.
- Key dependencies: what the team needs from the rest of the business and when.

All of this represents management decisions; the consultant simply provides the templates and integrates the output.

c. Finally, consultants integrate the output. This may include a GANTT chart. This does no more than show what has to be achieved in what order. It is normally put on a computer with some obscure program. Do not be intimidated: it could as easily be put on a large expanse of wrapping paper covered with Post-it notes, which can be moved around as and when timings change. This Post-it approach is much more user-friendly, and because this chart is visible and accessible to everyone, it has more meaning and relevance to the organization than a mystical GANTT chart hidden away on a consultant's computer.

3. Consultants support the project planning efforts of each work team. Project planning is straightforward. There are six steps in project planning:

   a. Identify where we need to get to. Project planning starts at the end (the desired outcome) and then works back to the beginning. You should be able to "size the prize" desired. The prize should be:
   - Relevant to the business.
   - High impact to make it worth working on.
   - Measurable so you know when you have achieved success.
   - Complete: the prize is not just monetary, there may be changed skills, behaviors, structure, processes.
   - Tangible: people should understand what it will mean for them personally.

   b. Understand where we need to get to. This is an honest assessment of current resources, problems, and strengths. It is also about understanding the expectations of the different relevant constituencies.

   c. Identify the obstacles that stand in the way of success. Each obstacle is essentially another management challenge to be overcome. Obstacles may be rational (lack of money, staffing, time, existing systems and processes) or they may be political and emotional (resistance to change, lack of cooperation). Both are real, and need managing by managers, not consultants.

   d. Identify the minimum number of steps required to get from the start to the end. There is a tendency to overcomplicate. Keep it simple. Break the problem down into small bits. Prioritize the bits in terms of risk/complexity versus impact. There will be some things that can be done fast: do them fast and build a sense of enthusiasm and momentum. Other bits are on long lead times: get them going early. Feed the rest in later. Generically, most projects go through four stages:
   - Start up: identify the problem, the prize and the team.
   - Understand the "as-is": really understand the problem, and begin to test likely solutions.
   - Develop the solution, the "to-be," and implement some early easy wins.
   - Implement the solution.

e. Ensure the right people are involved at the right time for the right reason. The typical roles include: the sponsor, a senior person to oversee and empower the team; a team leader with responsibility for delivering the result and implementing it; technical experts (IT, finance, marketing) who help develop the solution; and interested parties who will be affected by the result and should be kept informed.

f. Manage progress against the plan. This should involve regular updates and reviews to help primp, or to remove obstacles.

None of this is rocket science. But the scale of it, and its urgency, can make it seem a daunting and risky task to management. This is where consultants can make a killing.

4. Consultants monitor progress and identify problems. They call this project management. Four principles underwrite effective monitoring of progress:

a. Honesty in identifying problems early avoids much greater problems and delays later. If senior managers do not trust work teams to be open and honest about progress, they may use consultants as their eyes and ears. Managers would do better to either put people they do trust onto teams, or to create an environment in which openness and honesty is encouraged.

b. Frequent and early communication is essential. Speed and urgency drive the required level of involvement at all levels of the organization. In a merger that may mean that the executive committee needs to meet every day for half an hour, even by telephone, to keep on top of progress and unblock bottlenecks. For a long-term systems integration, the executive committee may hear no more than a summary of progress once a month.

c. Effective decision making. A good way to escalate costs, waste resources, and delay progress is to have slow decision making, decisions that are subject to appeal and reversal, and unclear responsibilities. This will also help demoralize and frustrate everyone on the project, except the consultants who simply bill you for the extra time spent. Effective decision making is a reflection of effective management and clear lines of control and responsibility.

d. Make progress visible and tangible. The fancy GANTT chart on the consultant's computer fails miserably in this respect. A large paper exhibit with the timelines and deadlines makes it clear to everyone what has to be done when and how their effort fits in with others. If it is put up in the reception area, it also helps put pressure on everyone to deliver, and gives recognition to teams when they do deliver.

Large-scale projects have a habit of looking big, nasty, and complicated. Management likes the comfort blanket of consultants to take away some of the perceived risk. This is a waste of money, it's bad for the organization, and it's unnecessary. This checklist provides the basic guide to project management. Follow these guidelines, and you will probably succeed. If you see a project being set up which does not seem to meet these criteria, quietly walk away.

PUNKS, HIPPIES, EXPERTS AND THE FUTURE

In early 1977 I left my hippie friends behind in England. I hit the hippie trail through Afghanistan to Nepal. Six months later I floated back to what I hoped would be a summer of love, only to find that my friends had in fact been punks for at least the last three years. I was baffled: neither they nor I had never heard of punk until then.

In 1987 reengineering hit the management world. We had never heard of it before. But this was okay because management told us that all our projects for the last three years had in fact been reengineering. We were therefore experts and could go and sell more reengineering work.

In 1997, I returned to my colleagues in New York after a six-month absence. I suddenly found that they were all Internet experts, and had been for the last three years. I had never heard the word before. There are some patterns in here somewhere:

- Big change happens in arbitrary 10-year intervals. Beware 2007.
- People lie. At least, they are creative about past reality. They regard past reality as thermoplastic: it can be molded to the needs of today.
- The future is genuinely unpredictable. You must move with the times. If you don't move you will end up like the managerial equivalent of a superannuated hippie lost in a time warp. This is not a recipe for managerial success.
- Expertise is relative.

Use relative expertise to your advantage. If you have seen part of a reengineering project and no one else has, you are the expert. And despite most of the consulting jargon and bluff that surrounds these fads, at heart most fads are simple. With a little experience, a good reference book and good judgment, you can lead one of these fads. This is what consultants do.

For instance, in late 1996 I returned to the UK. I decided to build a business helping banks prepare for the euro. At the time most banks did not know what EMU (European and Monetary Union) stood for. I did. I was the expert. I was probably never more than one step ahead of my clients, but what I learned from one client would help me keep ahead of other clients. We acquired 26 new clients in 18 months, which was exceptional. Never be intimidated by the professed expertise of consultants or others, especially if they are talking about a new fad.

QUALITY ZEALOTS

These are dangerous. The mantra is that quality is free, but the price is you have to sign up to the faith. This means documenting in great detail exactly how you meet voluminous quality standards that are arbitrarily set by a standards body that may or may not know your business.

The consequence of signing up is that all your management time and attention will be devoted to fulfilling these quality standards. Even worse, you will need to prove that you are maintaining these standards through endless documentation.

This is a favorite of government departments. They can use quality certification to show that they are doing a good job. By selecting suppliers that meet these standards, no one can accuse them of doing a bad job. Quality certification is a risk-free substitute for management judgment.

Quality bureaucracy could be tolerable if it was relevant. But the quality process becomes an end in its own right. Certification becomes the goal, not making a profit or serving the business. In its extreme form it is a way of ensuring that you take far too long to get exactly the wrong product out to the wrong market at the wrong time. But at least you will know that you were wrong in exactly the right way. You should be able to buy the quality certificates from your liquidators at a reduced price. Quality should be a servant of the business, not the master.

QUICK-FIX FIXATION

We see the snake oil salespeople coming. We know they are going to con us. We know that they will pitch us with the promise of some corporate quack medicine that will cure everything from a flagging share price, unhappy customers, demotivated staff, to personal and corporate health and happiness. We know it's nonsense. And yet we go on buying it.

We get our fix of each new cure-all: total quality, reengineering, kaizen, portfolio management, and time-based competition. We've been there and we've got the T-shirts to prove it.

And of course, the cures never quite deliver what they promise. We still have flagging share prices, unhappy customers, and demotivated staff. So we are all set up for the next snake oil salesperson who comes cruising into town. Either we are all terminally stupid, or there is something else going on. The real questions we should ask are:

- Why do we always fall for the snake oil salesperson?
- Why is it always certain not to meet our expectations?
- What can we do about it?

Why Do We Always Fall for the Snake Oil Salesman?

Managers are rationally making the right choice when they sign up for the latest snake oil, even if they know it will not deliver what it promises. Consider the possible outcomes for management. If a manager adopts a new fad, he or she cannot lose. If he or she opposes it, he or she can not win.

The snake oil might actually do some good. Any corporate initiative that gets people together to figure out how to improve things is likely to have some benefit. Each new fad gives a structure and focus for getting people together constructively. So if the manager brings in the latest fad, he or she has a chance of winning. He or she may be able to show some progress.

If the initiative does not succeed, the manager is unlikely to lose out. First, most of these initiatives are anchored at the top of the business. Once a CEO has signed up to a program and has devoted people and money to it, the CEO will not let it fail. The CEO will make sure something comes out of it. Even if the reality is poor, management will simply declare victory and move on.

If managers do not try the new snake oil, then they are exposed. If things start to go wrong in the business, then the finger can be pointed at the manager who failed to implement a reengineering effort or a quality program. Even CEOs do not want to be seen resisting change and best practices. If things go along well without adopting the fad, then there is absolutely no news.

We may be cynical about the fads, but for risk-averse management adopting the fad is lower risk than opposing it. The greater the marketplace momentum of a fad, the greater the visibility and risk of not adopting it. This is why fads tend to snowball and then die away. As momentum builds, fewer and fewer people want to be left off the bandwagon. Once everyone has been through their reengineering program, managers tick that off the list and wait for the next bandwagon to come rolling round the corner.

Why Are All the Quick Fixes Destined Not to Meet Expectations?

Quick fix fads are destined to fail:

- They are non-replicable. The fad is normally built on some case studies where it has had spectacular success. But the cases can not be replicated accurately, because:
  a. The best talent led the spectacular cases: your version of the quick fix will be led by people who have learned about it second- or third-hand. They do not have the same level of skill as the creators of the fad.
  b. The fad may be a great solution to someone else's problem.
  c. Your conditions are different from the original's. Kaizen may work in Japan, but it is part of a broader system that includes JIT, lifetime employment (sometimes), quality, unique corporate relationships and culture, and eating sushi. There is not much sushi in West Virginia.
- The fad is a zero sum game. Once everyone has reengineered and dropped their cost base by 20 percent, you are no better off in a relative way than you were before you started. At least operational fads are zero sum games. Strategy fads are negative sum games. To the extent that everyone adopts the same strategy prescriptions and analyses at the same time, they will all be attracted to the same markets. This competitive conformity is also competitive suicide, destroying industry profitability until there is an industry consolidation.
- The fad represents at best a partial solution. Quality, knowledge management, time-based competition, reengineering, are all great ideas in their own right. But they are not stand-alone solutions. They need to be integrated into the way the business works.
- Poor execution. This is common, and there are a thousand ways to

mess up. Most businesses are quite creative about finding new ways to mess it up. The fundamental problem is that managers are by definition trying something new where they do not have experience. This dramatically increases the chance of failure. The consultants do not help. They will throw in junior staff who have as little knowledge as the managers; the partner has picked his knowledge up second-hand. Your only hope is that in the middle there is someone managing the project who actually knows what he or she is doing.

These factors are more or less hardwired into any quick fix implementation, and guarantee that the results will not live up to the hype. So this raises a big question:

What Are We Meant to Do About It?

The solution is not magic. It is common sense.

- Focus on the problem, not the solution. When you understand the problem, you have a chance of finding the right solution, which may or may not include the fad.
- Go for a full solution, not a partial solution. The fad by itself is more or less certainly not the whole solution. Going for the full solution is high effort. Low effort is probably just wasted effort. You may need to implement not just the fad, but much more besides.
- Put the right people in place. The right people are probably the people you can least afford. This is about priorities. If the problem does not offer a big prize when fixed, then you probably should not be bothering with the solution or the fad. If it is worthwhile, it will need talent to make it happen. Getting the right people also requires giving the project the right political sponsorship, and finding the right external support if required.
- Size the prize. Know how big the opportunity is. Measure and track performance against the prize. The prize is not just financial. If it is a purely financial prize, then you will have people running round cutting budgets for the short term rather than trying to build the long-term capability you need.

RATIONAL, POLITICAL, AND EMOTIONAL MANAGEMENT

Business as it is taught is a rational science. This fundamentally misses the point of management. People quickly learn it is also a political art. Making things happen, achieving recognition, setting expectations, building alliances with peers, garnering resources, and agreement without power are the normal political and survival skills of middle management.

A few managers also discover that management is emotional. People have hopes; they have fears. They trust or distrust others. No one dares talk about emotional management, lest they are typecast as members of the tree-hugging community. But knowing how to work with people's emotions, how to gain their trust and cooperation, how to play to their hopes and fears is as hard-nosed as traditional management. It is about making things happen through other people.

Some managers work purely in the rational or the political domain. The great managers work effectively in the rational, political, and emotional domains all the time.

RECRUITING

The most intense competition between corporations is in the marketplace: the marketplace for customers and the marketplace for talent. The best talent and resources of the company focus on the customers. The HR department focuses on the marketplace for talent.

Put the best talent onto the talent hunt: this is the future survival of the business. The best talent can easily be spotted: they are the ones who are not available. Most big professional service firms have it about right. They send out a mix of recent graduates who have credibility and relevance to the campus recruits, together with some senior managers. Choose the senior managers with care. Do not just send the person with the biggest title. Students are unaware of all the fine nuances of your hierarchy, and are not impressed by it anyway. The test for the senior manager is whether the students would aspire to be like that person in 20 years time. A heavyweight, crusty old fart does not meet the bill.

Every company will give the same message: we are the fastest growing; we are the biggest and most individualistic; we are entrepreneurial but risk-free; we are hard-working and family-friendly. Students do sometimes appear marginally cynical because of this. Find a distinctive message that is true to what you are. It is possible to be both positive and honest.

Do not let recruiting professionals do the interviewing selection and follow-up. This is your decision, and you need to show your commitment to the recruits. The only question that flushes out the true opinion of fellow interviewers is the acid test: "Would you take this person on your team for next year?" Let them know that if they say yes, they are likely to get the person. Make managers live with their decisions.

REENGINEERING REENGINEERING

Reengineering is in urgent need of reengineering. Reengineering as sold by consultants is a deeply perverted form of reengineering as it was conceived. It has become little more than cost cutting with a smile. And the smile is optional. There are three distinct forms of reengineering being touted in the marketplace.

IT-Enabled Reengineering

This provides a technology fix to inefficient operational processes that wind through the business like a cowpath through a field. The technology may not straighten or simplify cowpaths, it may simply pave them over. High fixed-cost technology replaces high variable-cost labor. The system remains inherently inefficient, but now it is also inherently inflexible; adapting the processes to future requirements takes a significant technology cost.

Process Reengineering

In its traditional form, this is a charter for the consultants to go in and map out all the process flows of the business. It is simple, high margin, high leverage work for the consultancies. They like to sell it. If they do it well, they will straighten out the cowpaths, and the business will reduce its costs and increase its speed of operation. It looks successful. But it is based on a purely internal view of the world that assumes that the existing processes are the right processes delivering the right products and services to the right customers. If any of these implicit assumptions are wrong, process reengineering simply takes the business up a blind alley. Process reengineering focuses on doing things efficiently. This is useless if it enables the business to do the wrong things efficiently.

Business Reengineering

This is closer to the original vision of reengineering spelled out in *Reengineering the Corporation* by Hammer and Champy. Business reengineering starts with the marketplace. It is forward-looking and asks the basic questions about what is the very best way to go to market. It does not start with the status quo of today. It does not require hoards of analysts mapping what you already know. It requires the best brains thinking about how to design a business for tomorrow. It is less reengineering; it is more about creating the zero-based business. It is what the successful dot-coms like Amazon have done. It simply blows away the old way of doing things. It presumes that businesses do not shrink their way to success, but should grow their way to success. From the consulting point of view, this is high risk, low revenue and low leverage work. Do not expect to see much of it being sold.

Reengineering: Sheep and Wolves

Consultants and senior managers sell re-engineering as transformation. Others, when they hear the sales pitch, hear rightsizing, downsizing, redeploying, cutting and firing staff. Reengineering has earned itself a bad name. When you hear re-engineering is around, there are four possible survival strategies. These are common to all threatening initiatives, and threatening bosses:

- Ignore it and hide. This is called the "get lucky" strategy. It is the strategy of sheep: they hope that the wolf will pick another sheep. The sheep strategy identifies you as a potential victim. You are likely to land up as dead meat.
- Fight it. Sheep do not have a good track record of killing wolves.

But at least it is a more spectacular way to go. Re-engineering is normally driven top–down. Resistance is tough.

▉ Run. Find another shepherd, another department or company where there are no re-engineering wolves, or you can be protected. Good survival chances, but everyone else is also going to be running, so you need to run fastest.

▉ Join the wolves. Sheep in wolves clothing are not always convincing. But it is the safest place to be. You get to pick who the victims will be. Unless you have a strong death wish, you will not pick yourself.

REQUIRED RATES OF RETURN

The fundamental issue is how much should a project earn to justify investment? The theory does not help. Discounted cash flow is sound, provided you know what the discount rate should be. This is where things break down big time. A quick reminder. The cost of equity is: $COE = RF + B(RM)$ where:

▉ COE = Cost of equity.
▉ RF = Risk-free rate, normally represented by some form of government debt.
▉ B = Beta, or the specific risk of a stock or project.
▉ RM = risk premium on the market.

There are long arguments about how you measure beta (risk), and even what that right risk-free rate should be. Although these arguments are deep, they pale into insignificance compared to the debate about the risk premium. In one camp is the school that looks at historic data and shows that the risk premium should be somewhere between 5 and 8 percent. The historic camp is filled mainly with academics. In the other camp are stock analysts keen to justify ever-higher stock valuations, who use a forecast risk premium of 2 to 3 percent. Intellectually, both camps have internal logic on their side, which does not help the casual observer.

The difference between these two camps in a low inflation world is huge. Assume a risk-free rate of 5 percent (the yield on long-term government bonds). The historic camp will produce a cost of equity of 13 percent or so. The forecast camp will produce a cost of equity of as little as 7 percent.

For managers this means that an investment proposal would have to earn nearly twice as much to gain acceptance in the historic school of thought versus the forecast school of thought. In other words, either the historic school is passing up huge amounts of worthwhile investments, or the forecast school is making a lot of foolish investments.

This debate has a huge impact when deciding on big long-term investments like opening up new oil fields. In practice, however, management can afford to ignore this debate. Good investments normally have several obvious characteristics:

- The return is so attractive it breezes past any hurdle rate. If it is a close call and the figures have had to be massaged to get past the hurdle rate, the proposal is inherently unsound.
- The proposal will fit absolutely with the strategic direction of the business.
- The managers proposing it have a strong record of delivery; any financial risk is set off by reduced fulfilment risk.
- The plan is "de-risked" operationally: there will be clear staging posts that enable a go or no-go decision to be made about carrying on.
- For more marginal decisions, there will be a short payback period.

The financial case is important, but it is often best used as a structure for asking the right questions and examining the right assumptions, rather than being used as an answer in its own right.

RESISTING INSANITY

You do not have to succumb to the latest hare-brained initiative oozing its way out of the executive suite. There are plenty of ways of stopping it, without resisting it:

- Ignore it. Hopefully the executive achieves a moment of sanity and quietly kills the initiative. Or the executive will be promoted or moved, or you will get moved in the next reorganization before anything happens.
- Reinvent reality. If everything has to be e-commerce-based, show how all your work is now e-based. If you use a computer, then it must be e-based. This keeps everyone happy that the targets have been met without doing anything.

- Pass the buck. Agree it is a great idea that would be ideal for marketing or sales or engineering or whoever. Make sure they are too busy to deal with the idea.
- Agree with the idea. Set up a team to look at how to implement it. Come back enthusiastically with the recommendations that require doubling your budget, reallocate resources away from the bosses' other pet projects, and cause maximum harm and disruption.
- Delay, obfuscate, and confuse. Muddy the waters about who has to do what, when, where, and why. By the time this is sorted out, the idea should be past its sell-by date.

Whatever you do, don't resist openly. You will no longer be a team player. You will be a problem. Worse, it will force the issue into the open and bring about the exactly the actions you want to stop.

Apathy is the best resistance: it puts all the pressure on management to create the momentum. They probably lack the time, focus, resources, or energy to overcome corporate apathy. If they don't, then it is probably worth getting on board the bandwagon.

RESPECT FOR THE INDIVIDUAL

Respect for the individual is one of the most abused terms in management today. Respect for the individual often amounts to little more than window dressing for traditional command and control styles. Perhaps you have a wonderful organization where none of this ever happens:

- Turning commands into questions that only have one answer: "Will you work late tonight?" versus "You need to stay late." So much for balanced lifestyles and family-friendly policies.
- One-minute managing people, with trivial compliments that are meant to motivate: "Gee, you did that photocopying neatly."
- Artificial involvement in management proposals. This can take the form of questionnaires (results sanitized, perverted, or ignored), break-out groups in conferences (summaries to plenary sessions first garbled and then ignored), or documents circulated for suggestions (editorial changes included to show the writers are responsive while substance remains unchanged).

All of this is done with the best of intent. It is meant to involve people and show respect for them. The normal reaction is cynicism. Showing respect for the individual does work: it builds trust and commitment. Staff consistently rate as the best those managers who show that they care for them as individuals. They rate highest not just on caring, but on perceived effectiveness, results, analytical skills, and technical skills. But it will take more than one minute to build trust and respect. It takes real time and effort. And it means making the occasional painful choice, like letting people get back to their family even when it is awkward for the rush you are in. Respect comes from actions, not just words.

To build respect, build trust. Use the trust equation: $T = (S \times C)/R$ (*see page 3*). Respect, trust, motivation, productivity, and quality go together. Putting in the effort to show real respect and build real trust pays dividends to the business.

REVENGE

From time to time, we all get stiffed. Sometimes the other person has been a miserable, malicious, Machiavellian mismanager. Other times he or she has been plain incompetent, and you have been left holding the baby. It is tempting to seek revenge. It is not worth it, and it does not work.

If you try to get revenge, everyone sees what you are doing and all the individual and institutional defenses go up. You just discredit yourself. If you stay aloof, it is possible that days, months, or years later the chance for quiet revenge comes along. Take it if you want. But do not bother to wait for the opportunity. Revenge is immediate and at hand. It is called health and happiness. If you have those, nothing can touch you. Let the miserable Machiavellians wade in their own cesspool.

So to all those miserable mismanagers out there, and you know who you are, cheer up!

REVIEWING DOCUMENTS: THE ART OF READING

This is when the reviewer gets reviewed. A team fixes a time to review a document or a presentation they are preparing. They expect you to be smart and constructive and to add some value. You may quietly be judging whether they are any good. But they will certainly be judging whether you are any good, and will have no hesitation in telling each other what their verdicts are. Your competence as a manager is about to be assessed by the toughest group of all: your team.

Some people are naturally smart and brilliant and can look at the document in real time and add great insight. This is also a management ego trip: it shows that we are so busy, smart and important we do not have the time or need to do any preparation. For many of us, this is not a clever option.

Others ask for the papers in advance and carefully prepare lots of comments. Sometimes this just does not work logistically. And teams do not like it: it slows them down and then you cease to be their coach; you become their examiner. So, you may well end up having to do the review in real time.

The key to success is not to rely on having to react to what is in front of you. This simply lets you get trapped in its internal logic, which may or may not be great. Instead, prepare your own criteria for looking at what is produced. At this point, four minutes' preparation makes all the difference. Quickly jot down four things:

- Your argument or point of view on the subject they are seeing you about. This will give you something against which to test their ideas.
- The content headings you expect to see covered in the document. This will help spot the most difficult thing to spot, which are missing items.
- What next steps you expect to see to ensure momentum is maintained.
- Any coaching items you want to cover with the team on either substance or style.

With this is in your mind you have a proactive agenda to work with them, a distinct point of view to offer, and a yardstick against which to measure what they have done. Even if the document is sent to you in advance, it is still worth going through the four-minute test before opening the document and getting sucked into its logic. Do this, and you are in danger of looking naturally smart. Your office reputation might actually survive.

A similar method can be used in any meeting or at any presentation. Do not simply react to what is being discussed or presented. Jot down your own point of view and expectations before the presentation contaminates your mind. You will be able to make a much better intervention.

RISK AND THE MIDDLE LAYER

People hate losing. We are risk-averse animals. And the more we have, the more risk-averse we are, because we have more to lose. The great risk-takers, the entrepreneurs, tend not to be people in big management positions with big titles and big salaries. They do not give it all up to do some start-up in a garage, unless they suddenly lose their job anyway. The start-ups in garages are for dropouts. Bill Gates and Steve Jobs gambled when they had little to lose. Managerial risk has real life complications and opportunities:

- Where there is risk, there is resistance. The resistance is to the risk of loss. Managing resistance is often about managing risk.
- Resistance to big change often comes from the middle layer of management. The icing layer (top management) is in control of change. Since they are leading change they are reasonably confident they will be safe. The sponge layer (junior management) has less to lose, and more to gain from a shake-up of the business. The middle layer has most to lose and least to gain—and lacks control. Changing the loss, gain, and control equation is important.
- Risk is personal. Managers have no difficulty taking risks on behalf of the organization. That is what they are paid to do. It can be rationally managed. Personal risk is emotional, and theoretically off-limits as a management issue. Unless the emotion of personal risk is managed, resistance will appear under all sorts of rational guises. Trying to deal with the rational objections will miss the point and result in frustration all around.
- Risk is unequal. People have different risk appetites, and what is safe for one person is risky for another. Again, this means that risk management has to be customized to the individual.

There are three ways of dealing with risk:

- Take away or reduce the risk.
- Increase the reward relative to the risk; given people's risk aversion, an exponential increase in rewards equates to a linear reduction in the risk side of the equation.

■ Increase the individual's control over the situation. Most perceived risk comes from fear of the unknown. Give people control, the fear reduces and the perceived risk reduces.

RUSHING AND RELAXING

One of the smartest people I ever knew believed that if he did not miss at least one flight in ten, he was wasting too much time. He was always running from meeting to meeting at top speed, to fit everything in. He was a very stressed person. He smoked too much, drank too much, and died too young.

The best salesperson I know is not that smart. Whenever he goes to a big new client he goes outrageously early. Even if the plane is delayed, the taxi gets lost, and he has been given the wrong address, he still has enough time to get there.

This is not just about avoiding missing the meeting. It is about being relaxed and prepared. Because he knows he will be early, he concentrates on preparing the meeting, not on how he will get there. When the meeting starts he is 100 percent ready and focused. He does not go to many client meetings, but each one is a knockout.

Of course, he also drinks too much and smokes too much. But he is much less stressed, and he is still alive.

SALARIES AND SECRETS

There is an obsession with secrecy. Secrecy just encourages rumor, gossip, and misinformation. Blow it away. There should be a presumption of openness, not of secrecy. Secrecy belongs to the old command and control environment of the traditional hierarchy.

Salary is a sacred cow when it comes to secrecy. Kill it. Publish the salary information. It stops all the salary rumor and gossip, and gives staff useful information. It shows them clearly who is perceived as successful. It is a clear way for management to indicate who the successful role models are. Hopefully, it gives staff some aspirations in terms of their earnings potential. The dumb ones will ask: "Why can't I be paid 10 percent more than my peers?" The smart ones will ask: "How do I get paid 10 times as much, like the CEO?"

Publishing the salary information puts pressure on all the right people. Individuals who achieve a big salary increase will be under real peer pressure to show that they are worth it. Senior managers will have to show that they are worth it to the most demanding critics: their teams. Management will be under pressure to get the results right.

Publishing the salary data also brings true market forces into play. The competition and headhunters may find out. If they can poach the lower paid staff, no problem—provided management has rightly judged the capability of the lower paid staff. If the higher paid staff are being poached, that's a signal that management is underpaying the key talent.

SEAGULL MANAGEMENT

This is the preferred form of management for big bananas from other offices. They want to show they are pressing the flesh, in touch with the business, and adding value. So they fly by and drop poop.

The fly-by is the one- or two-day visit. They say they want to add value, so instead of having some internal meetings they demand to see all your most senior clients and add some value to them. They do not know the clients or the businesses, but have a simple faith that their innate brilliance will somehow rub off on the clients.

As they leave, they drop their poop. This is in the form of some gratuitous advice that they will expect to see followed up. They will also leave you with a big postdated check. They will tell you what a wonderful opportunity you now have at client X. The implication is that they have created the opportunity. So if the sale comes through, they get the credit. If it does not, you're a turkey.

Shooting seagulls is tempting. I prefer slowly boiling them. In Japan we always had big bananas coming through, normally with their families, on a company-sponsored holiday. We had a simple routine:

- From the moment the big banana stepped of the plane after a 14-hour journey, the day-planner would be filled for 16 hours a day with meetings, briefings, and dinners. Big bananas are normally macho, so a busy day-planner is a Good Thing. And they do not want to show weakness in front of their underlings. We, meanwhile, were covering the big banana in shifts to stay fresh.
- Most of the external meetings would be with Japanese clients. They do not speak English. This minimizes the chances for gratuitous advice, adds to the sense of confusion, culture shock, and jet lag the big banana is feeling.
- One or two meetings would be set up with tame Western clients. They all have the same big banana problem, and would know exactly what script was required. They would focus on how difficult and expensive business is in Japan, and what a wonderful job we are doing. We would return the favor later.
- Let the big banana pay for dinner. The big bananas probably will think they are buying the restaurant, not the dinner. Expenses do not get questioned again.
- Let them go from one meeting to another unaccompanied, just once. They will get lost and freak out, and will spend a fortune. And they will learn to respect the challenges of doing business in Japan.
- At the end of the allotted 48 hours, take them to the airport and ask for their advice. One big banana looked at me in despair and said: "They don't speak English!" At least he had learned something.

In every business there are similar defensive routines to deal with the big bananas who come flying through.

SECRETARIES

The Door to Power

Secretaries are often the gatekeepers to the high and mighty. They control access through the diary, and through handling telephones and e-mail. They are also busy people in their own right, and are often excellent judges of character. Most of my secretaries have been able to spot a good recruiting candidate from a bad one in the time that it takes them to escort the candidate up from reception. They consistently outperform the HR department in candidate assessment.

This means that it is worth treating secretaries as valuable and important people. Flowers and chocolates for the CEO's secretary may work with some and could be a disaster with others: it's obvious bribery, and condescending as well.

If you want to impress, treat them with respect, and as equals. Don't condescend. Help them do their job: don't ask for impossible meetings and impossible times; always return calls when you promise; if they are busy don't harass them. Equally, if there is a spare moment, chat and find out about them. Treat them with the respect that a professional deserves, and they will treat you with respect. And, when you do need the urgent meeting, they will be predisposed to rearrange diaries and to help. Without recourse to chocolate.

Use and Abuse

Secretaries are great productivity enhancers. They can take away all the routine administrivia that soaks up management time and energy. They also buttress the inefficient and ineffective. The solution is not to overburden the secretary, but to be more efficient and effective:

- Filing. Do it yourself. The number one file is the waste basket. Most files are kept "just in case". They clutter up and disturb. Fewer files means more focus, less administration.
- Telephone calls. Take them directly when you are not in meetings. Use voice mail when you are in meetings. You will need to deal with them at some point, so deal with them directly, not through a secretary.
- Diary. Juggle it yourself. Your secretary should not have to judge your priorities for you. Secretaries come into their own when you arrange a large meeting. Then secretary needs to speak unto secretary to try to coordinate diaries.

■ E-mail. E-mail was invented especially for dealing with flight and train delays.

■ Letters. A handwritten response commands much more attention than the standard corporate letter. And it is quicker, and can be written anywhere.

SELL-BY DATES: WHEN TO MOVE ON

We all have a sell-by date, which is when it is time to move on. There is an ultimate sell-by date, which is beyond our control. It's the same date that will appear after "best before . . ." on our gravestones.

It's worth knowing when you are reaching your professional sell-by date. There are five warning signs:

■ The job is boring or unenjoyable. You know this as you struggle into work each day. Listen to your instincts.

■ You are not learning or developing any more. Ideally, the job would always be stretching. There should be moments when you feel that you are outside your comfort zone. If the whole job is well within your comfort zone, you are going nowhere. This drift can carry on a long time, until you wake up one day and find the world has passed you by.

■ You cannot see clear progression ahead. I use a simple benchmark: can I see a way of earning 10 times as much in 10 years? If I can, I know I can see a way of stretching and developing: I will be doing something totally different and more challenging at the end of the 10 years. I started at 50 cents an hour. It's worked since then. Everyone will have a different way of looking at progress.

■ How will I remember the next one or two years when I retire? This is the test of are you doing something that is intrinsically memorable and exciting today. It helps if you feel that you would not only remember the next two years, but that talking about them would be of interest to other people. Going into the office and having meetings fails this test.

■ Performance is declining and the politics are moving against you. These may well go hand in hand, and are probably a sign of burn-out and demotivation. Read the signals early and act on them before you go into a death spiral in the current job. You do not want to become damaged goods on the market. The stress and excitement of a new start in a new environment will be energizing.

SELLING

One-to-One Tactics

Managers do not like to be thought of as salespeople. But good managers are always selling. They are in the business of selling ideas to bosses, peers, and staff. They are trying to motivate, enlist support, and get action.

Bad managers do not see the need to sell. They hope that traditional command and control is enough to tell people what to do. Command and control is for administrators seeking compliance, not for managers seeking commitment.

Perhaps the most important thing for salespeople to remember is that we were born with two ears and one mouth, and they should be used in that proportion. Effective selling is not about making a pitch. It is about listening intently, and understanding the expectations, prejudices, and concerns of the other side. Once you really understand that, you have some chance of communicating in a way that will be well received. The blind pitch is an invitation to disaster.

Having said that, it is worth having a model of how to sell. I was taught a method of selling soap in Northern Scotland. I also used it to sell diapers to drugstores in Birmingham. And I used it to sell multi-million dollar projects to CEOs in America, Japan, and Europe. And I have used it to sell my bosses and staff on ideas for the business. The principles are the same the world over. The most important steps of the seven-step model are the first and last. The steps are:

1. Agree on the problem or situation. You cannot do this unless you understand it from the buyer's point of view. That means preparing and listening. If you both totally agree on the problem, the chances are that the solution will pop out easily. The rest of the sale is easy. And you cannot sell a solution to a problem that does not exist.

2. Agree on the benefits fixing the problem: they should be tangible, relevant, and credible. Benefits are not simply financial and business-focused. They are sometimes intangible, non-measurable, and personal. Removing risk can be a huge benefit to individuals. From the start you want buyers excited about some good outcomes they can expect to enjoy. This will put any concerns they may have into perspective.

3. Suggest the solution. This should be short, sharp, and simple.
4. Explain how it works. Show the suggestion is practical. This should address the questions you know will be asked. Avoid unnecessary detail. The more detail you give, the more likely you are to get bogged down in discussion about the detail, not about the big idea. Brevity is good.
5. Preempt any big concerns. You should know what they are, especially if you have been listening. By preempting the concerns you show that you are positive, you understand their situation, and you are responsive to their needs. Handling objections reactively always appears defensive and can degenerate into an unnecessary conflict.
6. Reinforce the benefits of the suggestion. This is the time you want the buyer focused on the prize.
7. Close. This is crucial. It is where you get their agreement. A good close is not an open question such as "What do you think?" Open questions invite buyers to start acting as judge and jury, and they may come up with the wrong verdict. You want them to be moving into action with you. A good close focuses on action. Typical examples could include: the alternate close: "Shall we start this week, or would you prefer for us to start next week?" or the action close: "Would you like me to draft the memo announcing this?"

The close can be brought forward. If the buyer is ready to buy, close and stop selling. You will only frustrate the buyer, and you create the risk of unselling the sale if you continue selling.

This sales process can take place over weeks for the more complicated and risky sale where you need to build trust and intimacy. The longer it takes, the more listening you probably have to do. It can also take place over a few seconds for an easy sale to people you know, for example, getting your team to go for a drink at the end of a long day:

- State the problem: "Tough day today."
- Preview benefits: "We should relax."
- Make suggestion: "Let's go down to the bar."
- How it works: "It's just next door, we can talk things over there."
- Preempt objections: "Just a pint and we can still get the last train home, I'm buying."
- Reinforce benefits: "It's better than sticking round here getting more frustrated."
- Close: "Last one out, turn off the lights" (action close).

If you are getting nowhere with a sale, go right back to step one. If there are objections, listen and listen again. Show you understand the objections by paraphrasing them back. If the objection is simple, it will go away. Do not get into a conflict trying to handle objections. The conflict will only destroy trust and make the sale harder.

Disagreement over the problem or the situation is probably at the root of your difficulties. And the nature of the problem may well be personal: how the individual will be affected by what you are suggesting. It does not matter that his or her fears appear to be irrational, they have to be overcome. Only when you have shown that you understand and respect the other person's situation will you have the trust to start the sales process over again. And you have the knowledge about how to preempt his or her concerns. When you first use this, it will feel awkward and clumsy. Eventually it is as easy as breathing air.

The Big Complex Sale

As a junior manager, selling can be simple. You only need to persuade the boss and maybe one or two other people that your idea is good, and you have succeeded. As managers gain seniority, the selling task becomes much more complicated. There are multiple constituencies with different agendas, over whom you have no power, that need to agree with what you want to do. These sales always take longer and are much tougher.

But at heart, the same principles apply as one-to-one selling. You are applying the same selling skills, not just one to one, but to a whole network of people in one-to-one situations. The big sales meeting may happen at the end, but that simply confirms the outcomes of all the one-to-one sales you have already done. To identify the network you need to sell to, spot the following:

- The authorizer of your initiative. Probably a senior executive who is above all the constituencies you need to align. The authorizer will rely on the views of all the different constituencies, and may not be deeply involved. Authorizer opposition is fatal. Access can be difficult and intimidating. Get access early to understand the authorizer's agenda. Align your proposal with that agenda, and your conversations with the rest of the network will be transformed.
- User buyers. This is the person who day to day will live with the

consequences of your proposal and may have to implement it. This could be you. Users should be turned into a champions of the proposal. The benefits to users are not just rational business benefits. They must also be personal benefits, where the career opportunities are great and the risks are neutralized in your proposal. It is an emotional and political sale to the user, not just a rational one.

- Economic buyers. This will largely be a rational sale to the bean counters in finance or accounting. Give them the chance and they like to act as judge and jury. Do not let this happen: it is a game where you are guilty until proved innocent. Co-opt them early: seek their input and get them to build the business case with you. Then, when the user or authorizer asks the statutory awkward financial question, let an economic buyer respond. The economic credibility of your proposal will not be questioned again.

- Technical buyers. These are people who have special technical expertise, who will need to be convinced that the proposal hangs together. It may also include a purchaser or buyer who is desperately keen to see that lots of little forms are filled in neatly. It is a cross to bear, unless you have a good relationship with the CEO. Then the functionary will get back into his or her box and do as he or she is told. Do not let technical buyers take over: they can unravel any deal through death by detail. Make sure that the decision remains a management decision, not a bureaucratic decision.

- Key influencers. These people are hard to spot. They have no formal role in the decision. But often they are the people whom the CEO or other executives will turn to for informal advice. They might be in planning, or have a non-executive position, or perhaps be an old friend from a previous job. Find them. They are a great way of informally selling, and normally they are delighted that someone else is taking the time and trouble to speak to them.

- Coaches. In among this network, you should find some coaches. The ideal is to position each of these people as coaches. In other words, do not go to them trying to sell them, go to them asking for advice on your idea. Seek their help. This turns potential adversaries (finance department) into advocates. Generally, people love being coaches. It plays to their sense of self-worth and importance to be consulted. It also establishes the right, mutually supportive relationship in which you sell by listening, not talking. Good coaches will knock down technical obstacles for you, give good advice, and give you access to constituencies you are finding hard to reach.

■ Gatekeepers. This is a dangerous role. Some people appear as coaches, promising to get you access to other key people. Then you find they are simply acting as gatekeepers preventing access other than on their terms. This is their way of gaining control over your initiative. Bypass them as gently as you can.

As you build your network, monitor it. Keep tabs on each person. The key things to note are:

■ The basics. Name, title, location, contact numbers, secretary's name and number.
■ Role in the buying process.
  Hot buttons. What turns this person on? What does he or she like and dislike about the proposal? These are not just rational hot buttons, but personal ones as well. Understand their ambitions and fears and how your proposal may affect them.
■ Key relationships. Who does this person appear to influence, and is this a risk or opportunity?
■ Contact history. What happened when.
■ Personal style. Is this person a people person, a numbers person, an assertive talker, or more of a thinker and listener. Adapt the tone of your approach to suit his or her style.
■ Next steps. Promises made, next meeting.

People often try to keep all this in their heads. For a small simple sale this is possible. For a big complex sale with lots of moving parts, this is not possible. If you have a small team helping you build this network sale, then keeping tabs on where you are with different parts of the network is essential.

SEX AND DRUGS AND ROCK AND ROLL

■ Sex in the office. Not worth it. May be fun at the time, but it just leads to endless complications and always ends in tears.
■ Drugs. Compulsory in some businesses. Power is addictive and should be classified as a Schedule 1 drug, but we all got hooked on it anyway. Otherwise, Just Say No.
■ Rock and Roll. Grow up and get out of your time warp. As managers age, most of them get stuck in a time warp. It can happen when they are 20 or 60 or anywhere in between. In private, their tastes in

music and fashion, their sporting heroes, the films and celebrities they admire all get frozen around a certain time. They lose interest in new stuff, which always seems to pale by what happened before. This personal ossification is matched by professional ossification. The rules of the game they learned at that time are the rules of the game they stick by. The old dog will not learn new tricks. Even if the new is shocking, successful managers maintain a lively interest in it and always learn and adapt.

Sex and drugs offer a shortcut to ruin. Rock and roll is the slow and easy road to ruin.

SHAKESPEARE AND MANAGEMENT

Shakespeare wrote three sorts of plays: comedies, histories, and trage-dies. Most management reports, management time, and managers fall into one of those three categories. It is worth knowing which sort of play you are in, and to act your part appropriately. But whichever type of play it is, it is drama and it is the stuff of life. So enjoy it.

SHERIFFS AND COWBOYS

Accountants and auditors are the sheriffs of the corporate world. It pays to have them on your side, especially if you are a cowboy. In-stinctively, it's easy to hate the sheriffs. They spoil all the fun, stop you doing what you want to do, and generally get in the way. Unfor-tunately, they have authority on their side. Because so many people get frustrated by the accountants, it is easy to make them into allies; they are not used to being treated well.

Look at the world through their eyes. They are meant to keep every-thing in order, often with recalcitrant and uncooperative managers. At the end of the month, they need to get all their numbers to balance out, and they have to spot any risks, fraud, or potential problems. If there are any banana skins out there, they have to spot them. They hate surprises.

The worst accountants get into pettifogging detail and believe that the business is there to serve them, not vice versa. But many accoun-tants will help, if you help them. Once you have the sheriff on your side, you can really go to town. Bringing them on side is basic stuff:

■ Talk to them at the earliest stage of new proposals. Find out how the idea will be assessed, and what the rules of the game are going to be. Give them a feeling of control. They will be grateful.

■ Co-opt them into helping draft or at least validate your proposal and its numbers. Let them avoid surprises. Let them look in control and let them be seen to be doing a good job by their boss.

■ Make their life easy: if they need certain data at a certain time, give it to them ahead of time packaged the way they need it. They will return the compliment when it is their turn.

■ Never pick a fight over numbers with them in public. Even if you are right, they will use enough smoke and mirrors to confuse everyone, delay everything, and knock you off course. You will have an unnecessary battle and enemy on your hands. Preview data with them in private, sort out disagreements then.

SKILLS: STUFF AND PEOPLE

Most people start their careers learning technical skills. It may be cutting code, balancing books, doing pricing analyses, or designing promotions. If you are still cutting code 20 years later, you have probably failed.

Narrow technical and functional stuff become proportionately less important over time. People skills and general management skills become more and more important with seniority. But as people get more senior, they retain the bias of their original functional training. CEOs with accounting backgrounds always look to the financial ratios and performance figures first. Marketing-bred CEOs look to the marketplace, customers, and market share performance first. Engineers look to the product first. This has some basic implications:

■ Personal development depends on building people and general management skills. Business schools help with the general management perspective. They offer no preparation for the messy reality of people management.

■ Too much functional excellence and enthusiasm is career-limiting. People who are functionally excellent are often asked to do more and more of their functionally excellent work. They are typecast as the expert for designing promotions or doing pricing analyses. And this is a box from which it becomes ever harder to escape. The company wants you to do your excellent work. You increasingly become seen as a bit of an nerd in your specialist area and will not be trusted with broader responsibilities.

■ Choice of leader is not just about managerial excellence: it is about fit. A growth company may need a growth-focused marketing CEO. A company in a declining market may need a more control-and-accounting-led CEO. The leadership team as a whole need balance between these skills.

SORRY

"Sorry" is a powerful word. Said early enough and with honesty, it draws the anger and emotion out of a situation. People can move on from blame to action. Some people seem to be pathologically incapable of saying this word. Some of them may be so perfect that they are never wrong and never need to say sorry. Others would rather fight tooth and nail to protect their dignity by redirecting the blame. Sorry is good business sense.

SPEND, SPEND, SPEND

Make your accountants weep. Ignore the cost savings and go on a spending spree. Here are the 10 top cost savings to ignore:

■ Cheap chairs for secretaries who need them all day: only executives get fancy chairs; maintain the caste system.

■ Poor quality coffee machine: make it a pay machine, not free; real coffee, china cups for executives only.

■ Cheap office party to show you don't care about the staff.

■ Lights and air-conditioning that turn off automatically at 6 P.M. to make sure no one works hard.

■ Second-class post: show your suppliers and customers how much you care.

■ Cheap stationery to project the right company image.

■ No hot water in the bathroom: stop people cleaning their hands.

■ Cheap fluorescent lighting: make sure no one gets too comfortable.

■ Skimp on the cleaning and maintenance contracts: show you care about costs, not quality.

■ Replace the canteen with a vending machine: watch everyone leave for lunch and take longer—the smart ones never come back again.

STAFF AND THE MASTERS OF THE UNIVERSE

Two hundred years ago business survived without much staff. Good-bye to consultants, lawyers, investment bankers, accountants, PR and marketing, recruiting and HR departments, and goodbye to the high priests of information technology.

Now these same people represent the corporate life support systems of any large business. Managers only discover how important the staff are when they leave the firm and are denied the oxygen of all the support services.

But the servants of the business are acting above their station. In the twenty-first century they want to be the masters of the house. Fire them, shoot them, stuff them. Never let them take over. They make wonderful servants, terrible masters. When they take over disaster looms:

- The business becomes internally focused, not focused on the marketplace. Managers spend time on getting budget codes for paper clips and worrying about the ensuing variance analysis of paper clips.
- Decision making is slowed down. Decisions are vetted, previewed, reworked, and analyzed by all the worthy staffers in finance, strategy, HR, IT, and elsewhere. They all need to add value, so they all add comments and questions that need to be dealt with. The goal should not be to jump through staff hurdles, but to make the right decision.
- The wrong decisions are made. An IT implementation designed by IT may be technically exquisite. A simpler but less technically beautiful solution is often what the business needs.
- Responsibility is diffused. Once staff start to get involved in decision making, it takes away responsibility from line management. There are more people to blame. Politics escalate.
- Reporting and coordination costs increase. More people need more information on more subjects. And when they get the information, they want to do something about it, so there are more meetings and more discussions and more internal focus.
- Costs escalate. More staff costs money and causes more indirect costs as a result of all the extra internal work they create.
- Morale drops. By this stage the business is in the death spiral as it becomes ever more internally focused; everyone is blaming everyone else for problems. Instead of putting out the fire, they argue

about who started it and who is responsible for filling the water buckets.
- Competition wins.

Good staff functions are worth their weight in gold. They understand that they are there to serve the business. They give the business leverage and help management focus on what is important by taking away from them the routine and the complicated.

STATUS

Everyone craves status. But the more senior you are, the less it is necessary. For junior managers, every little sign of status is another way of giving them some recognition, giving them some confidence that they are advancing. It costs little and does more good than harm.

But status is as addictive as crack. Managers cannot kick the habit. Every year the office and the desk must be bigger, but the PC and mobile phone must be smaller. And then there are the demands for golf club memberships, boxes at all the big sporting events, first-class travel and ultimately the chauffeur-driven car and corporate jet. All justified on the basis of meeting clients and saving time. And it is all nonsense.

Focus on status is in inverse proportion to focus on the business. And it serves to alienate management from the rest of the business: it creates a "them and us" situation. It reinforces the strongly hierarchical nature of the business. Not that senior management will notice: they will be cocooned in their first-class cabin, their big corner office, and their executive box. They will not be in touch with the reality of their organization. There are three solutions to the status problem:

- Get rid of the status symbols. Share an open office, perhaps with the rest of the leadership team. These are the people you need to talk to most often, and with no walls in the way, talking is easier. Make it easy for staff to stop by. Most of them are not stupid: they will not seek to waste time. You may have less status but better communications and faster decision making, and it is easier to stay in touch with the business.
- Monetize the status. Figure out how much all the perks cost, and offer 50 percent of the value in cash instead. The business saves a fortune, and the executives end up with greatly increased income. Curiously, when it is their own money they will not have quite the same need to spend it on first-class travel.

▆ Give them all uniforms. A five-star general's outfit for the CEO through to sergeant's stripes for the frontline supervisor. At least the status and the hierarchy is now clear for everyone to see. And you can even start awarding medals for good conduct and bravery in the face of the competition.

STEWARDSHIP AND VALUES

Stewardship is for success and failure. Stewardship should mean leaving something in better condition than you found it. Stewardship applies as much to the two or three years that managers spend in each job as it does to the two or three hours managers spend each day on helping staff, going to meetings, or any of the other daily activities of management. As a value, it is powerful.

In some businesses the idea of stewardship is corrupted. It means being seen to leave things in better condition that you found them in. This is the survivalist approach to stewardship. It requires careful positioning and expectation setting more than performance. Examples of the survivalist approach to stewardship:

▆ On taking a new job show that you have inherited a disaster. Things can only look better when you leave.
▆ On leaving a job paint a picture of imminent victory. If your successor wins, claim the credit. If he or she fails, it's because he or she screwed up.
▆ On new initiatives offer lots of advice, take no responsibility. If the initiative succeeds, jump on the bandwagon and claim the glory. If it fails, let the turkeys roast.

The corporate version of stewardship is a powerful driver of performance and of making the organization work together. The survivalist version is a recipe for politicking, internal strife and poor performance. The values of the business are not in the values statement. They are in the daily rules of survival and behavior of management, starting with the leadership.

STRATEGY: WAR AND PEACE

Part One: War

Strategy is very important. But no one knows what it means. Every professor in the world has a different version of what strategy means.

This keeps academics in business but does not help management. In answer to the professorial question "What is strategy?", there is only one universally accurate answer: "It means exactly what you want it to mean to make your point."

There are broadly two schools of thought that battle it out on the bookshelves and conference circuit. First, the intellectual and analytical school, led by Michael Porter. Proponents of this school are the ones that come up with lots of diagrams and analytical tools that only brainy people like them can really understand. This means you have to pay them lots of money to take your data and rearrange it insightfully for you. The good news is that they can come up with good insight, and using facts is better than blind guesswork. The challenges are that much of what they do is either not useful, or is positively dangerous:

- Data only exists about the past, not about the future. Strategy is about the future. Looking into the rear mirror to drive forward is rarely smart.
- Most strategy tools are prescriptive: they tell you what you should do. But everyone has the same tools, which means that much strategy leads to everyone settling on similar strategies. This is competitive suicide. You cannot build advantages by being the same as everyone else: competitive advantage involves being different.
- The analytical focus ignores the importance of creativity in seeking original solutions and the importance of engaging and mobilizing the organization behind a new way of thinking. Most strategy reports wind up as expensive door stoppers. They may have provided some comfort to senior management and the board, but they are not living, actionable documents.

On the other hand, the process school, led by Hamel and Prahalad, is the revolt against the intellectuals. The essential argument is that good strategy is about stretching the organization and leveraging its resources to achieve the unachievable. It is a call to arms for the organization. It emphasizes ambition, stretch, creativity, and mobilization of the business. This is all good stuff. And it is extremely dangerous if misapplied.

There is a fine line between goals that stretch and goals that break the organization. For every cited case of a business that has set outrageous goals and achieved them, there are many more for which the ambition has been pie in the sky.

Ambition that is not rooted in an understanding of the market, that lacks the fact base of the intellectual school, is free from constraints in terms of ambition. It may also be free from reality.

All of this would not matter if it were simply a matter of business school professors arguing over abstract theory. Unfortunately, it matters hugely. The methods of these two schools of thought permeate senior management and consulting firms. In practice, this means that strategy is not built around the needs of the business. Strategy is determined by the person you ask and the approach he or she uses. Ask the wrong person, get the wrong strategy.

Part Two: Peace

Given the cacophony of noise from all the experts on strategy, managers are on their own in terms of figuring out what strategy is and how they build and implement it. Ask five different experts for advice, get six different replies.

There are no hard answers. But there are questions that will let you know whether you are on the right track. And by answering the questions, you have a fighting chance of getting a strategy that will work for your company:

■ Is the strategy distinctive? If it is the same as your competition or it is easily copied you are heading either for competitive stalemate or a game of never-catch-up.

■ Is it stretching? A strategy that is essentially an extrapolation of past financial performance is not a strategy. A stretchy strategy will force the business to find new ways of doing things, new ways of competing, and new ways of using limited resources. Business as usual is a criminal waste of internal capabilities and external opportunities. Strategy should match the capabilities to the opportunities.

■ Is the strategy relevant to everyone in the business? The test of relevance is whether it helps people make choices and focus on the right things. Each part of the business may have odd-sounding things like a floor space strategy, or customer satisfaction strategy, or euro-conversion strategy. Purists are appalled by this use of the strategy word. But provided people are developing their local and departmental strategies in line with the corporate one, it is helping focus priorities and resources the right way.

- Is the strategy reality-based? This is not the same as having it proven 300 different ways in some big strategy report. It may be based on some insight about how the market or the competition is inefficient, or customers are dissatisfied. The insight should have some justification, but it should be future-focused, not backward-looking. Unless you have a good crystal ball, do not bet on getting too much data about the future.
- Is it actionable? The strategy should be owned by all managers, not just the executive committee. Everyone will have to live with it and implement it. A process that involves management in developing the strategy is more likely to get managers to buy in, to "own" it, than a process that simply informs them after the event.

STRESS IS GOOD

What sort of environment brings out the best in you?

Option A: The Laid-Back Environment: The Walking and Sleeping Business

Here everything is nice and comfortable. You have easy responsibilities, a light workload, pleasant offices. There are dark creative rooms with funky furniture where you can listen to whale music while you meditate and think your creative thoughts. This is a great lifestyle. But how good is your work and how much are you developing?

Option B: The High Commitment Environment: The Running Business

People are in a rush. People run to meetings, run to pick up the phone. Everyone is stretched, and a little stressed. There is a bit too much for everyone to do: you have to prioritize ruthlessly, cut out all the dross work, and delegate like crazy to make things manageable. Tough lifestyle. But how great is your contribution and how much are you developing relative to the laid-back environment?

Every business should have a stress counsellor, to make sure there is enough stress in the business.

TEAM PLAYERS

There are three sorts of team player.

Team Players

These people actually play for the team, rather than for personal glory. Provided they are good, they are invaluable team members. But they rarely get the recognition. Other people are better at claiming the credit. They are not alpha males who lead from the front and get all the best pickings, they are the beta males who are always the second in command.

Flat organizations depend on team players who are prepared to work outside their boxes and support other people. Reward and measurement systems are rarely geared up to recognize this sort of effort. Annual evaluations often come down to the boss looking at what each individual has done for him or her, not for the business as a whole.

Non-Team Players

These players were useful in the traditional hierarchy. They could accept their own area of responsibility and get on with it. But with more and more business requirements crossing functional requirements, the non-team player is an endangered beast. Except at the CEO level, where the focus is on captaincy and leading the team, not being a team player is unhelpful.

"My Team" Players

These people abound in flat organizations, and claim to be great team players. Their basic premise is that either you are on their team, or you are not a team player. In this context, disagreeing with them or failing to follow their instructions without question is taken as proof positive that you are not a team player. This is the traditional hierarchy disguised as team playing. Under these circumstances the traditional hierarchy has greater honesty and clarity.

TEFLON-COATED MANAGEMENT: TURNING LOSSES INTO INVESTMENT

Investment is good, spending is OK, and losses are bad. This is a problem when you are given a hospital pass: a loss-making business. The art is to turn losses into investment. Do this and you turn from a leper into an Olympian.

Essentially, this is about managing expectations and perceptions, and about demonstrating that you are in control. If you can do all of these, you acquire a thick coat of Teflon.

For example, you are asked to run the business in Japan. You arrive to find it has no sales, no income, and no prospects of any sales. But it does have an expensive office and expensive staff. You could close it down, but you have been sent to build the Japanese business, not kill it. And you know that you are heading for big losses:

- Rule one: take control. Do not let the corporate executives get ahead of you with the bad news. Their spin on the bad news is unlikely to be helpful. This means you have to get to corporate management before they do; do not try to hide. They will find out, and then you will appear not to be in control of the situation.
- Rule two: get all the bad news out. You do not want bad news to keep on trickling out. If there is bad news, get it all out. If necessary, overestimate the extent of the financial damage. This gives you some leeway later, and management might even be relieved that you pull the projected loss back from $6 million to a mere $5 million. If you have set their expectations that they will only lose $4 million, then $5 million looks like a failure. Same financial result, different expectations, and different career result.
- Rule three: have the solution. Do not go to corporate management with only the problem: you then become part of the problem. Come with the solution. This then shows you are in control. And the corporate executives are unlikely to have a better idea than you about what should happen.
- Rule four: find a positive spin. The losses need not be losses. Instead, propose a three-year investment program to build a success-

ful business in Japan. Be clear about the great outcomes: skilled staff, profitable business, and happy clients. The investment simply represents the excess of costs over revenues for the first three years. The executive committee may underwrite your investment plan, even if it does not tolerate losses. They are, of course, the same thing.

- Rule five: build a coalition. You know who the key decision makers are. Get them on board as soon as possible, and in private. Try to co-opt one or two of them into being your coaches. You are certain to come under fire. Identify the potential problem makers, and try to preempt them personally or through your coaches.

- Rule six: deliver on your new plan. You have just used up several of your corporate lives. Do not risk disappointing people again; they will not be so generous next time round.

TELEWORKING: MYTH AND REALITY

Reports of the death of the office are premature. Technology allows us to do more on the move, but we will remain anchored to an office. Teleworking was a reality for hundreds of years through to the industrial revolution. The cloth trade was based on putting work out: individuals would be paid a piece rate for working the wool in stages from the sheep to the shirt. The work would be done at home to supplement the income from farming.

Eighteenth-century teleworking succeeded because the teleworkers needed no human interaction, there was no complex co-ordination required, and the output measurements and rewards were transparent. Teleworking did not require broadband telecommunications and high technology. It required the right sort of work.

All the technology for teleworking is in place. But teleworking will remain an eighteenth-century, not a twenty-first-century way of doing things. The twenty-first century may be high tech relative to the eighteenth century, but it becomes ever more high touch. Twenty-first-century work needs personal contact and:

- Trust. We need to trust the people we work with. So far, human nature has not changed enough for us to be satisfied with a purely remote contact. Air travel grows even as e-mail and voice mail grow. We need to be able to see our colleagues, clients, and business partners in person.

■ Complexity. Business is becoming more, not less, complicated. This means that the depth and frequency of coordination efforts are rising. It also means that it is becoming harder to measure the contribution of many management jobs. The eighteenth-century piece worker needed little coordination: produce the goods by a certain day. In a more complicated world, direct high touch contact helps blow away some of the ambiguities of business, coordination and performance contribution. Seeing is believing.

■ Motivation. The basic discipline of turning up for work, free from domestic transactions, makes a huge difference to productivity.

■ Communication. The water cooler and the open office door remain the best tools for communication. E-mail and voice mail help, but cannot replace the immediacy and intimacy of office contact.

Teleworking will arrive as fast as the paperless office has arrived.

THANK-YOU

Nice to receive. Easy to give. Much underused.

THINKING

Thinking and Responsibility: The Outsourcing Options

Thinking is painful and risky. It's painful because it is about making choices. It is risky because choices lead to actions, which may be wrong. This is why management avoids serious thinking. Continuing the current status quo, the current trajectory is the safe option. Even if the trajectory leads to disaster, the failure is absolute, not relative. In other words, everyone has failed, not just the person who stepped out of line with some fresh thinking and a new perspective.

Ultimately, thinking is about responsibility and dealing with reality. Managers have four choices when it comes to thinking and responsibility. They can:

■ Outsource their thinking and their responsibility.
■ Outsource their responsibility, but keep the thinking.
■ Outsource their thinking, but keep the responsibility.
■ Keep both the thinking and the responsibility.

Outsource Thinking and Responsibility

This is the pass-the-buck game. It is also consistent with the follow-the-herd game. You do not think, you follow. It is the course that most managers follow most of the time. It is easy and low risk, it makes for a quiet life for both the business and the individual. It keeps the wheels of the business turning, without moving the business forward.

This is a sustainable approach in the civil service and other risk-averse monopolies where doing nothing (and not making any mistakes) is preferable to doing something. In businesses that are intended to compete and move forward, it puts all the pressure on the leadership to come up with the great ideas that move the business forward. This approach is consistent with that of junior management in traditional hierarchies.

Outsource Responsibility, But Keep the Thinking

This is the classic role of the staff function. They go away and analyze, criticize, and recommend. But they have no responsibility for doing anything. And the line managers have no responsibility for thinking. This sets up a classic blame game.

Staff can show that managers are messing it up and recommend changes. If management then succeeds, staff can claim the credit. If management fails it was because it did not follow the recommendations, or implemented them poorly. Either way, the staff cannot lose and management cannot win.

Outsource the Thinking, But Keep the Responsibility

This is an unusual, but potentially high-performance choice. It can be done well or badly. At worst, this is the management version of pass the buck and avoiding doing anything. Set up a task force or a committee, hire in consultants, and then managers have someone to blame if things go wrong.

If the manager truly retains responsibility, then he or she may still set up a task force or committee. But this is in pursuit of both getting the best ideas, and of building the commitment across the organization to make something happen. The manager retains responsibility, but personally commits to moving the business forward, not just to spinning wheels.

Keep the Thinking and the Responsibility

This is a trap. It appears to be what management should do, but it is not. It is the paradigm of leadership in the traditional hierarchy where leaders did the thinking and workers did the working, with managers in the middle doing the communicating.

This paradigm is still strong. Organizations like to think that the leaders have all the answers. They delegate the thinking upward. And some leaders like to be seen as all-powerful and all-wise, so they go along with this paradigm. The downside of this is that:

- The thinking is rarely as good as it could be: one leader cannot be expected to have all the answers.
- There is a gap between the thinking and the action: apathy and resistance are more common than committed enthusiasm to someone else's idea. The leader has a job to do to sell the idea.
- Decision making gets slowed down as it filters its way through the hierarchy, and this creates a low-empowerment, low-commitment culture.

Thinking and Writing

More thinking, less writing. Convincing the CEO does not require a 3-kilogram report with charts, tables, and appendices he or she does not have time to read. It requires a well-thought-out argument.

The argument should be expressed on one sheet of paper. Good writing is evidence of good thinking. Less writing is better than more. If less writing is better, no writing is best. There are three reasons for not writing:

- The proposal should be capable of clear, simple expression in a few spoken words.
- Talking gives you flexibility in responding to the CEO's comments, instead of defending the phrasing of the paper. It allows a conversation to develop.
- Peer groups tend to discuss things: bits of paper invite others to act as the schoolmaster. It invites them to assess you and the paper.

Thinking Versus Doing

In an ideal world managers think, then do. Some think and do nothing; they are called staff. A few try neither thinking nor doing. Many prefer to do without thinking. This is the easy way of simply following orders. But it leads to wheel spinning, not progress.

Clear thinking normally depends on good questions. The easiest question to ask is why. Keep on asking it until everyone gets sick of trying to answer it. By about the sixth answer to the question why, you may be getting to a real answer. Asking why is a luxury for consultants, staff, and senior managers who wish to interrogate hapless line managers.

The way for managers to help themselves is to have a very clear model of how their business or department works. The model should not produce prescriptive dumb answers that your competition will have. The model should help ask all the right, pertinent questions, which will lead you to the right answers. These models tend to be highly context-specific, which is what makes them useful. If you are sick of the why question, think of the model of how your business makes money.

The simplest model is the pyramid of ratios, which accountants use to understand financial performance of the business. It does not give answers, but it helps highlight where some of the problems and opportunities lie. Every part of the business can have its own model. The following is a case study of a sales organization.

Sales: Thinking Versus Doing

Sales were slack. People thought it might be a sales productivity problem rather than a product or advertising problem. So the sales business went into overdrive: there were bonuses, competitions, promotions, hiring and firing of staff, new campaigns, and pep talks. Each effort produced a small peak in a downward-sloping sales graph. The harder they tried, the less each effort had an impact in the noise of all the other initiatives.

After lots of doing, they decided to start thinking. They realized that their sales were the function of a very simple formula, which could show them where there might be opportunities. The formula is: $VS = NS \times CD \times HR \times CS$. The equation says that there are four management levers that can affect the value of sales. The issue for management was to see which could yield the best results:

■ VS = The value of sales.
■ NS = Number of salespeople. This asked the basic question of coverage density. A further look at coverage patterns showed that some parts of the country were inadequately covered relative to market potential, others were covered too densely (which led to low sales productivity per person). The higher the density of coverage, the higher the total sales and the lower sales per salesperson. Obvious, but rebalancing coverage helped raise both total sales and productivity per salesperson.

■ CD = Number of calls per day per salesperson. This is a function of how the salesperson spends the day and how the business supports the sales effort. We found that on average, less than 10 percent of the salespeople's time was spent face to face with the customer. This would be fine if each call was effective and the rest of the time was spent preparing for the call. The rest of the time was spent largely on administrative activities and client-servicing activities that other staff could handle. Doubling the amount of client-facing time transformed productivity, and raised morale of salespeople. They had less administrative rubbish to deal with and were earning more by selling more.

■ HR = Hit rate or conversion rate of calls into sales. Further analysis showed this was driven by three factors:

– Salespeople's effectiveness varied by a factor of 5 overall, and by a factor of 12 for individual products. Some salespeople were beyond hope. The broad mass were good at something, and were able to raise productivity by learning best practices, or tips of the trade, of the best salesperson in each category through a structured program.

– Client targeting had a large impact: some customer groups were three times as likely to buy as others.

– Warm versus cold selling. The cold sales had a hit rate of about 1 in 20. Warm leads converted at closer to 1 in 3.

■ CS = Contribution per sale. The size and margins of each sale varied widely by product. This is a function both of the product strategy and the sales force compensation and measurement system. Sales people are rational. They will sell what yields the most benefit for the least effort. The incentive scheme was realigned with the economics of the business, and some products were dropped altogether.

Clearly, none of this is magic. It is not even clever. It is simply about driving clear thinking into clear action. It is about achieving forward motion without spinning wheels.

TIME: ACTIVITY, EFFICIENCY, AND EFFECTIVENESS

Time is not on our side. We do not even know how much our allotted time on earth is. We have to make the most of what we have. Basically, there are three ways of making the most of our time.

Run Around Ever Faster in Ever-Decreasing Circles

This is the most popular form of time management. Senior managers are addicted to it. They tend to believe that a full planner, 200 e-mails a day, and dinners every evening show that they are important and busy. Being late for each appointment is a way of reinforcing the point that they are busy and important. This is not time management; it is an ego trip where activity is a substitute for efficiency or effectiveness. Because senior managers do this, junior managers copy them and the office is full of people chasing each other's tails.

A standard study is to look at what managers do during the day. This is old-fashioned time and motion. It is worth doing to yourself. In one case I found a middle manager who was well respected as someone who got things done and sorted things out. Over the course of eight hours he had the following profile:

- Eighty-two phone calls. Seventy-four of them were either inbound calls, or outbound calls to fix the issues raised by the inbound calls.
- Sixty-three face-to-face interactions. Fifty-nine were fixing inbound issues (fire fighting). Four were arranging travel for the following week.
- Three formal meetings, which were not his. They were other people's agendas. He was late for each.
- He never had more than two minutes between phone calls, a face-to-face interaction or a meeting. This time was used to read or respond to some of the 70-plus e-mails he received.

At the end of the day, the wheels had not fallen off the business, but it had not moved forward. The question for management is: "Are they simply stopping the wheels coming off or are they moving the business forward?" The danger signs are:

- Fragmentation of time: lack of focus on a few things.
- Reactive not proactive agendas.
- Internal versus external focus.
- Reporting and fixing versus proposing and doing.

Test your own time against these four criteria.

Efficiency

This ranges from the trite to the useful. Anyone who has been one-minute managed knows how irritating it is. The trite and insincere morning compliment, which is meant to be your one-minute motivation for the day is a small example. The concept of quality time is a fiction: spending fifteen minutes showing a three-year-old flash cards is not a substitute for parenthood. Some things demand time if they are to be done well.

Other efficiency savers make sense. For the individual some basic rules help. Handling each piece of paper once, doing things right the first time, saves time. But the greatest efficiency in the world does not help if you are doing the wrong thing.

Effectiveness

An old friend from California visited President Reagan at the White House. They had a leisurely lunch. They played golf. The President then invited the friend back for the evening. The visitor was astonished: "Don't you need to get to any meetings? Don't you need to be running the nation?" he asked. The President looked surprised and said, "No, I've plenty of good people doing all that for me."

Working all day and all night is not prerequisite for success. We all know of someone who is apparently lazy and still successful. The lazy way to success depends on three things:

■ Being very good at something (Reagan, the great communicator). This requires real focus effort and commitment.

■ Delegating like crazy. Know what you are not good at, and let other people do it. Give them the glory. The business will be better for it, and so will you.

■ Focusing on what is important. Have clear personal objectives, which will help you prioritize what you will do.

Time management is 10 percent about being efficient in what you do, 90 percent about knowing what you will not do.

Businesses have a duty to help staff manage their time properly. At a trivial level, this can mean things like a concierge service to stop staff being distracted by the administrivia of home life. At a more fundamental level, it is about organizing work well.

A standard study I do on sales forces looks at how salespeople spend their time. Rarely do salespeople spend more than 10 percent of their time face to face with a client. If the other 90 percent of the time was well spent on call preparation and prospecting, this might be justifiable. Normally the other 90 percent of the time is spent on internal meetings and reports, travel and client administration activities. Salespeople often go along with this. It is not as tough as the key job, which is selling. Most non-sales activity can be eliminated or reassigned to administrative staff.

TITLES

Titles are about human dignity and vanity. At junior levels, titles are about dignity. Salespeople hate being called salespeople. They want to be known as account managers, relationship managers, business or market development executives or managers. Anything but salesperson. This is a cheap way of giving people dignity and status. Give it. A little title inflation can go a long way.

Further up the organization, titles are about vanity and power. Everyone is a vice-president. The real competition is to become a senior vice president or executive vice president. Title inflation may be fine at the bottom of the organization. It is not acceptable at the top of the organization.

Always keep a gold standard title, which everyone can aspire to. The VP must want to become an SVP, and the SVP must want to become an EVP. Outsiders probably neither know the difference nor care. Internally, people care passionately. At some level, the title signals that the manager has finally arrived in corporate Valhalla. This is in the land of the gods. Give this title out sparingly: keep people hungry. Make sure that the few that get into Valhalla really do represent the role models for the business. If vanity counts so much, make it work for the business.

TRAINING VERSUS EXPERIENCE

There are three sorts of formal, off-the-job training:

- Technical training.
- People training.
- The training you want, but never get.

Technical Training

This is useful. Most of the technical training that people actually use is professional training such as law or accounting. This provides the fundamental skills and frameworks of the profession.

Formal off-the-job technical training rarely achieves as much as it should. It is not normally customized enough to the needs of the individual, and it arrives at the wrong time. To be effective, training needs to be of immediate relevance, so that the new skills can be applied in practice at once. The best sort of Just in Time (JIT) training that can be customized to individual needs is always going to be on the job, not off the job.

People Training

This suffers the same problems as off-the-job technical training: lack of immediate relevance. It also suffers because it is difficult to change people. Even if people want to change, it takes them years not days. In practice, however, task-driven people remain task-driven and assertive people remain assertive. They cannot be transformed into tree huggers. At best the people training gives people a bit more self-awareness, a bit of insight into other people, and a temporary high fueled by the conference drinks bar and freedom from the office.

The Training You Want But Never Get

What people really want to know is how to succeed in their own organization. This is not a manual that any organization writes. And people want to learn it not from some training functionaries, but from successful people they admire and trust. This sort of training is possible.

Basically, success training is about sharing best practices. Most people are successful at one aspect of their jobs, and want to learn more about other aspects. Everyone has part of the answer to the question of how to succeed. Everyone can contribute to, and learn from, best practices. Most people have enough vanity to enjoy being seen as a best practitioner and are willing to give time and effort to sharing their experience.

Delivering a best practices program takes effort from the training functionaries as well. They cannot simply buy an off-the-rack training program and send everyone the diskette or book the conference center. They have to build a program that systematically codifies the learning in a structure that makes sense, and create a program in which knowledge is consistently shared, spread, and codified. The knowledge has to be made a living beast.

Then the training has to be delivered by the most credible people at the right time. In other words, it needs to be provided on a JIT basis by the best practitioners themselves. This takes time and effort.

The choice is between an expensive but good training program, which is used, versus a cheap off-the-rack training program, which is not used. Most companies prefer to invest less and lose the value of the whole investment, than to invest more and get a return.

THE TRUST EQUATION

Trust goes to heart of all the decisions we make. Budgets and business plans are worth only as much as the people standing behind them; if we trust the authors, we trust the plan. We only go into new departments or businesses if we trust the managers that will lead them. We will accept change if the change is being led by someone we trust. The extent of trust between two people can be assessed through the trust equation $T = (S \times C)/R$ where:

- T = Trust.
- S = Shared goals. If both of us have common goals and common interests, we are more likely to want to work together and succeed together. If we have different interests, the art of trust building is to find those areas of common interest where we can work together.
- C = Credibility. It's no use having common goals if one of the parties can never deliver on promises and can never make the awkward decisions and compromises needed to succeed. People have to walk the talk.
- R = Risk. This is the great test of trust. You may trust me to post a letter, but will you trust me with a million-dollar discretionary budget?

In business, the greatest risk that anyone faces is career risk. This makes the relationship between an individual and his or her manager critical. The risk to the individual of a bad or unsympathetic manager is huge. The challenge to both sides is to build trust. This is not just about results (credibility), it is about listening and understanding and establishing truly shared goals.

Shared goals are not a formal document. They are a psychological contract in which there are implicit expectations on both sides. That contract exists from day one in any relationship. The problem is that both sides may have totally different understanding of what is in the contract. Make sure you understand what the other person thinks is in that contract.

UNDERSTANDING AND PARAPHRASING

How often do you hear people say something like "I hear you"? You know that is a shorthand code for: "I can hear your babble, and I wish you would just shut up, but I can't say so because I need to show that I am being kind, considerate, and that I understand your point of view." They are hearing but not listening.

Of course, if you really can understand the other person, see the world through his or her eyes, you are in a powerful position. You can start to talk a language he or she will understand and respect, you build trust and cooperation. But understanding is more than saying "I hear you." It takes effort. The best way to achieve understanding, and to show that you understand, is to paraphrase. When someone says something that you think is important, paraphrase it back in your own words. This has several advantages:

- It demonstrates to the other person that you are really listening. This encourages him or her to open up more.
- If you get it wrong, you get immediate feedback. You then find the correct message, and future misunderstanding is avoided.
- If you get it right, the other person will be delighted: you are building trust and the basis for cooperation.
- Paraphrasing forces you into active listening. You will become a much more alert, better listener. You will pick up much more information than through passive listening.
- Paraphrasing helps you remember what happened in the conversation much better. With passive listening the substance of any conversation is easily and quickly forgotten.

Paraphrasing is simple, low cost, low effort, and big impact.

UNFAIR COMPETITION

The competition is only unfair if it is winning. If we are winning, it is because we are smarter than they are. Managers will never say we are losing because we are no good. It is always someone else's fault. Denial is natural. But it stands in the way of reality and recovery.

In 1995, the big three US auto companies launched a huge campaign to build their presence in Japan. Most companies seeking to build market share worry about things like product, pricing, promotion, service, and quality. This was irrelevant to the Big Three. Instead, they argued that the Japanese government should arrange to give them more dealerships across Japan, to counteract the unfair competition of the Japanese.

The evidence that the Japanese were unfair was the very low sales of the Big Three in Japan. At the time, the Big Three were selling cars with the steering wheels on the wrong side of the car. The cars were totally outsized for Japanese roads. They cost twice as much as Japanese cars. Quality sucked. Even the British Mini, produced by one of the world's smallest and worst auto manufacturers, had sales in Japan greater than the combined sales of Ford, GM, and Chrysler. The Mini filled a niche. But the US manufacturers could not conceive that the solution lay with them. They were losing. It had to be someone else's fault.

If the Japanese had gone to the US government and demanded that the US government arrange for them to be given extra dealerships to sell cars with steering wheels on the wrong side of the car at high prices and low quality and in the wrong size, they would have been laughed out of town.

But government intervention is a legitimate business tool. As long as there are politicians desperate enough for popularity, there will be opportunities to get a free lunch: the extra subsidy, soft loans, start-up grants, import protection, sanctions on competition. If governments are dumb enough to give all this, businesses should be smart enough to take it. It may be bad economics, but as long as it is good politics, it may as well be good business as well.

UNREASONABLE MANAGEMENT

Reasonable management is dangerous. Good managers are not reasonable. They are, selectively, unreasonable. Reasonable management would have told Virgin that they were crazy to take on British Airways. Toyota and Honda were insane to take on the Big Three U.S. auto manufacturers. President Kennedy was way out on a limb when he promised to send a man to the moon within 10 years, and bring him back again alive.

Reasonable managers listen to all the logical, rational reasons why a 20 percent cut in costs and working capital while maintaining revenues can not be achieved. They then cut the targets back to more reasonable goals for each business.

The reasonable managers are the ones that land up in the quiet backwaters of underachievement. They are weak. The unreasonable managers are the ones that demand, and enable, an organization to stretch and achieve previously unthinkable goals.

Somewhere, there is a dividing line between stretching and breaking a business, between unreasonable and insane management. Goals that are not backed up by a real focus of corporate effort are simple daydreaming. In setting the unreasonable goals, management should:

- Build a coalition in support of the goals.
- Make the goals an inescapable reality for all management.
- Line up all the rewards and measures behind the goal.
- Focus the resources of the organization behind the goal.
- Be flexible about how the goal is achieved, inflexible about the goal itself.

But having done that, they will not hear excuses. Any setbacks simply represent another challenge to be overcome on the way to success. We remember Alexander the Great, not Alexander the Reasonable.

UPWARD MANAGEMENT

Careers depend on upward management. Flat organizations make upward management a minefield of ambiguity and contradictions. In the traditional command and control organization, the rules of engagement are clear. The boss said what needed to be done, and the underling went away and fulfilled those obligations. Underlings knew where they stood, even if they did not like it. There was no ambiguity. And in many organizations, this remains the case today.

In the flat organization, the culture is that everyone acts as a peer to everyone else. Culturally this is attractive. It encourages openness, communication, flexibility, and responsibility. But the rules of the game are totally ambiguous.

Three Hundred and Sixty Degrees of Ambiguity

The evaluation process is at the heart of the ambiguity. In command and control environment, the boss rates you, and that's it. Flat organizations encourage the 360-degree evaluation. But this 360-degree circle is a mathematical mystery. It is a circle with distinct and uneven sides. The boss's evaluation will still determine your bonus, pay, and promotion prospects. Your evaluation will be useful feedback to the boss, but will at best have limited impact on his or her prospects.

So how honest should you be? The bosses suck. If you tell them, will they extract revenge? The organization may be flat, but there is a distinct slope to it at evaluation time. This nagging awareness of the power and decision-making hierarchy affects the day-to-day behavior of everyone in the flat organization. To make it worse, there are no clear rules of behavior.

Flat Organizations and Rules of Engagement

The first thing to do is to find out what the rules of engagement are. Every boss has different rules and different expectations, which even they may find hard to articulate. Some rules of upward management are universal, others will be specific to the style of the boss. Universal rules of upward management include:

■ Understand the rules of engagement: the behaviors that do and do not work with the boss.
■ Focus on what is of most value to the boss: understand his or her agenda.
■ Always, always, always keep promises and avoid surprises. This is central to trust building.
■ Deliver the results.

Other rules of upward management will vary according to the boss:

■ Initiative: how much initiative are you really meant to take? Control freaks want everyone on a short leash; elsewhere failure to lead and take the initiative is terminal for careers.
■ Debate: some bosses want their ideas to be tested and challenged, others want them obeyed.

- Formality: do you drop by the boss's office when you need to or do you have to make an appointment?
- Risk: is this a risk-taking high performance environment, or is it a no errors compliance environment?

A decent boss in a flat organization will go out of the way to make these rules of engagement clear. Setting or asking for an expectations discussion at an early stage is a useful start. The expectations are not about performance. They are about behaviors and what both individuals want to achieve personally. Requesting an expectations meeting quickly gets the boss to reveal the informal rules of engagement:

- Defensive command and control types will avoid the request.
- Traditional bosses struggling to get into the new world will have the meeting, and use it to focus on performance goals, not on mutual rules of engagement.
- Some bosses may actually have a useful discussion about rules of engagement.

VENTING

This is an art I learned from Professor Chan Kim, a great professor at INSEAD. The message is simple and powerful. In a crisis, managers have long political and emotional agendas that stop progress. These agendas are about denial of the problem and spreading the blame for the problem. Any amount of rational argument is doomed to failure. In a crisis, management get very creative and eloquent in putting forward rational arguments to deny the problem and spread the blame. You may not be convinced, but they will be. People need to vent before they can start dealing with reality. It is a painful process for everyone.

How It Works in Practice

We were responsible for leading three-day workshops for a major multinational in crisis. And the management hated being there. They suspected the workshops would either be irrelevant, or a vehicle for forcing them into making unwise performance promises. And there was deep antagonism between departments, countries, and layers of management. They were all gathered together for the first time and they all felt the problems were the result of the others. Of course, collectively they were the others: there was no one else.

Leading these sessions can be suicidal. Managers may hate each other, but they are not going to declare warfare in front of 50 of their most senior colleagues. There was an obvious outlet for all their anger and frustration: the outsiders leading the program.

The solution was to let them vent. They would do this over the first day, into the evening and through to the early hours of the morning. Allowing them to vent was about letting their anger and frustration surface, and about listening, not preaching. For consultants, academics, and CEOs, this tends to lead to blood blisters on the tongue. Talking and challenging the B.S. is tempting, but fatal. The managers needed to talk themselves into submission.

At about 2 A.M. there was a valley of death where everyone was in total despair. At around this time they made several discoveries:

- The business was in real crisis: denial was no longer an option.
- They were the enemy: spreading the blame would not work. Between them, they were the management and there was no one else for them to blame.
- They needed to start dealing with reality.

After passing through the valley of death, there was a catharsis, and enthusiasm for tackling the road to recovery. In practice, venting is good daily management exercise. The more creative rational arguments become, the more they are likely to hide political and emotional issues that do not lend themselves to rational argument.

VICTIMLESS CRIMES

The best crimes are those where the victims do not know that they have been victims. If no one knows there has been a crime, the criminal can never get caught.

Businesses are full of criminals who have got away with appalling crimes. The worst of these is missing market opportunities. No one can be pinned with the blame. The only sign of missed opportunities is when new competitors suddenly emerge out of the ether to challenge traditional industry players.

Canon entered Xerox's market through distributed, non-leased copying; Apple created the PC market, not IBM; CNN, not the established networks, created 24-hour news broadcasting; Microsoft created and owned the operating system business; the Japanese redefined the market for motorcycles and small cars in the United States, displacing incumbent American companies; FedEx, not the long established UPS, created the overnight delivery business. The list is endless.

Innovation within an established company is risky. Get it wrong, you're fired. Naturally, managers shy away from big risk, and play the percentage game instead. The incremental improvements to existing products bring visible results and recognition at low risk. No one at

Xerox got fired for missing the distributed copying market; no one at IBM got fired for missing the PC market.

This logic can be turned on its head. If businesses have the courage to take risk and innovate they can commit the perfect crime: they can take a market before it is contested. This takes a notion of strategy, risk, and organization that is wholly alien to most businesses. The traditional solution of the corporate skunk works is valid: give it money, a powerful political patron, good talent, and an office far away from headquarters out of reach of all the corporate executives who may help it to death.

VISION STATEMENTS

These are excellent for dysfunctional management. Give them the challenge of writing a vision statement and it should keep them happily occupied for months, and out of harm's way. The end product will use up some space in the annual report, and otherwise be quite harmless.

Vision statements can be created through the original vision machine. All you need to do is put the following statements into a random number generator, and then assemble the vision statement in the order the numbers come up. Here are the statements you need:

1. We will be the best at what we do.
2. We will be the market leader in all the markets we serve.
3. People are our most important asset.
4. Our business is built on respect for the individual.
5. We aim to exceed the expectation of all the constituencies we serve: our customers, shareholders, employees and their families, government, and the local community.
6. We will never compromise our ethical standards.
7. Diversity is where it's at, man.
8. We care passionately about caring passionately.
9. We care particularly passionately for the environment.
10. We seek to make above average returns for our shareholders over time.
11. We will all live happily ever after.

Note that this is a non-discriminatory vision statement. You can use it for any industry in any country, in any order. Should your dysfunctional managers produce the vision statement too fast, confuse them by asking them to produce a values statement to go alongside the vision statement. There will then be long discussion about vision versus values and what values really are, and is it culturally biased to have the same values across the world. Don't worry. The same statements used in the original vision machine can also be used for the values statement.

Visions and values are not about crafting elegant statements for the annual report. They are about guiding the daily business and behavior of the company. They are about what people do, not say. It is about the walk, not the talk.

WHAT DO YOU DO?

Answers to this question are normally inaccurate and revealing in equal proportions. The dull but truthful answer for many managers should be: "I sit in meetings, talk to people, write e-mails, and answer the telephone all day." This is not an inspiring vision of a life. The most inspiring and accurate answer is when people say something like "I am setting up a new widget business." Even "I sell diapers to pharmacies in Chicago" is at least accurate and revealing. Most people answer the "What do you do" question in one of three ways:

- The status seeker's answer: "I am a partner, vice-president, big banana at Megacorp." This may impress underlings, but cannot impress outsiders. It says nothing about what the person does: it simply shows an interest in status.
- The professional's answer: "I am an accountant, lawyer, doctor, consultant, etc." Again, this does not say what the person does. What do consultants really do? But it shows that the person's first loyalty is to their profession, not to their company.
- The company person's answer: "I work for Megacorp." This is now rare in the West, but is still standard in Japan. It shows that the person is less concerned about what he or she currently does. Instead, loyalty is to the business.

WHY WORK?

If work was so wonderful, the rich would have found a way of monopolizing it. For most of us, work is not so wonderful. Listening to another boring presentation, writing yet another report, dealing with the daily grind of management is not wholly uplifting.

The most basic answer is that we work to eat. This may be why young professionals are prepared to work all night and all day as they build their careers. This impressive display of passion and commitment is totally unconnected to passion and commitment to the employer. High staff turnover rates give the lie to that assumption.

The passion and commitment is more about instant gratification. Working hard has two immediate benefits. First, it allows for the work-hard, play-hard lifestyle in the short term. Second, it holds out the hope that within a few years the staff can acquire enough money to no longer have to work to eat. They can then move on and set up their own business, become artists, raise a family or whatever their dream is.

The passion and commitment is to themselves, not to the business. The underlying proposition of most businesses is that employees work hard to make someone else richer. The most highly committed workforces are those where there is a strong link between the performance and rewards of the individual. There are exceptions in the voluntary sector and arts where people are not working to eat. But for the majority of management in the majority of businesses, working to eat remains a powerful motivation. This is perhaps cynical, but it is healthy for the individual and the business. The individual has a clear focus. The business gets a hardworking workforce. High attrition allows for flexibility.

WISHFUL THINKING

The smarter people are, the more likely they are to indulge in wishful thinking in more catastrophic ways. Because they are smart, they trust their judgment, and believe that they will win. We all like to think of ourselves as winners; we do want to be seen or act as losers.

Nowhere is this wishful thinking more dangerous than in career choice and managing money, the two most important financial decisions people make.

Wishful Thinking Career Choices

Professional service firms and banks suck up most of the best talent from campuses. Recruits are smart people. And because they are smart, they think they will win. They believe that they will get to the top, get to be a partner. Typically, about 10 percent of them will succeed. They have a 90 percent chance of failure. And yet they always believe that the 90 percent are the other people. Objectively, they could look around and see that their peer group is exactly that: their peers are their equals and they are more likely to be part of the 90 percent than the 10 percent. It is probably this mindset that encourages young men to go to war or drive fast: it is the other person that will get killed.

By the time it comes for the 90 percent to leave, they have normally rationalized in their own minds why they did not want to be part of that firm anyway, and would rather compete to win elsewhere. But the disappointment in their faces as they reach that conclusion over months or years is always visible.

Wishful Thinking Investors

As smart people, we like to think that we are smart with our money. We are all smart investors. We like to think we can beat the market. By definition, not everyone can beat the market, especially after trading costs.

One private bank offered its clients an options and futures trading facility. This private bank had a minimum investment of $1 million, so its customers were wealthy and presumably fairly comfortable handling money. And because of this, they thought they were smart. Options and futures represent a great way to back your judgment against the market and make money fast, or to lose it fast if your judgment is poor.

Eighty-six clients signed up for this service. We decided to look at how many of them made money, and how many of them lost money on this service. We found that all of them lost money. And the more they traded, the more they lost. They were not stupid, but spreads and dealing costs are stacked against the private investor as surely as the roulette wheel is stacked against the gambler. The more you play, the more the house wins. Wisely, the bank withdrew the service. It was making money, but losing customers.

Ultimately, everyone has to take risks. But when wishful thinking blinds smart people to a cool assessment of the odds, disappointment follows.

WORKING HOURS

For the manager, working hours should be an irrelevance. The issue is not about time put in, but about results that come out. So, if people want to turn up late, and need to disappear in the middle of the day, that's fine. As long as there is clarity about what needs to be achieved, by whom, and by when. Most people, when trusted, will respect this. The working hours may be unusual, but they will go out of their way to repay the trust and get the results. In return, they get the flexibility to manage their personal lives as they need. There will be some who abuse the system. But they will not get the results either. The normal evaluation system will catch them.

The fly in the ointment of this flexible approach is regulation. This creates an environment long on rights and short on responsibilities. Regulating working hours and family-friendly policies puts the focus on time and rights, not results and responsibilities. It also fosters resentment from non-family types who have to fill in for family types. Eventually, the dead hand of bureaucracy will take over. Until then, smash the office clock and make sure it is not repaired.

WRITING SKILLS

None of us can be Shakespeare. But we should spare our colleagues the standard jargon-filled drivel that passes as writing in too many organizations.

The best editor I ever had distilled effective writing down to five principles:

- Write for the reader. Understand who you are writing for and why they need to read your memo. This will focus your writing, and help to keep it short and relevant.
- Tell a story. A good memo does not include everything that may be relevant. It corrals all the facts and figures, and then presents only those that tell the story, that make the point you need to make. This makes reading the memo easy, avoids diluting the key message, and minimizes the chances of misinterpretation.
- Keep it short. Churchill once wrote a long letter to his wife, Clementine. At the bottom he added a note: "I am sorry I wrote such a long letter, I did not have time to write you a short one." Writing short is difficult. It means clear focus on the key messages only. It also means using short words, avoiding jargon. Finally, it means using short sentences. Short words and sentences are easier to understand then long ones. A busy executive probably does not have the time or inclination to wade through a long-winded document. Twelve words per sentence is a good average.

■ Make it active. Avoid the passive tense, avoid the impersonal. It sounds dull and bureaucratic. Dull may be fine for the civil service and insurance companies, but is not so great for other businesses.

■ Support assertions with facts. Just because you believe something is right, don't assume that everyone else will make the same assumption. Make sure the facts are there. This also implies that you should make few, not many assertions to keep the writing short. That means focus on the key messages by telling a story.

Finally, make use of visuals: use diagrams, charts, and pictures. People are much better at remembering pictures than they are at remembering words. A well-judged cartoon will be better remembered and more persuasive than reams of prose, even at CEO level.

To make this simple, write out the following five principles on a piece of card and put it on your desk. Use it when writing, editing, reviewing or coaching other people. It works. It remains a standard to which I always aspire, and always fall short.

Writing and Editing Skills

1. Write for the reader.
2. Tell a story.
3. Keep it short.
4. Make it active.
5. Support assertions with facts.

THEORIES X, Y AND Z

Theory X has three underlying assumptions, which lead to a strong command and control business:

- People hate work.
- Formal rewards (bonus promotions) and sanctions (firing, withholding bonuses) are required to make people perform.
- People hate risk and like security. This implies they like to be led and directed, even if they grumble about it.

Theory Y takes the contrary view, which focuses on building a high commitment workplace:

- People like work: it gives structure and purpose to their lives.
- People need more than money: they need recognition. They have egos that need to be fed, as well as bellies. They will work for a higher purpose.
- People will be flexible and take risks to the extent that it is worthwhile (for money, ego, vision).

Most organizations display deep schizophrenia over which model of human motivation and management they believe in. They want to believe that theory Y is correct, and this is what all the gurus urge in talking about high commitment, and passionate organizations. The twenty-first century is meant to be about theory Y. But theory X is going to be around. Ultimately, we probably land up with a fusion of theory X and Y, call it theory Z:

- People need money both for today (to eat) and for their egos (big pay means big car means big ego; big pay means retire early and do your own thing). Formal rewards and sanctions are powerful motivators and demotivators.

■ People crave recognition and status. They want to be valued as an individual both formally (titles) and informally (my boss shows that he or she cares about me personally).

■ People are schizophrenic about responsibility: they want freedom and power, but like security. Security tends to come from leadership and direction.

To make matters more interesting, businesses and individuals vary widely in character from theory X to theory Y. It helps to know what sort of business and manager you have got.

YGWYD

Ygwyd (ee-goo-ihd) is a Welsh word. It is an important one for managers to understand. Next time things go wrong, use it. In English, it means: "You Got What You Deserve."

If you work for a lousy, dispiriting business with bad management and no prospects, ygwyd. You can complain. Or you can do something about it: leave. If you run a lousy business, the staff are lousy, the consultants are lousy, the information systems are lousy and the results are lousy, ygwyd. You can make excuses, or you can do something about it. Ygwyd is about management responsibility and taking control. If we do not accept responsibility and we are not in control, we are not managers.

THE YOGI AND THE COMMISSAR

The great manager is an impossible creature: a combination of the yogi and the commissar. The yogi has deep insight. The greatest yogi understands all of human nature, understands the world, sees the future, and can provide solutions to even the deepest problem. Such is his wisdom that he attracts devotees that will follow him with enthusiasm to the end of the world. The yogi probably lives on a mountain in Shangri-La rather than in the office next to you.

The commissar is the paragon of efficiency. He can equip, supply, and move an army overnight. Everything happens where and when and how it is meant to happen. Nothing is left to chance. He makes good decisions fast, gets them obeyed. No one dares to disobey. His troops have learnt to follow him wherever he goes. Every office is full of aspiring commissars who lack only the military uniform to go with their aspirations, if not their capabilities.

Most of us struggle to be anything like a yogi or a commissar. But the assumption is that we can be both at the same time. Like being Buddha and Genghis Khan, or Plato and Alexander the Great all rolled into one. We can't do it.

Luckily, everyone else is as deficient as we are, more or less. The trick is not to try to be a yogi if you are a commissar, or vice versa. The trick is to make sure that yogis are in yogi positions and commissars are in commissar positions. If you are in a position that requires both talents, get someone else to support you in the other role. The managerial yogi needs a commissar and vice versa. Like Marx and Lenin.

ZONES OF COMFORT AND DISCOMFORT

Everyone has a comfort zone. And no one should operate completely within it. Within your comfort zone, you know that you are capable of doing all the tasks for which you are responsible. This is efficient and leads to a secure and easy life. It is comfortable. It also means that you are not stretching yourself, not building new skills and capabilities, not achieving all that you can for either yourself or your business. Long term, operating inside the comfort zone alone is unsustainable.

The results of operating in the comfort zone can be seen throughout any organization: there are gray people sitting in corners doing the same dead end jobs that they have had for the last 10 or 20 years. If new technology or new skills come along, they are dead meat.

Long term, taking controlled risks by developing new skills and taking on new challenges is a lot less risky than sitting on your hands and hoping the status quo survives. There are typically four stages in competence growing:

1. Unconscious incompetence. Most of us are terrible at most things: it's only when we try them we discover just how bad we are. Try a simple task like juggling. Luckily, we do not need to be good at most things, like juggling.
2. Conscious incompetence. This occurs when we actually try a new task, like juggling. It is far better to be aware of how bad we are than unaware. At least we can then make the decision about whether we want to acquire that particular skill.
3. Conscious competence. This is where we are learning and it tends to be where people get most frustrated and give up. It's like speaking a foreign language: every word and phrase has to be thought about and it is very tiring to sustain. Having a good coach at this point helps.

4. Unconscious competence. By this stage we have mastered the new skill and no longer have to think about it. At this point, we no longer think about the foreign language we are speaking: it comes naturally to us.

As an exercise, identify all the skills you need and want. Then identify your capabilities in those areas against the categories above. If the portfolio consists purely of skills where you are consciously incompetent, you are in trouble. You are probably drowning in your current position. If all your skills are in the unconscious competence category, you are complacent and going backward in your career. Time to wake up. Ideally, you will have a balanced portfolio: some strong skills that allow you to excel in your current role, and other embryonic skills that allow you to grow in the future.

Summary

This is not a universal theory of management. It is no simple formula for instant management success. And that is, perhaps, the most important lesson: there are an infinite number of ways to succeed and fail. Do not trust or follow one simplistic management theory.

The challenges that managers face on a daily basis are consistent around the world and across industries. They are the familiar challenges of inadequate resources, wasted meetings, difficult bosses and staff, mountains of administrivia. Just as the challenges are the same the world over, so too are the patterns of managerial success and failure. The most important guidelines are:

- Understand the rules of the game. Every industry and every company has different rules by which competition is played out. There are, however, different attitudes to risk-taking, career progression, hierarchy, dress codes, and even use of language. These rules are rarely written. If you understand the rules by which you are expected to play, you can decide if that particular company and industry represents a good fit with how you like to live and work. And, once you understand the rules of the game, you will know when you can profitably break the rules. Breaking the rules is a vital part of the rules.
- Get the basics right. All managers spend a large amount of time in meetings and preparing or reviewing documents and presentations. This is common to all industries and all managers, and yet very little training or guidance is available on how to do these well. Not surprisingly, most management documents, meetings, and presentations are deadly dull. This means power to those managers

who stand out from the mediocrity around them. Excellence is not necessary: competence is sufficient.

- Manage people, not things. Management is about human nature, and human nature is not always rational. People and management are naturally political. That means that core management skills have to include politics like building and using alliances to secure support or resources you require. People are also emotional. They crave recognition, they normally dislike risk. Understanding and managing this requires being able to see the world through their eyes, not yours. Most training focuses on technical skills such as accounting, IT, or marketing. These are important at the start of a career. As managers gain seniority, the people skills become more important relative to the technical skills. But, if there is any training on managing people, politics, or emotions it is normally some flaky psycho-babble.

- Focus on what's important, not just what is necessary. Most management time is spent dealing with the necessary: the flood of daily e-mails, routine meetings, preparing reports. This administrative work is more or less necessary to keep the business going. But it does not move the business forward. If managers are to make a mark, they have to move the business forward. They have to make a difference. Projects that make a difference are what is important. The challenge for managers is to have a clear picture of these objectives, and to ensure that they have the time to achieve them.

Nearly all of this is common sense. This is a commodity that is in short supply. Little of this is available through training; it is assumed that either you have it or that you pick it up by some magic form of osmosis. And you will certainly not find any of this taught at business schools, although common sense is what you need to survive in business.

Index

ABC, *see* activity-based costing
abstraction (of feedback), 96–97
abuse, computer, 39–40
accountability, 34, 81
accountants, 56, 193–194
accounting, 77–80, 120–122
acquisitions, *see* mergers and acquisitions
activity-based costing (ABC), 4, 48–49
acts of God, 87
advantage, competitive, 35–37
advertising, 22–24, 59–60
agreement, 1–2, 18–19
aids, presentation, 152–153
air-conditioning, 195
alliances, 135
allocation, resource, 165
alphabet soup, 3–7
altitude sickness, 7–8
Amazon.com, 36, 119, 176
ambiguity, 1, 70–71, 218–219
annual reports, 84–86
Apple Computer, 36, 104, 221
appraisals, performance, 8–12, 131
argument, agreement and, 1–2
Ariel Automatic, 157–158
association with success, 11
assumptions, 27
atomic power, 82
attendance (at meetings), 126–127
attitudes, 57–58
attrition, 11–12
authorizers (of initiatives), 190
automatic voice response (AVR) systems, 60
averages, statistical, 12–13
AVR (automatic voice response) systems, 60

bad news, 203
balance sheets, 79, 85
balloon, squeezing the, 49–50
baselines, 14–15, 15–16
battles, corporate, 16–17

Bayliss, Trevor, 103
B2B (business to business), 4
BBC, 104
B2C (business to consumer), 4
behavior, 53, 57–58
bell curves, 28–29
benchmarking, 17
Benetton, 24
best practices, 213–214
beta, 177
big complex sale, 190–192
blame, 19–20, 220
bluffing, 17–18
boards of directors, 18–19
bookkeeping, double-entry, 77–78
boundaries, organizational, 20
branding, 21–24, 33, 78, 154, 160
Branson, Richard, 55
break-out sessions, 41
bribery, 46–47
British Airways, 217
British Parliamentary Select Committee, 82
Brooks Brothers, 87
B.S. detector, 117–118
budgets, 24–26, 144
Buffet, Warren, on reputations, 64
bureaucracy, 80
business
    change equation for, 29–30
    and entrepreneurs, 70–72
    reengineering of, 176
business schools, 26
Business to Business (B2B), 4
Business to Consumer (B2C), 4
"but," 113

calculators, 26–27
Canon, 104, 221
capacity, 30, 31, 72–73
career choices, wishful thinking, 225–226
caring, 70
cartels, 158–159

cash flow statements, 79, 85
caste systems, 64–65
cautious recovery, 69
centralization, 80
chairs, 195
Champy, James, 176
change, 28–31, 51–54, 68–69, 168–169
chaos, pricing, 153–155, 159–160
charts, organization, 140–142
Chrysler, 216
Churchill, Winston, 8, 227
claims to fame, 31–32
cleaning, office, 195
clients, 33, 163
CNN, 104, 221
coaches, 191
coalitions, 204
Coca-Cola, 35
coffee machines, 195
comfort zones, 233–234
commercial confidentiality, 33–34
commissar, the yogi and the, 231–232
commitment, 45–46
committees, 18–19, 34
common sense, 5, 173
communication
    and empowerment, 61–62
    and flat organizations, 80–81
    and information inflation, 100–101
    and jargon, 4
    of knowledge, 112
    and organizational culture, 53–54
    and power games, 150
    project, 167
    and teleworking, 205
competence, 233–234
competition
    and cartels, 158–159
    copying the, 107–108
    non-price, 160
    unfair, 216
competitive advantage, 35–37
competitive intelligence, 37–38
compliance, 45–46
compounding, 38–39
computer abuse, 39–40
computers, 82
conditional guarantees, 88
conferences, 40–41, 81, 150
confidentiality, 33–34, 43
conscious competence, 233
conscious incompetence, 233
consultants, 29, 41–44, 101–102, 158, 169

contempt (for customers), 59–60
continuous improvement way, 39
contracts, 44–45, 108
control
    of infrastructure, 92
    of losing situations, 203
    management levers of, 45–46
    and risk, 183
    of your destiny, 98–99
controlled pricing chaos, 153–155
*Control Your Destiny or Someone Else
    Will* (Noel Tichy and Stratford
    Sherman), 98
corporate branding, 21–22
corporate herd instincts, 95
corporate life support systems, 71–72
corruption, 46–47
cost(s)
    allocation of, 121
    cutting of, 47–49, 195
    drivers of, 121
    of equity, 177
    of the guarantee, 87–88
    management of, 121–122
    of staff, 196
courtesy, 51
cowboys, sheriffs and, 193–194
credibility, 3, 89, 214
crimes, victimless, 221–222
culture, organizational
    change in, 51–54
    control of, 46
    and diversity, 63–64
    and dress codes, 64–65
    and enthusiasm, 69–70
    entrepreneurialism fostered in, 72
    and expatriates, 74
    and flat organizations, 80–81
    and humor, 98
customers
    accountants *vs.*, 56
    advantages for, 35
    and computers, 40
    contempt for the, 59–60
    and guarantees, 87–88
    lies of, 57–58
    loyalty of, 54–55, 88
    making it easy for your, 66
    and marketing, 7
    and pricing, 156
    and profitability, 55–56, 143
    research about, 57–58
customer service, 58–60
cycle of change, emotional, 68–69

death, the valley of, 68–69
death spiral, 68
DEC, 104
deception, 61–62, 79–80
decision making, 34, 121, 167, 196
delegation, 61–62, 67, 211
Dell Computer, 36, 104
democracy (at work), 62–63
depersonalization (of feedback), 96
destiny, controlling your, 98–99
devil, the pact with the, 70–72
diaries, 186
dictatorship (at work), 62
diligence, due, 65
direction, 70
discomfort zones, 233–234
disillusionment, 87
diversity, 63–64, 105–106
documents, reviewing, 180–182
doing, thinking vs., 207–209
Domino's, 88–89
dot-coms, 78, 80, 95
double-entry bookkeeping, 77–78
dress, 64–65, 151, 198
drugs, 192–193
due diligence, 65
duty of care, 44
Dyson, James, 103

easy, making choices, 66–67
eating power, 150
e-business, 66, 67
economic buyers, 191
Edison, Thomas Alva, on record play-
    ers, 82
editing skills, 228
effectiveness, 211–212
efficiency, 210–211, 231
electric lighting, 82
e-mail, 187
emotional cycle of change, 68–69
emotional management, 174
empowerment, 55, 61–62, 120, 164–165
engagement, rules of, 218–219
Enron, 79, 80
enthusiasm, 69–70
entrepreneurs, 70–72
entropy, 72
environment, 201
equity, 3, 177
etiquette, telephone, 51
euphoria, 68, 69
excellence, 72
excess capacity, 72–73

excuses, 73, 85
executive apartheid, 138
executive committees, 18–19
Exodus Communications, 80
expatriates, 74
expectations, 67, 108
experts, 23, 81–82, 168–169
explicit knowledge, 111
external drivers of advantage, 37
external headhunters, 90–91
eyes of management, 75–76

facility (of head office), 93–94
fads, 168–169
    knowledge management, 110–111
    and quick fixes, 170–173
    resisting, 178–179
fame, claims to, 31–32, 85
Fast Moving Consumer Goods
    (FMCG), 155
Fear, Uncertainty, Doubt (FUD) Factor,
    129–130
FedEx, 88, 104, 221
feedback, 88, 96–97
filing, 186
financial accounting, 77–79, 79–80,
    85–86
financial data, 124
first steps, practical, 30, 31
Fisher, Irving, on stock market, 82
fitter, cutting costs to get, 48–49
Flash Gordon, 69
Flash (product), 27
flat organizations, 80–81, 116, 145, 202,
    217–219
flow, presentation, 153
flyers, frequent, 82–83
FMCG (Fast Moving Consumer
    Goods), 155
focus, 67
forced ranking, 13
Ford, 33, 216
forecasting, 14–15, 81–82, 121
Fortune, 133
frequent flyers, 82–83
FUD Factor, see Fear, Uncertainty,
    Doubt Factor
Fujitsu, 104
future, predicting the, 168–169

games, power, 148–151
gatekeepers, 186, 192
Gates, Bill, 182
General Motors (GM), 216

Global Crossing, 80
global management, 74, 131–132
GM (General Motors), 216
goals, 147, 166, 214
governance, corporate, 18–19
government intervention, 216
"grass is greener on the other side of
   the fence," 86–87
Greenspan, Alan, on infectious greed,
   79
growth, 38–39
growth maturity evaluation, 10
guarantees, 87–89

Hamel, Gary, 199
Hammer, Michael, 176
Hayes, Rutherford on telephones, 82
headhunters, 90–91
head office, 91–94
help (from head office), 91–93
herd instincts, 94–95
hierarchy, 45, 139
high-commitment environment, 201
hippies, 168
Honda, 36, 217
honest feedback, 96–97
hot water, 195
hours, working, 226–227
humor, 97–98
hustle, 71, 98–99

"I," 114
IBM, 36, 104, 221, 222
ideas, killing, 109–110
infectious greed, 79
information and reporting model, 45
information inflation, 100–101
information technology (IT), 5, 102–103
infrastructure control, 92
innovation, 103–104, 124, 221–222
innovation index, 36–37
insanity, resisting, 178–179
In Search of Excellence, 5, 122
insight, 231
intangible advantages, 35
intangible assets, 77–78
intellectual and analytical school, 199
intellectual property, 78
intelligence, competitive, 37–38
intermediate technology, 102–103
internal drivers of advantage, 37
invention, 103
inverted qualifiers, 113
investment, 104–105, 203–204, 226

investment analysts, 94–95
investment banking, 78
Irish Republican Army (IRA), 118–119
"-ists," 105–106
IT, see information technology
IT consultants, 101–102
IT-enabled reengineering, 175

Japan, 107–108
Japan Inc., 156, 160
jargon, 3–4
JIT (Just In Time), 5
job descriptions, 108
Jobs, Steve, 182
"just," 113
Just In Time (JIT), 5

kaizen way, 39, 172
Kennedy, John F., 217
key influencers, 191
killing ideas, 109–110
Kim, Chan, 220
Kissinger, Henry, on leadership, 115
knowledge management (KM), 5,
   110–112

laid-back environment, 201
language, 113–114, 228
lawyers, 114–115
leadership, 8, 28, 115–117
learning, 117–118
letters, 187
lies, 118
   annual report, 84–86
   and averages, 12–13
   customer, 57–58
   and promises, 87–89
lifestyle brands, 21
lighting, 82, 195
logic, 27, 127–128, 157–158
losses, 203–204
Louis Vuitton (brand), 21
loyalty, customer, 54–55, 88
luck, 118–119

M&A, see mergers and acquisitions
management, 120
   and accountability/responsibility, 34
   of advertising, 22–24
   and altitude sickness, 7–8
   and annual report lies, 84–85
   of attrition, 11–12
   and baselines, 15–16
   behavior of, 53

and blame, 19–20
and consultants, 44
control levers of, 45–46
and corruption, 46–47
eyes of, 75–76
leadership tests for, 115–117
myths of, 133–134
by numbers, 6–7
and Parkinson's Law, 144–145
and power games, 148–151
project, 162–168
rational/political/emotional, 174
of risk, 182–183
seagull, 184–185
Teflon-coated, 203–204
time, 209–212
unreasonable, 216–217
upward, 217–219
management accounting, 120–122
management alphabet, 4–6
Management By Walking Away,
    122–123
Management By Wandering Around
    (MBWA), 5, 122–123
management herds, 94–95
management information systems
    (MIS), 123–125
management reports, 193
mandated services, 93
margin-driven approach, 155–156
margins, 56
market-based assumptions, 147
markets, 33, 103–104, 124
market segmentation, 160
Mars Bars, 125
Mazda, 63
MBWA, see Management By Wander-
    ing Around
McKinsey, 56
McleodUSA, 80
meetings, 81, 125–128, 149
mergers and acquisitions (M&A),
    128–130
Metromedia Fibe Network, 80
Microsoft, 104, 221
the Midas Touch, 130–131
middle management, 2–3, 44, 182
mineral water, 158
Mini (automobile), 216
Mintzberg, Henry, 7
MIS, see management information sys-
    tems
mistakes, 117–118
MLAs (Multi-Letter Abbreviations), 3

monitoring, progress, 167–168
Moore's Law, 102
morale, 196–197
motivation, 205, 229–230
moving on, 86–87, 187
Multi-Letter Abbreviations (MLAs), 3
multilocals, 131–132
multinationals, 131–132
multiple advantages, 35–36
"my team" players, 202–203
myths of management, 133–134

Napoleon Bonaparte, 8, 118, 119
Navy (Royal), 61
negotiation, 135
Nelson, Horatio, 16, 61
Net Present Value (NPV), 55
new economy blues, 135–136
Nike, 21, 24, 35, 78
Nissan, 63
non-price competition, 160
non-team players, 202
NPV (Net Present Value), 55

obstacle identification, 166
office parties, 195
offices, 137–139, 149
Olson, Ken, on computers, 82
one-firm approach, 63
one-minute management, 6
one-to-one tactics, 188–190
one-way options, 139–140
"only," 113
OPEC, 158, 159
opportunities (of moving on), 86–87
organizational culture, see culture, or-
    ganizational
organization charts, 140–142
organization data, 124
organization(s)
    boundaries of, 20
    client rule in the, 33
    flat, 80–81, 218–219
outcomes model, control of, 46
output integration, 165–166
outsourcing, 205–207
overhead costs, 78–79
overpay people, 142

Pacioli, Luca, 77–78
pact with the devil, 70–72
pain, 30, 31
Palmer, Arnold, on practice, 118
paraphrasing, 215

parcel delivery service, 104
Pareto, Vilfredo, 143
Pareto Principle, 143–144
Parkinson, C. N., 144*n*
Parkinson's Law, 144–145
partnership, 138–139
pastime power, 150–151
patents, 78
pay, 142
PC, *see* political correctness
people, change equation for, 30–31
people training, 213
Pepsi, 35
perfect predators, 145–146
performance appraisals, 8–12, 131
performance averages, 12–13
performance metrics and rewards, 34
persistence, 118–119
personal branding, 22
personal equity, 3
pharmaceutical companies, 78
phonographs, 82
photocopiers, 104
planning, 146–148, 166–167
plenary sessions, 41
political correctness (PC), 83, 148
political management, 174
Porter, Michael, 199
positive spins, 203–204
postage, 195
power games, 148–151
power words, 114
practice, 118
Prahalad, C. K., 199
predators, perfect, 145–146
preparation, 119, 127
presentations, 151–153
price wars, 160–161
pricing, 153–161, 155–158, 158–161
pricing chaos, 153–155, 159–160
pricing signals, 159
problem identification, 163, 167
process identification, 163–164
process reengineering, 175–176
process school, 199
Procter & Gamble (P&G), 13, 21, 23, 38, 157–158, 159
product branding in action, 21
products, 143
professional service firms, 161–162
professors, 162
profit(s)
    and accounting, 79
    and annual report lies, 85

and customers, 55–56, 143
    management of, 121–122
    pricing for, 155–158
    and products, 143
progress monitoring, 167–168
project management, 162–168
promises, 87–89
promotion, job, 32, 52–53
psychological contracts, 108
punks, 168
purpose
    of meeting, 126
    of presentations, 151
    sense of, 70
pyramid charts, 141–142
pyramid structures, 161–162

qualifiers, inverted, 113
quality, 170
quick fix fixation, 170–173

radios, 82
rates of return, required, 177–178
rational management, 174
reactionaries, 29
reading, art of, 180–182
Reagan, Ronald, 211
reasonableness test, 27
record players, 82
recovery, cautious, 69
recruiting, 90–91, 142, 174–175, 225–226
red dollar syndrome, 49–50
reengineering, 175–177
Reengineering the Corporation (Hammer and Champy), 176
relaxing, 183
relevance (of guarantee), 88
remoteness (of head office), 93–94
reporting
    and empowerment, 61–62
    by gigabyte, 40
    and information model, 45
reports, annual, 84–86
required rates of return, 177–178
research, customer, 57–58
resistance, 182
resisting insanity, 178–179
resource allocation, 165
respect, 179–180, 186
responsibility
    and committees, 34
    and customer service, 55

and staff, 196
and thinking, 205–207
return on investment (ROI), 105
revenge, 180
reviewing documents, 180–182
reward systems
   and the Midas touch, 131
   and motivation, 229, 230
   and one-way options, 140
   and organizational culture, 52
   and overpaying people, 142
   and status, 197
risk(s), 3, 182–183
   and cost of change, 30, 31
   and entrepreneurs, 70–71
   and herd instincts, 94–95
   and innovation, 221–222
   and motivation, 229, 230
   of moving on, 86–87
   and rates of return, 177
   and trust, 214
rock and roll, 192–193
ROI (return on investment), 105
Roman Empire, 45
Roosevelt, Franklin, on directing people, 104
rules and hierarchy model, 45
rules of engagement, 218–219
rules of the game, unclear, 86
rushing, 183
Rutherford, Ernest, on atomic power, 82

salaries, 184
sales formula, 208–209
salesperson, 125, 144
scepticism, 86–87
Schiffer, Claudia, 24
scoreboarding, 50
seagull management, 184–185
secrecy, 184
secretaries, 186–187
segmentation, market, 160
Self-Help (Samuel Smiles), 117
sell-by dates, 187
selling, 188–192
senior management
   and advertising, 22–23
   and altitude sickness, 8
   and consultants, 44
   and frequent flying, 82–83
   and head office, 91–92
   and humor, 97–98
sense of humor test, 97–98

sensitivity testing, 147
service(s)
   customer, 58–59
   effective guarantees of, 88
   from head office, 92–93
   mandated, 93
seven habits of highly effective people, 5, 7
sex, 192–193
Shakespeare, William, 193
shared goals and interests, 3, 214
sheriffs and cowboys, 193–194
Sherman, Stratford, 98
sickness, altitude, 7–8
signals, pricing, 159
silo mentality, 141
single point advantages, 35–36
skills, 78, 86, 194–195, 227–228
skills and standards model, 46
skulduggery, 46–47
Smiles, Samuel, on mistakes, 117
Smith, Adam, 78
solutions, 203
Sony Walkman, 119
"sorry," 195
spending, 195
squeezing the balloon, 49–50
staff, 196–197
   and budgets, 25
   caring demonstrated to your, 70
   and customer service, 59–60
   making it easy for your, 67
   support, 51
standard contracts, 44–45
standards, 46
stationery, 195
statistics, 12–13
status, 82–83, 138, 197–198
stewardship, 198
stock market, 82
storytelling, 97, 227
strategy, 198–201
stress, 201
style, presentation, 151–152
substance, presentation, 152
success, association with, 11
success training, 213–214
Sun Tsu, 16
support networks, 86
support services (of head office), 92–93
support staff, 51
symbols, 53

tacit knowledge, 111
tangible advantages, 35

task forces, 34
"tea lady," 53
team players, 202–203
teams, project, 163, 167
technical buyers, 191
technical training, 212–213
technology, 102–103, 135–136
Teflon-coated management, 203–204
Telcos, 79
telecom industry, 95
telephones
  and customer service, 59–60
  etiquette for, 51
  Rutherford Hayes on, 82
  pricing rates for, 154, 159–160
  and secretaries, 186
teleworking, 204–205
"thank you," 205
Theory X, 6, 229
Theory Y, 6, 229
Theory Z, 6, 229–230
thinking, 205–209
thinner, cutting costs to get, 47–48
Three-Letter Abbreviations (TLAs), 3
3M, 103
Tichy, Noel, 98
Tide, 21, 35
time management, 209–212
titles, 212
TLAs (Three-Letter Abbreviations), 3
Toyota, 217
traditional hierarchy, 139
training, experience vs., 212–214
transactions, volume of, 55–56
travel, 83, 149
trust, 3, 123, 180, 204, 214, 227

unconditionality (of guarantee), 88–89
unconscious competence, 234
unconscious incompetence, 233
uncontrolled pricing chaos, 155
understanding, 215
unfair competition, 216
uniforms, 198
Unilever, 159
unreasonable management, 216–217
UPS, 104, 221

upside down thinking, 141–142
upward management, 217–219
user buyers, 190–191
utility, 125

the valley of death, 68–69
values, 198
values statements, 52
vending machines, 195
venting, 220–221
victimless crimes, 221–222
virgin, 21–22
Virgin Atlantic, 54–55, 217
vision, 30, 31
vision statements, 222–223
volume of transactions, 55–56

Watson, Thomas J., on computers, 82
"we," 114
"we know how to get there" myth, 134
"we know where we are going" myth,
  133–134
"we know where we are" myth, 133
Wells, H. G., on radios, 82
"What do you do?", 224
win, negotiate to, 135
wishful thinking, 225–226
women (in corporate world), 105–106
Woolite, 21
working, reasons for, 224–225
working hours, 226–227
work stream design, 165
world of jargon, 3–4
writing skills, 207, 227–228

Xerox, 104, 221, 222
XO Communications, 80

Ygwyd (You Got What You Deserve),
  231
yogi, the commissar and the, 231–232
You Got What You Deserve (Ygwyd),
  231
yourself, making it easy for, 67

Zero Based Budgeting (ZBB), 48
zones of comfort and discomfort,
  233–234